Move Beyond 3

TEACHER'S EDITION PACK

macmillan education

Anna Cole
Michael Terry

	AFTER SCHOOL			
	Grammar (2): *wh-* questions, *like* + *-ing*		**Vocabulary (2):** Classroom phrases and free-time activities	

LISTENING & VOCABULARY	GRAMMAR (2)	LANGUAGE & BEYOND	SPEAKING	WRITING
Raspberry Pi ***Listen for the main ideas*** **Vocabulary (2):** Computer parts	Articles: *a/an*, *the*, and zero article ***Use a/an and the to refer to things***	Get organized ***Use lists to help you organize your time***	Say what you think ***Ask for and give opinions***	Could you live without your cell phone? (website answers) ***Use the correct word order***
Soap opera ***Understand a situation*** **Vocabulary (2):** Free-time activities	Present progressive for future arrangements ***Talk about arrangements in the future***	Get thinking ***Identify the cause of a problem***	On the phone ***Check that you understand on the phone***	My status update (status updates) ***Use and, also, and too***
Wonderful wildlife photos ***Take notes*** **Vocabulary (2):** Wildlife	Past progressive and simple past ***Talk about actions in progress and finished actions in the past***	Get organized ***Use mind maps to organize information for a speech***	I have a suggestion ***Make and react to suggestions***	A vacation story (vacation story) ***Write a story with time expressions***
What a waste! ***Recognize facts and opinions*** **Vocabulary (2):** Containers and amounts PRONOUNCE Word stress in phrases	Indefinite pronouns ***Use indefinite pronouns***	Respect others ***Consider other people's needs and preferences***	At a restaurant ***Express preferences when you order food***	My favorite recipe (recipe) ***Order ideas***
Where do I belong? ***Recognize when speakers need time to think*** **Vocabulary (2):** Countries, nationalities, and languages PRONOUNCE Stress changes in words	Hopes, plans, and predictions ***Talk about your hopes and plans, and predict events in the future***	Know yourself ***Recognize what you're good at***	Can I help? ***Offer help and express spontaneous decisions***	Time capsule (informal list) ***Use because and so***

IRREGULAR VERBS page 74 **EXTRAS** pages 75–76

CONTENTS

WELCOME TO THE *MOVE BEYOND* TEACHER'S EDITION

Move Beyond is an exciting eight -level course for teenagers, covering CEFR levels from A1+ to B2. Its scope and sequence is meticulously mapped to the CEFR and international exams. The course offers comprehensive coverage of the four language skills through the incremental and cumulative development of subskills. It equips students with transferable linguistic strategies to use in the English classroom and beyond. The inclusion of age-appropriate 21st-century skills adds an inspiring new dimension to language teaching. The life skills lessons create a learning environment that's relevant and accessible to teenagers.

The course is flexible and works in a number of teaching contexts. Lessons are clearly labeled so that you can choose to prioritize material that's relevant in your teaching contexts. The extensive online materials present you with a variety of teaching and practice alternatives to enrich the learning experience.

With eight levels, your school's needs can be met with one single course – be it for streaming, multilevel entry, or a program that takes your students from A1+ all the way up to B2.

The material has a creative and dynamic approach to topics that motivates students and makes language learning more meaningful and successful. Units provide constant opportunities for students to express themselves, while the pages are brought to life through a series of specially produced videos. Throughout the course, language is recycled and reviewed, allowing students to assess and consolidate their progress.

The course's combination of language skills, life skills, and motivating material prepares students for success in and beyond the classroom.

A message from the authors

Secondary teaching is a rewarding but demanding profession. With this course we have tried to make your role as a teacher as easy as possible. The material is clearly organized and can be taught with little or no preparation time. We have also provided resources to help you test and evaluate progress, review material, and work with mixed-ability classes.

Having enthusiastic and interested students also makes the teaching role easier, so throughout the creation of this series we have considered the teenagers' perspective on learning and come up with materials that teach them about the world and allow them to express their views of the world.

When producing the course we used the following key principles to guide our writing:

10 KEY PRINCIPLES OF *GO BEYOND*

1 Subskills: learning how to read, listen, speak, and write

All reading, listening, speaking, and writing lessons have an integrated subskills focus that teaches students linguistic strategies to maximize their learning. This comprehensive subskills syllabus is a key part of *Move Beyond*'s goal to develop literacy.

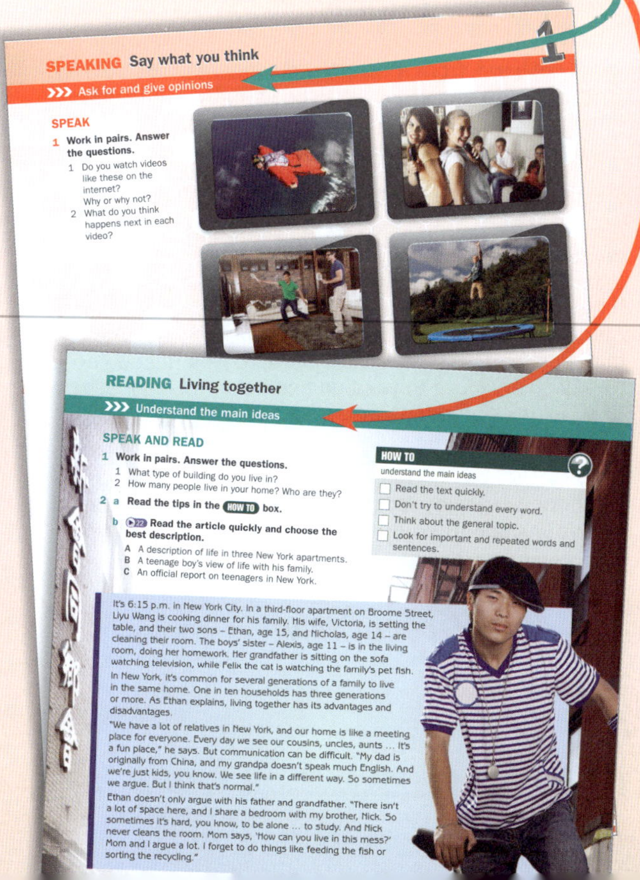

2 Life skills: learning for life

To be successful at school and in life, students need to learn skills that go beyond pure academic knowledge. In order to thrive in today's global market, they need to become aware of and acquire a range of life skills, such as learning to deal with stress, communicating effectively, and understanding different cultures. One lesson in every unit is dedicated to developing a life skill under one of five umbrella headings: Get organized, Get thinking, Respect others, Know yourself, and Communicate & cooperate.

3 Original content and striking images

The cross-curricular focus of *Move Beyond* helps students learn about the world around them. The original material sustains students' interest. The striking images create a strong visual impact and engage students with the content.

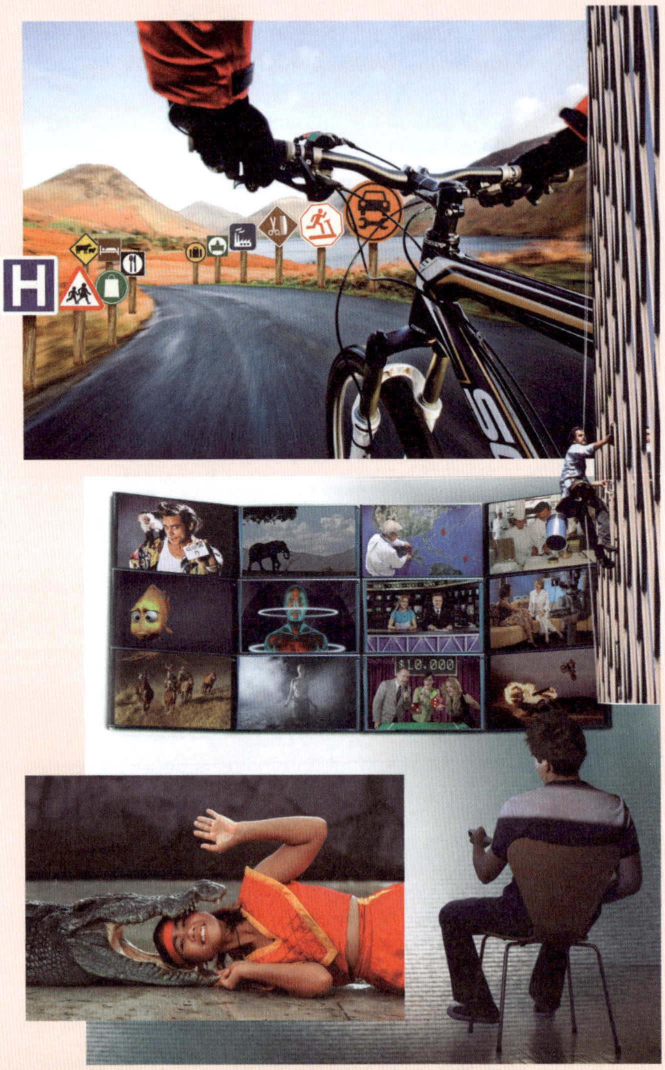

4 Varied and adaptable approach

Move Beyond has adaptations for students' differing learning styles and levels. There are ideas and prompts for students who need more help and a varied approach to dealing with topics and language. To help with differentiation in the classroom, the Teacher's Edition suggests alternative procedures for more confident or less confident students and for fast finishers.

5 Clear and easy to use

All lessons in *Move Beyond* are easy to teach directly from the page. Goals and stages are clearly marked so that teachers can quickly see the objectives and structure of each lesson.

6 Opportunities for personalization

Throughout the course, students are encouraged to relate what they have learned to their own experiences. This personal investment in the course is motivating and rewarding, and it makes the learning process more memorable and the content more relevant.

7 Strong communication focus

In *Move Beyond*, the pairwork discussions, functional speaking tasks, presentations, and variety of writing tasks all encourage students to produce meaningful and real communication.

8 Language in context

All new language in *Move Beyond* is contextualized so that students can see its function and form in realistic situations before studying the grammar rules.

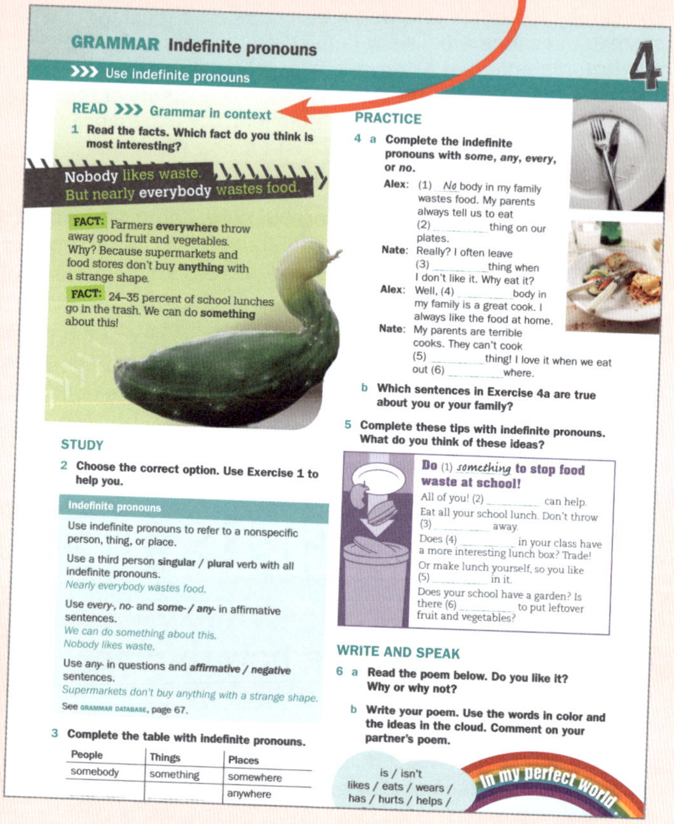

GRAMMAR Indefinite pronouns

4

››› Use indefinite pronouns

READ ››› Grammar in context

1 **Read the facts. Which fact do you think is most interesting?**

Nobody likes waste.
But nearly everybody wastes food.

FACT: Farmers **everywhere** throw away good fruit and vegetables. Why? Because supermarkets and food stores don't buy **anything** with a strange shape.

FACT: 24–35 percent of school lunches go in the trash. We can do **something** about this!

STUDY

2 **Choose the correct option. Use Exercise 1 to help you.**

Indefinite pronouns

Use indefinite pronouns to refer to a nonspecific person, thing, or place.

Use a third person **singular / plural** verb with all indefinite pronouns.
Nearly everybody wastes food.

Use *every-*, *no-* and *some- / any-* in affirmative sentences.
We can do something about this.
Nobody likes waste.

Use *any-* in questions and ***affirmative / negative*** sentences.
Supermarkets don't buy anything with a strange shape.

See GRAMMAR DATABASE, page 67.

3 **Complete the table with indefinite pronouns.**

People	Things	Places
somebody	something	somewhere
______	______	anywhere

PRACTICE

4 a **Complete the indefinite pronouns with *some*, *any*, *every*, or *no*.**

Alex: (1) *No*body in my family wastes food. My parents always tell us to eat (2) ______thing on our plates.
Nate: Really? I often leave (3) ______thing when I don't like it. Why eat it?
Alex: Well, (4) ______body in my family is a great cook. I always like the food at home.
Nate: My parents are terrible cooks. They can't cook (5) ______thing! I love it when we eat out (6) ______where.

b **Which sentences in Exercise 4a are true about you or your family?**

5 **Complete these tips with indefinite pronouns. What do you think of these ideas?**

Do (1) *something* **to stop food waste at school!**
All of you! (2) ______ can help.
Eat all your school lunch. Don't throw (3) ______ away.
Does (4) ______ in your class have a more interesting lunch box? Trade!
Or make lunch yourself, so you like (5) ______ in it.
Does your school have a garden? Is there (6) ______ to put leftover fruit and vegetables?

WRITE AND SPEAK

6 a **Read the poem below. Do you like it? Why or why not?**

b **Write your poem. Use the words in color and the ideas in the cloud. Comment on your partner's poem.**

is / isn't
likes / eats / wears /
has / hurts / helps /

In my perfect world...

9 Learner autonomy

Students are encouraged to work independently in a variety of ways, from a carefully guided inductive approach to grammar to self-study worksheets in the Student's Resource Center. This approach makes learning more memorable and supports learner autonomy.

10 Flexible multimedia material

Move Beyond can be used by teachers with limited or no access to technology. But for those wanting to use technology both inside and outside the classroom, the course includes a projectable digital version of the Student's Book as well as a large bank of additional materials and tests in the Online Teacher's Resource Center. Every *Move Beyond* unit contains an original video to supplement the lessons.

"We hope you enjoy teaching with *Move Beyond* and that your students enjoy learning with it. We wish you a successful and productive academic year."

The Move Beyond Team

Lesson 1 – In the picture

> "The first two pages are a single **vocabulary lesson** that serves as an introduction to the unit and its central theme."

Unit themes appeal to teenagers and provide interesting, unusual, and informative material.

1 The lesson starts with a Recall exercise that activates prior knowledge of vocabulary. Recall words are listed in the Words & Beyond section at the back of the book, where students learn and practice a related Vocabulary Tip.

2 New vocabulary is clearly visible in a word box and is presented and practiced with the support of the images on the pages. Lexical sets are recorded for ease of presentation. Once introduced, vocabulary is recycled throughout the unit and reviewed in the Unit Review and every two units in a Progress Check.

3 The Moving Picture feature on the opening pages brings a dynamic element to the spread by introducing a video and an accompanying task connected to the lesson.

UNIT 4

WHAT'S COOKING?

IN THE PICTURE Inside the kitchen

>>> Talk about food and cooking

WORK WITH WORDS

1 RECALL **Work in pairs. Write lists of food words under the headings. You have three minutes.**

Vegetables	Fruit	Meat & Fish	Dairy	Other	Drinks
onion	*lemon*	*chicken*	*milk*	*bread*	*orange juice*

2 44 **Listen and order the photos.**

1 ___ 2 ___ 3 ___ 4 ___ 5 ___

3 45 **Find these things in the photos. Listen and repeat.**

1 a saucepan *b*
2 a frying pan ___
3 a bowl ___
4 a cutting board ___
5 a knife ___

4 46 **Listen and repeat the words.**

beat chop cut fry heat pour stir

5 47 **Use words from Exercises 3 and 4 to complete the sentences. Then listen and check.**

So first you beat the eggs in a large (1) *bowl* like this.
After that, you (2) ___ an onion – carefully. Don't forget to do it on a (3) ___ .
Then you heat some oil in a (4) ___ and (5) ___ the chicken.
You (6) ___ the lemon juice into a (7) ___ and stir slowly.
Now, with a (8) ___ you cut some bread.

6 a **Work in pairs. Match the verbs in Exercise 4 to some of the words on your food list in Exercise 1.**

Chop tomatoes.

Beat eggs.

b **Work in pairs. Mime some of the actions. Can your partner say the correct phrases?**

7 THE MOVING PICTURE **Watch the video. Would you like to go to Passport NYC? Why or why not?**

40

The unit opener is supported by a video that brings the pages to life. Audio and video are located in the Presentation Kit for ease of access in the classroom and easily available for students on the DVD-ROM.

SPEAK

8 In pairs, read the advertisement and answer the questions.

1 What is a "foodie"? Are you a foodie?
2 What is your favorite food?
3 Which of these things can you do: chop an onion, fry an egg, make a salad?

MOVE BEYOND

Do the Words & Beyond exercise on page 72.

Workbook, page 120

41

4 The final exercises consolidate language with communicative activities in a personalized context.

5 The Move Beyond extras provide material for fast finishers, homework, or additional class activities. The Move Beyond extras refer students to the additional exercises on the Words & Beyond pages at the end of the Student's Book section.

USING THE *MOVE BEYOND* STUDENT'S BOOK

Lesson 2 – Reading

"After the double-page opening spread, each individual page is one complete lesson. The **reading and listening** lessons include an integrated but explicit subskills focus designed to teach students how to read and listen to a variety of text types successfully over the course of a level."

1 The first exercise gives students the opportunity to say what they know or think about the topic of the lesson. This increases confidence and helps students focus on the lesson.

2 The HOW TO box provides tips for applying the subskill. Students read the tips, carry out a related task, and then reflect on which tips they used to complete the task.

3 Students read a variety of text types and learn the subskills they need to deal successfully with each genre. Reading texts include unusual and original perspectives on familiar topics.

4 The React exercises encourage students to share opinions on the text and relate to it in a personal way.

5 The Move Beyond task provides a further activity related to the content of the reading text.

READING Zach's favorite recipe

>>> Use headings to find specific information

Subskills are clearly identified.

SPEAK AND READ

1 Work in pairs. Answer the qu

1 How often do you cook?
2 Are there any recipe books in your home? Do you use recipes? Why or why not?

2 a Read the tips in the HOW TO box.

b Look at the recipe. In which sections can you find the following information?

1 How do I make it?
2 How long does it take?
3 What things do I need?
4 Is it hard?

3 Which tips in the HOW TO box did you use for help with Exercise 2b? Check (✓) them.

...d specific information

- ☐ Decide what information you need.
- ☐ Read the headings (and first sentence if necessary).
- ☐ Find the correct heading and read the information under this heading.

Zach's Spanish Omelette

Level of difficulty	Time	Serves
easy	40 minutes	four people

ABOUT THIS RECIPE

I love food, but I don't have much time to cook. This is one of my favorite recipes because there aren't many ingredients and it doesn't need a lot of preparation. All you need are some potatoes, an onion, a few eggs, and some oil. It's easy. Try it and see.

Ingredients

500 g potatoes
one onion
150 ml oil
six eggs

TIP Don't cut the omelette when it's very hot. Wait for it to cool (about 10 minutes).

Directions

1 Cut the potatoes into small pieces. Chop the onion.
2 Heat the oil in a large frying pan. Add the potatoes and onion and fry for 20–30 minutes. Stir occasionally until the potatoes are soft.
3 Beat the eggs in a bowl.
4 Add the potatoes and onions to the bowl and stir with the eggs. Before you pour the mixture into the frying pan, add some salt and pepper. Then cook on medium heat.
5 To cook the top of the omelette, put the frying pan under the broiler for a few minutes. Or turn the omelette in the frying pan.

ZACH'S FOOD FACTS

Many countries have their own kinds of omelette. The Italian frittata contains cheese, vegetables, and sometimes pasta. A Chinese omelette ... Do you know any egg recipes?

Reading texts contain examples of the next lesson's grammar point in context.

4 (48) Read the recipe again to decide if each statement is correct (C) or incorrect (I).

1 You can make the omelette in under an hour. C
2 Leave the omelette to cool before cutting it. ___
3 Add salt and pepper when you beat the eggs. ___
4 You need three different vegetables to make the omelette. ___
5 A Chinese omelette has vegetables and pasta. ___
6 The chef likes the recipe because it's quick to make. ___

REACT

5 Work in pairs. What do you think? Tell your partner.

1 It's a good/bad recipe because ...
2 After reading the recipe I think / don't think I can make a Spanish omelette.
3 I know some / don't know any egg recipes.

MOVE BEYOND

Work in pairs. Close your books and explain the recipe to each other. How much can you remember?

42

>>> Workbook, page 121

All texts are recorded to provide extra classroom and self-study opportunities.

There are links to the corresponding Workbook pages (that can be found at the end of the Student's Book) at the bottom of each page.

Lesson 3 – Grammar (1)

> The target **grammar** is always presented in context, and students are encouraged to figure out rules from examples.

GRAMMAR Expressions of quantity 4

»» Talk about quantity

READ AND LISTEN »» Grammar in context

1 (49) **Read and listen to the conversation. Which omelette can Tanya and Leo make for lunch – Spanish, Italian, Chinese, or Mexican? (See the recipe on page 44 to help you.)**

Tanya: There isn't much food. There are a few eggs. And there's some pasta – about half a package.
Leo: How many eggs are there?
Tanya: Three. And there's a little cheese too – but not much.
Leo: Is there any bread?
Tanya: No, there's no bread. But there are a lot of vegetables.

STUDY

2 **Complete the table with the words in the box. Use Exercise 1 to help you.**

large quantity   not large or small quantity
small quantity   zero

Expressions of quantity

Expression of quantity	Quantity
a lot of	....
some	....
a few, a little, not much, not many	....
no	....

See GRAMMAR DATABASE, page 67.

3 **Look at the table. Which expression can you use before all nouns and in all kinds of sentences?**

Countable and uncountable

	Countable *egg(s)*	Uncountable *pasta*
+	*some, no* *a few, a lot of*	*some, no* *a little, a lot of*
–	*any, many, a lot of*	*any, much, a lot of*
?	*any, many* *a few, a lot of*	*any, much* *a little, a lot of*

See GRAMMAR DATABASE, page 67.

PRACTICE

4 **Write short descriptions. Use the words in the box.**

a few   a little   a lot of   no   ~~some~~

1 ___some___ bread

2 .... vegetables

3 .... apples

4 .... pasta

5 .... rice

5 **Choose the correct options.**

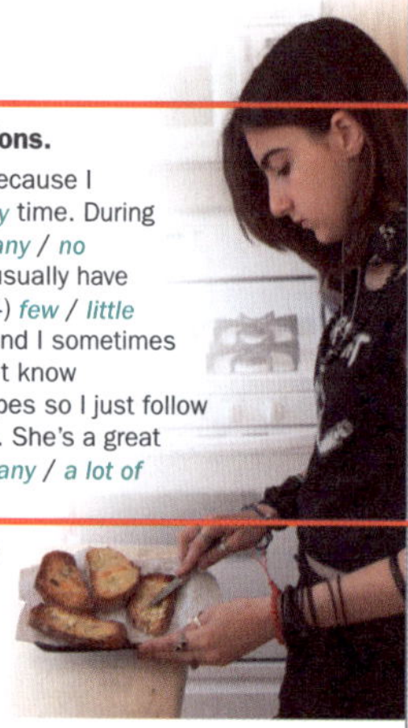

I'm not a very good cook because I don't have (1) (much) / many time. During the week I don't make (2) any / no meals except breakfast. I usually have (3) a / some toast and a (4) few / little orange juice. On the weekend I sometimes help make lunch, but I don't know (5) much / many good recipes so I just follow my big sister's instructions. She's a great cook and she makes (6) many / a lot of really nice food.

6 **Complete the questions with one word.**

1 You're hungry but you have ___no___ time to cook. What do you eat?
2 How .... take-out food do you eat?
3 Do you hate .... vegetables? Which ones? Which ones do you like?
4 A .... friends are watching a movie at your house. What snacks do you offer them?
5 Do you eat a .... of fruit? What's your favorite fruit?
6 You need to make .... food for a picnic. What do you make?

SPEAK

7 **Work in pairs. Answer the questions in Exercise 6. Who makes healthy choices?**

»» Workbook, pages 122–123

43

1 Target grammar is always presented in context. Students either read or read and listen to a conversation or short text that expands on the theme of the unit.

2 Practice exercises start with more controlled task types and then become progressively freer, preparing students to talk about their own lives and experiences in the Speak or Write and Speak exercise at the end of the lesson.

3 In the Study section, students are guided to notice grammar structures from the text and then to complete explanations or examples in the Study box.

4 The target grammar is practiced in a controlled but meaningful context that often also provides opportunities for personalization.

5 The final tasks focus on speaking and/or writing for accuracy of the target structure within a communicative context.

Lesson 4 – Listening and Vocabulary

> **Listening** comprehension tasks are designed to support understanding and not to test. They progress from a focus on global understanding to an understanding of specific details. The exercises are designed to give practice in a specific listening subskill. Students are always asked to react personally to what they hear.

1 As on the Reading page, the first exercise ensures that students access their relevant knowledge and experiences before they listen. In the Work with Words section, students focus on the second lexical set of the unit. In some units, the Work with Words activity comes before the listening activity in order to introduce new target vocabulary first.

2 The HOW TO box provides tips that help students focus on the subskill.

3 Listening texts contain examples of the grammar point found in the next lesson, allowing students to hear the language in context before looking at it in depth.

4 The React activity encourages students to give their personal opinions about the listening text.

5 The Move Beyond task allows students to do a further task related to the new vocabulary set.

LISTENING AND VOCABULARY What a waste!

»» Recognize facts and opinions

SPEAK AND LISTEN

1 **Look at the picture. What do you think the people are doing? Choose A, B, or C.**
- A They're throwing leftover food in the trash can.
- B They're looking at what the supermarket threw away.
- C They lost something in the trash can, and now they're looking for it.

2 (50) **Emma is one of the people in the picture. Listen to an interview with her and check your answer to Exercise 1. What's on her list?**

3 a **Read the tips in the HOW TO box.**

b (50) **Listen again. Which sentences are facts (*F*) in the interview? Which are opinions (*O*)?**
1. Every year the world wastes a lot of food. *F*
2. Europe and North America waste 100 kg of food per person each year. ___
3. Supermarkets throw away a lot of food. ___
4. Supermarkets have to throw away all the food that they can't sell. ___
5. It's wrong to waste food. ___

HOW TO
recognize facts and opinions
- ☐ **Facts:** Listen for numbers and percentages (%).
- ☐ **Opinions:** Listen for phrases like *I think ...*, *In my opinion ...*, and for words meaning "good" or "bad" like *OK*, *wrong*.

4 **Which tips in the HOW TO box did you use for help with Exercise 3b? Check (✓) them.**

REACT

5 **Work in pairs. What do you think? Tell your partner.**
1. Is it wrong for supermarkets to throw away food?
2. Is it OK to take food from supermarket trash cans?

WORK WITH WORDS

6 (51) **Match the phrases for containers and amounts to the pictures. Listen and check.**
1. a bottle of water *a*
2. a box of chocolates ___
3. a package of pasta ___
4. a can of soda ___
5. a carton of milk ___
6. a jar of jam ___
7. a loaf of bread ___
8. a piece of meat ___

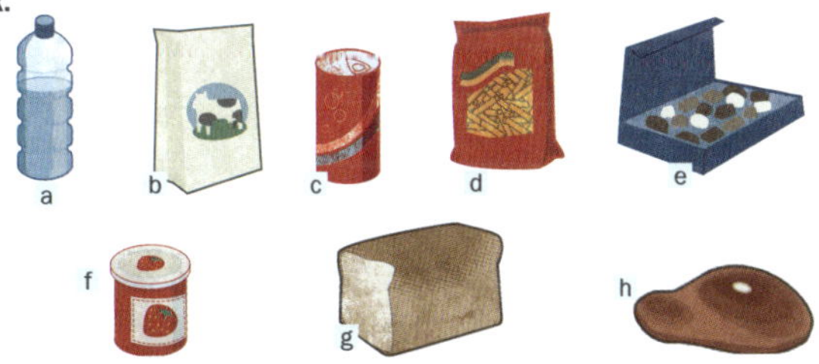

7 (52) PRONOUNCE **Listen to the phrases in Exercise 6 again. Underline the words that aren't stressed. Then listen again and repeat phrases.**

8 **Look at the pictures in Exercise 6 then close your book. Make a list of what you remember. Check your list with a partner.**

Is there a can of soup?

No, there's a can of soda.

MOVE BEYOND
Do the Words & Beyond exercise on page 72.

44

»» Workbook, pages 124–125

Lesson 5 – Grammar (2)

When applicable, a pronunciation section focuses on misunderstandings that commonly occur when English is used between speakers of different first languages. Pronunciation sections can appear in any lesson, depending on the content, and focus on key sounds and stress patterns in words and sentences.

> "The second **grammar** lesson follows the same structure as the first **grammar** lesson of the unit – see page 13."

GRAMMAR Indefinite pronouns 4

»» Use indefinite pronouns

READ »» Grammar in context

1 **Read the facts. Which fact do you think is most interesting?**

Nobody likes waste. But nearly everybody wastes food.

FACT: Farmers **everywhere** throw away good fruit and vegetables. Why? Because supermarkets and food stores don't buy **anything** with a strange shape.

FACT: 24–35 percent of school lunches go in the trash. We can do **something** about this!

STUDY

2 **Choose the correct option. Use Exercise 1 to help you.**

Indefinite pronouns

Use indefinite pronouns to refer to a nonspecific person, thing, or place.

Use a third person **singular** / **plural** verb with all indefinite pronouns.
Nearly everybody wastes food.

Use *every-*, *no-* and **some-** / **any-** in affirmative sentences.
We can do something about this.
Nobody likes waste.

Use *any-* in questions and ***affirmative*** / ***negative*** sentences.
Supermarkets don't buy anything with a strange shape.

See GRAMMAR DATABASE, page 67.

3 **Complete the table with indefinite pronouns.**

People	Things	Places
somebody	something	somewhere
....	....	anywhere
....	everything	....
nobody	....	....

PRACTICE

4 a **Complete the indefinite pronouns with *some*, *any*, *every*, or *no*.**

Alex: (1) *No*body in my family wastes food. My parents always tell us to eat (2) ....thing on our plates.
Nate: Really? I often leave (3) ....thing when I don't like it. Why eat it?
Alex: Well, (4) ....body in my family is a great cook. I always like the food at home.
Nate: My parents are terrible cooks. They can't cook (5) ....thing! I love it when we eat out (6) ....where.

b **Which sentences in Exercise 4a are true about you or your family?**

5 **Complete these tips with indefinite pronouns. What do you think of these ideas?**

Do (1) *something* **to stop food waste at school!**
All of you! (2) .... can help.
Eat all your school lunch. Don't throw (3) .... away.
Does (4) .... in your class have a more interesting lunch box? Trade!
Or make lunch yourself, so you like (5) .... in it.
Does your school have a garden? Is there (6) .... to put leftover fruit and vegetables?

WRITE AND SPEAK

6 a **Read the poem below. Do you like it? Why or why not?**

b **Write your poem. Use the words in color and the ideas in the cloud. Comment on your partner's poem.**

is / isn't
likes / eats / wears /
has / hurts / helps /
fights / tells me
there's / there are

In my perfect world ...
Nobody is hungry.
Everybody smiles.
Nothing hurts.
Everything is peaceful.
Everywhere there are happy faces.
(...ura, 15)

45

There are frequent opportunities for students to talk about themselves and to express their views.

The Grammar Database is a useful reference section where all the grammar points of the level are covered in further detail. You can find additional tips and suggestions for using the Grammar Database in the Teacher's Resource Center.

Target vocabulary is recycled throughout the unit.

Lesson 6 – Language & Beyond

> The **Language & Beyond** page is the life skills lesson. The goal of these lessons is to equip students with the necessary transferable skills for life beyond the classroom, especially in college and in the workplace. The life skills lessons are grouped under five umbrella headings: Know yourself, Get organized, Get thinking, Respect others, and Communicate & cooperate.

1 A wide range of texts and images is used to raise students' awareness of a particular issue or challenge in their everyday lives. In the first stage, they read or read and listen to texts or conversations about situations that are common among teenagers everywhere.

2 Students are then directed to carry out a practical task in the Do stage. Often working in small groups, they put themselves in the situation described and think about what they would do.

3 The Reflection Point feature encourages students to pause and think about what they've just done and guides them toward drawing their own conclusions.

4 The life skills in *Move Beyond* are transferable to other situations and contexts. The exercises in the Extend section enable students to apply the skills they have learned to a realistic situation, which builds a classroom-to-real-life bridge.

LANGUAGE & BEYOND

Asha ____________. She doesn't eat any meat or fish, but she eats dairy products like eggs, milk, and cheese.

Carmelo ____________ so he can't eat any food with them in it, especially cake and cookies.

Lucy ____________. That means she can't eat anything with flour in it, like bread, pasta, or pizza.

>>> Consider other people's needs and preferences

READ

1 A group of American students are visiting your school. Three of them have special diets. Read the information about them above and complete their profiles with the correct phrase.

can't eat gluten | is allergic to eggs | is a vegetarian

2 Work in pairs. Make a list of the food you can see in the photos. Then write A (Asha), C (Carmelo), or L (Lucy) next to the food they can't eat.

DO

3 Your class ... he group of American st...
- In groups, ...
- Include opt...
- Consider the needs and preferences of other students in your class.

REFLECT

4 Discuss the questions with your class. Do you agree with the REFLECTION POINT?
1 Whose special diet was the hardest to consider – Asha's, Carmelo's, or Lucy's? Why?
2 Do you know anybody with a special diet? Describe it.
3 How do you think people with special diets feel when they can't eat anything at a meal or party?

EXTEND

5 Work in groups. Make a music playlist for the welcome party. Think about the preferences of other people in your class.

RESPECT OTHERS

PHRASE BYTES
Let's bring ...
Why don't we make ... ?
What could we bring for ... ?
Do we have anything for ... ?
We need something without ... in it.

REFLECTION POINT
It isn't always easy to consider other people's needs and preferences. But when you consider them, people feel better.

46

Workbook, page 129

Working with other students is a key part of the life skills lesson.

The Phrase Bytes boxes provide language support and build students' confidence when planning and carrying out speaking tasks in English.

Lesson 7 – Speaking

> Using real-life scenarios, the **speaking** page provides students with the language they need to communicate effectively in a range of everyday situations. Each speaking lesson helps students develop a specific speaking subskill. Every speaking page has an audio conversation with teenagers using new language in context.

SPEAKING At a restaurant 4

»» Express preferences when you order food

SPEAK

1 Work in pairs. Answer the questions.

1 What kinds of restaurants are near your home or school?
2 What's your favorite meal when you eat in a restaurant?

LISTEN

2 (53) Listen to the conversation. What do Rick and Sandy order? Complete the sentences.

Server: Hi. Are you ready to order?
Rick: Yes. I'd like the (1) *chicken sandwich*, please. Can I have it without onions?
Server: Of course. Would you like some fries with it?
Rick: No, thanks. I'd rather have (2) ______ .
Server: OK.
Sandy: I'd like the (3) ______ , please. And I'd prefer (4) ______ with it.
Server: OK. Would you like anything to drink?
Rick: Do you have any fresh orange juice?
Server: No, but we have milkshakes and sodas.
Rick: Um … I'll have some (5) ______ .
Sandy: I'd like a (6) ______ , please.

3 a Read the tips in the HOW TO box.

b Write the polite versions of the sentences from the conversation in Exercise 2.

1 Give me a milkshake. *I'd like a milkshake, please.*
2 I don't want onions. ______
3 Drink? ______
4 I don't want fries, I want salad. ______
5 What do you want to eat? ______
6 Water! ______

HOW TO
be polite

- Use polite requests like *Can I have … ?* and *I'd like …*
- Say *please* and *thank you*.

ACT

OUR SPECIALS
Chef's Sandwich (chicken with onions, lettuce, and tomato)
Cheeseburger (100% beef burger with cheese, onions, and ketchup)
Spanish Omelette (eggs, potatoes, and onions)
Chef's Salad (lettuce, tomatoes, peppers, and eggs)

SIDE DISHES
Salad, Fries, or Fried Rice

DRINKS
Selection of delicious milkshakes and cool sodas.
Ask your server for today's specials.

PHRASEBOOK (54)

Order food
I'd like …
I'll have …
Can I have a / some … ?
Do you have any … ?

Express a preference
I'd rather have …
I'd prefer (to have) …

4 Work in groups of three or four.

- Choose something you'd like to eat and drink from the menu.
- Choose one person in the group to be the server.
- The server takes the order. What do you say? Use the conversation in Exercise 2 to help you.

»» Workbook, page 127

47

1 The lesson starts with speaking exercises, which give students the opportunity to describe photos and speculate about a situation. New vocabulary is often introduced.

2 Audio tracks of conversations present students with the context for key functional language. Students listen to the conversation and complete an initial gist exercise before focusing on the speaking function or subskill.

3 A variety of exercise types focuses students' attention on the speaking subskill.

4 Each lesson ends with an Act section in which students prepare a conversation of their own to present in groups or to the rest of the class.

5 A PHRASEBOOK with relevant functional phrases is provided for use with the Act section of the lesson. This is part of the audio material provided and also serves as a review for speaking functions.

Lesson 8 – Writing

> The **writing** lesson in each unit allows students to put everything they've learned in the unit into practice. Each writing lesson also develops a specific writing subskill. Students are systematically guided to discuss, write, and share their writing.

1 The lesson opens with a short speaking and reading exercise to introduce the topic. Students read a model text and complete a task to check that they have understood the text.

2 The HOW TO feature focuses on a writing subskill and offers tips on how to structure writing and link ideas more effectively.

3 After practicing the subskill, students are given a topic for a writing task and instructed to discuss their ideas in pairs or groups first to help them prepare for writing.

4 Students follow a three-step writing plan that guides them to organize their ideas, use the grammar from the unit, and follow the tips in the HOW TO box.

5 In the final exercise, students share their work with each other and either write a reply or discuss what they have written.

WRITING My favorite recipe

>>> Order ideas

SPEAK AND READ

1 **Look at the photo in the recipe for pancakes. Would you like to eat this? Why or why not?**

PHRASE BYTES

Yes, it looks delicious!
No, I don't like fruit / sweet things.
No, I can't eat things with flour.

MY FAVORITE RECIPE: *pancakes*

Ingredients
225 g flour, a little salt, two eggs, 580 ml milk

Directions

- After that, pour in the milk and beat it with the flour and eggs.
- Finally, heat a little oil in a frying pan. Pour in some mixture and fry the pancakes on both sides until they're golden brown.
- Next, make a hole in the middle of the flour. Add the eggs and stir together with the flour.
- First, put the flour in a bowl with a little salt.
- Then leave the pancake mixture for 15–20 minutes.

MY TIP
Eat the pancakes as dessert with fruit and cream, chocolate sauce, or lemon juice and sugar.

2 a **Read the tips in the HOW TO box.**
b **Underline words to order ideas in the recipe.**

HOW TO
order ideas

- Use *first* for step 1.
- Use *next*, *after that*, and *then* for the next steps (in any order).
- Use *finally* for the last step.

3 **Read the recipe and put the directions in the correct order. Use the HOW TO box to help you.**

PRACTICE

4 **Use words from Exercise 2 to order the recipe for Black Bean and Corn Salad.**
(1) ___*First*___ , chop some small tomatoes, an onion, and some cilantro. (2) ______ cut one small hot green chili. (3) ______ stir the tomatoes, the onion, the cilantro, a can of beans, and a can of corn in a bowl. (4) ______ mix some oil and lime juice with a little salt and pepper. (5) ______ pour it over the salad.

DISCUSS

5 **Discuss a simple recipe that you know how to prepare.**

WRITE

6 **Write the recipe you discussed. Make a list of the ingredients. Write the quantity and the ingredient.**

1 Use a number or a quantity: *three eggs*, *a little salt*.
2 Write the instructions. Use order words. Use *first*, *next*, *then*, *after that*, and *finally* to state the instructions. See the HOW TO box.
3 Include a tip. When do you like to eat this? How do you like to eat this? Is there a secret ingredient?

SHARE

7 **Take turns reading your recipe. Listen to your classmates. Which recipe would you like to try?**

48

>>> Workbook, pages 128–129

Lesson 9 – Unit Review

> The **Unit Review** page allows students to check and assess their own progress in vocabulary and grammar.

UNIT REVIEW 4

VOCABULARY Kitchen equipment and cooking verbs

1 Choose the correct options to complete the instructions.

Phil: (1) *Chop* / *Stir* a large onion into small pieces. Use a big (2) *bowl* / *knife* and a (3) *cutting* / *frying* board. Then (4) *beat* / *fry* them in the (5) *cutting* / *frying* pan.

Sue: (6) *Cut* / *Heat* a liter of milk in a big (7) *knife* / *saucepan*. When it's hot, (8) *heat* / *pour* in the cake mix. Remember to (9) *fry* / *stir* all the time to mix it well.

Lynn: (10) *Beat* / *Chop* eight eggs in a (11) *bowl* / *saucepan*. Then (12) *cut* / *pour* some bread for sandwiches.

___ /12

Containers and amounts

2 Complete the words on the shopping list for a party.

A large onion
(1) A c________ of milk
(2) A b________ of cookies
(3) A j________ of jam
(4) 2 c________ of eggs
(5) 8 l________ of French bread
(6) 8 p________ of chicken
(7) 4 c________ of fruit juice
(8) 12 c________ of soda

___ /8

GRAMMAR Expressions of quantity

3 Complete the phone conversation with the words in the box.

any few little lot many much no some

Sue: Hi, Tom. Everything's ready for the party.
Tom: So how (1) ________ food is there?
Sue: Well, we've made a (2) ________ of sandwiches. About 30! There are a (3) ________ different omelettes too, (4) ________ pieces of spicy chicken, a big salad, cake, and a (5) ________ ice cream too, but not much.
Tom: Are there (6) ________ tomatoes in the salad? You know I hate tomatoes.
Sue: No, there are (7) ________ tomatoes in it. I remembered!
Tom: How (8) ________ people are coming?
Sue: About 15.
Tom: Great. See you at 6 p.m.

___ /16

Indefinite pronouns

4 Complete with the correct indefinite pronouns (*__body, __thing, __where*).

"OK, the party's over, so I want (1) ________ to help clean up this mess. (2) ________'s going home until the house is clean again. To start with, (3) ________ needs to take the food to the kitchen. Can the rest of you put (4) ________ else into this plastic bag and check that there's (5) ________ under the sofa? There's food (6) ________ in the kitchen too. And one more thing, does (7) ________ know where the cat is?"

___ /14

Your score: ___ /50

SKILLS CHECK

✓✓✓ Yes, I can. No problem!
✓✓ Yes, I can. But I need a little help.
✓ Yes, I can. But I need a lot of help.

I can use headings to find specific information. ____
I can recognize facts and opinions when I listen. ____
I can consider other people's needs and preferences. ____
I can express preferences when I order food. ____
I can order ideas when I write. ____

Workbook, pages 130–131

49

1 The Unit Review starts with two exercises to test the two lexical sets covered in the unit. Each exercise has a space for students to record their scores.

The exercises in the Unit Review are all set in a single context and reflect the way language is used in real life.

2 Two grammar exercises test the two grammar points covered in the unit.

3 After completing all the exercises, students calculate their total scores. Each review has the same overall score so that students can assess their progress across units.

4 Students are encouraged to self-assess their progress using CEFR "can-do" statements that refer directly back to the objectives of the skills pages.

Progress Check

> After every two units there is a two-page skills-based **Progress Check** that allows students and teachers to see how well the learning objectives in the preceding two units have been met. Tasks on these pages reflect those that students will see on standardized English tests. The Progress Checks also include tips on how to deal successfully with the various tasks.

1 Progress Check tasks consolidate the language from the preceding two units.

2 The Test-Taking Tips help students prepare for standard exam-style tasks.

PROGRESS CHECK

READ

1 The people below are going on a vacation together. You're organizing the vacation and want everybody to enjoy it. Read the descriptions of activities. Decide which activity would be the best match suitable for each person.

1 **Victor** loves being by the coast with his friends, but he hates going in the water because he didn't learn to swim when he was child. He doesn't like any sports or being active.

2 **Sienna** likes sports and outdoor games, especially water sports. Last year she learned to kayak at summer camp. She also loves animals.

3 **Salvatore** hates busy places where there are a lot of people. He likes being in the countryside. He's a good photographer, and last year he won a wildlife photography competition.

4 **Yoko** worries about environmental problems. Last month she organized a *Save Our Climate* campaign at school, and it was a great success. She's scared of swimming and insects.

5 **Ted** is a foodie and a fantastic cook. His parents bought a restaurant a few years ago, and he often helps in the kitchen. He thinks it's important to eat fresh, healthy food.

TEST-TAKING TIPS

do a matching exercise (people + texts)

- Read all the people profiles carefully.
- In the people profiles, underline important words or phrases.
- In the activity descriptions, look for ideas that match the important words.
- Make sure all the information about the people matches the description.

Vacation activities

A Forest visit
Learn about the different species of animals and flowers in the forest. Find out about the lives of ants, bees, owls, snakes, and spiders and how tourists are destroying their habitats. Small groups only and no loud music or phones.

B Walk by the ocean
A five-kilometer group walk along the beach. We'll tell you about the history of the area. Learn how important the ocean was for local people in the past when most people worked on fishing boats. Wear comfortable shoes and appropriate beach clothes.

C Cooking class
In this class, we cook very easy dishes with fresh local foods. Are you a beginner in the kitchen? Can't fry an egg or chop an onion? Can't even remember the last time you used a saucepan or a cutting board and knife? Then this class is for you!

D Tree planting
A great way to have a fun day but also do something for our world. Trees clean our air, but every year we cut down 3–6 billion to build houses and roads, to clear land for farms, and to make furniture. Help us plant new ones.

E Boat trip
Join us on an exciting boat trip on the ocean. During the two-hour stop on a small island, you can go swimming, diving, or water-skiing with our trained instructors. Maybe we'll see some turtles or dolphins somewhere on the trip. Good swimmers only.

F Market day
Visit the local market – it was Market of the Year this year. There are clothes, bags, shoes – everything you can think of. There's also a lot of food, of course – vegetables, meat, fruit, fish, cake, and bread … And the great thing is, you can try everything!

G Beach trip
Lie on the beach all afternoon! Listen to the sound of the ocean and dream. Or enter our sandcastle competition and make a big castle with your friends! Later we'll sit around the campfire and talk about our day.

H Games day
Do you enjoy quizzes? Do you want to win super prizes – for example, a big bottle of soda, a box of chocolates, or a jar of candy? Play games in our new indoor community center with space for 200 people. A fun afternoon for everybody!

Reading: _____ /10

50

PROGRESS CHECK 3&4

LISTEN

2 (55) **You'll hear a restaurant owner talking to some guests at a restaurant. Listen and write the missing information.**

Type of restaurant:	(1) ________
Owner's opinions:	Important to know where food comes from
	Bad for the (2) ________ to transport food a long way
Lunch menu	Soup
	Pancakes with vegetables in a cream sauce with (3) ________ (or rice)
	OR
	Omelette with onions, tomatoes, and spices with a bowl of salad and bread
	(If you're (4) ________ anything, they can make something different)
Drinks	Apple juice from restaurant's own apples
	Milkshakes
Price of lunch menu	(5) $________

Listening: ______ /10

TEST-TAKING TIPS

listen and complete notes

- Read the information carefully before you listen.
- Decide what kind of information is missing.
- Listen for the words before the missing information.
- Write the exact words that you hear.

WRITE

3 Write a story (80–100 words) with the following first sentence:
I was eating dinner with my parents when something strange happened.

Writing: ______ /10

TEST-TAKING TIPS

write a story

- Read the task carefully.
- Think of the main events in your story and make notes.
- Use the simple past and past progressive to tell your story.
- Use time expressions to order the events in your story.
- Check the number of words.

Progress check score ______ /30

51

3 Overall scoring is the same in every Progress Check, so students can monitor both their overall progress and their progress in specific skills.

Other features

At the end of the Student's Book material, you'll find the following resources:

Grammar Database
The Grammar Database provides detailed, additional explanations of the grammar points of each unit, as well as grammar tables and common errors to watch out for. It's a valuable reference section for students.

Words & Beyond
These pages contain lists of the main lexical sets from each unit, as well as other important vocabulary from the unit, vocabulary tips, and additional tasks.

Irregular verbs
A list of common irregular verbs is provided for students' reference.

Extras
The material for pairwork activities (with Student A and Student B) from the units is provided here, as well as answers to quiz questions.

USING THE *MOVE BEYOND* WORKBOOK

The *Move Beyond* Workbook lessons recontextualize, review, and recycle target items from the corresponding lesson pages of the Student's Book and offer comprehensive practice for homework and class use.

- Two vocabulary pages per unit practice the target vocabulary in new contexts.
- Intuitive instructions make it easier to complete each exercise.
- Puzzles and games add an element of fun and variety.

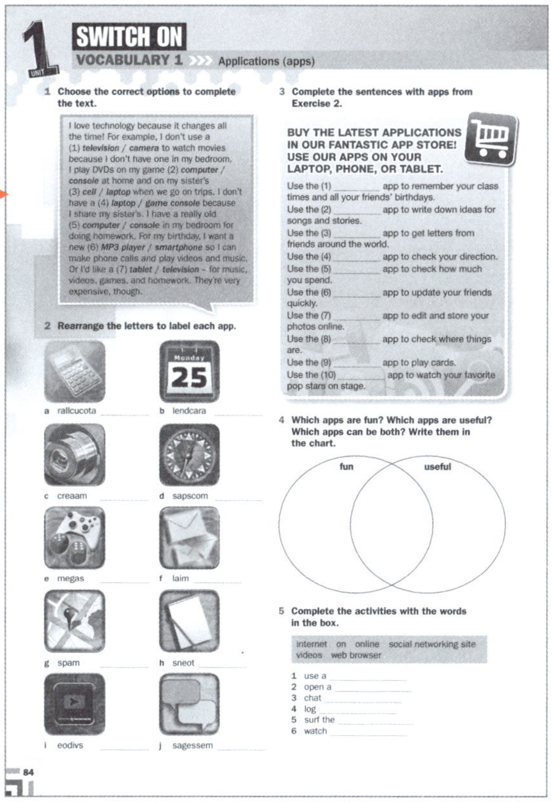

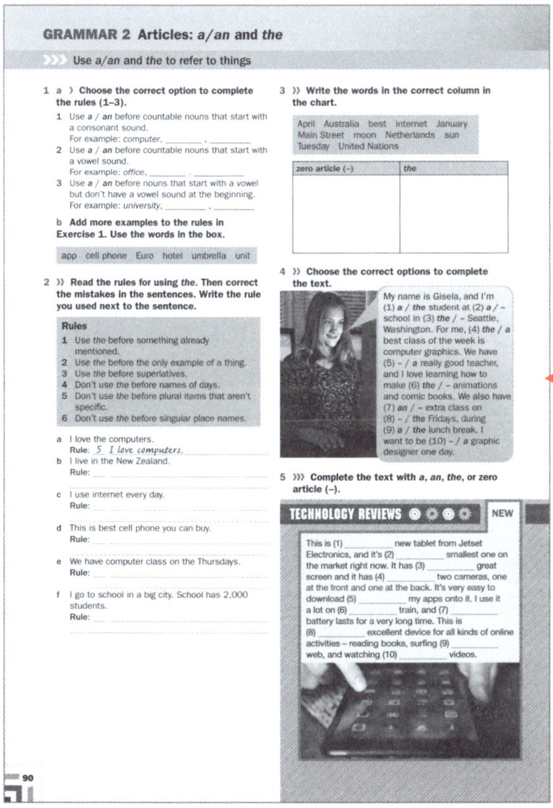

- The Workbook contains three pages per unit for practicing target grammar.
- Grammar Study boxes review the form and use of key grammar.
- Students then practice through contextualized grammar exercises.
- Exercises on the Grammar pages are presented in order of difficulty, shown by chevrons (❯ = easiest, ❯❯ = medium challenging, ❯❯❯ = most difficult).

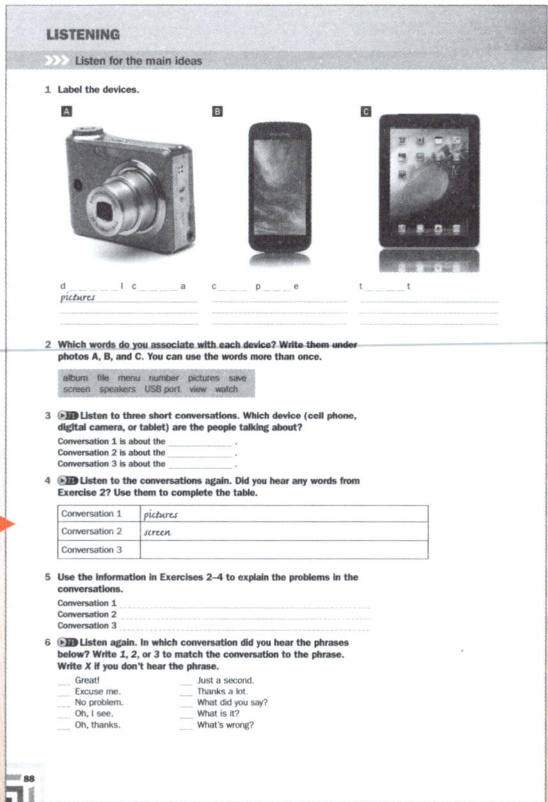

- Key listening subskills from the Student's Book are reintroduced and reexamined.
- Exercises put these skills into practice and review target language.
- Additional listening exercises focus on the theme of the unit, often through test-style tasks related to the subskill in the lesson.

USING THE *MOVE BEYOND* WORKBOOK

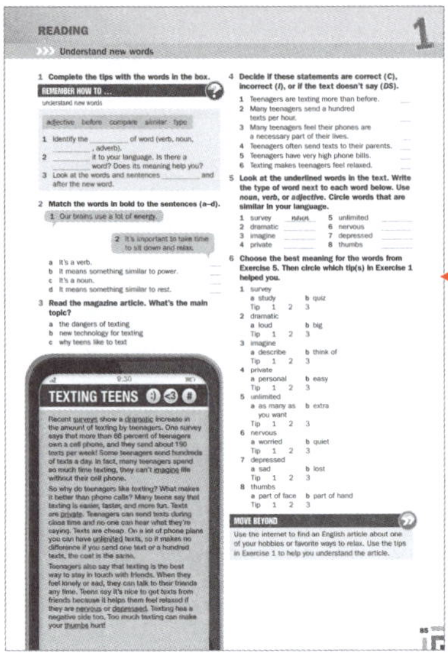

- REMEMBER HOW TO boxes focus on key subskills from the Student's Book lessons.
- Texts build on the themes introduced in the Student's Book.
- Tasks focus on putting reading subskills into practice, recycling key language, and exposing students to test-style tasks.

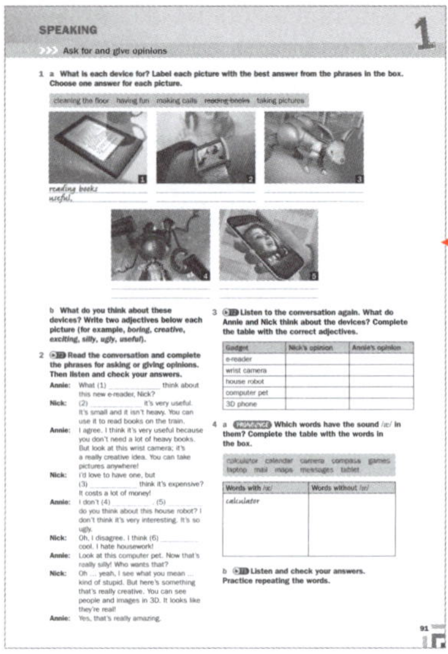

- The Speaking lesson focuses on reviewing key lexical items.
- Target items are presented in context and recordings are frequently used to focus on important aspects of speaking, such as register, stress, and intonation.

- Key writing subskills from the Student's Book are developed in exercises carefully designed to practice the skill.
- Emphasis is put on the planning and structuring of texts, and students are guided through final exam-type writing tasks.

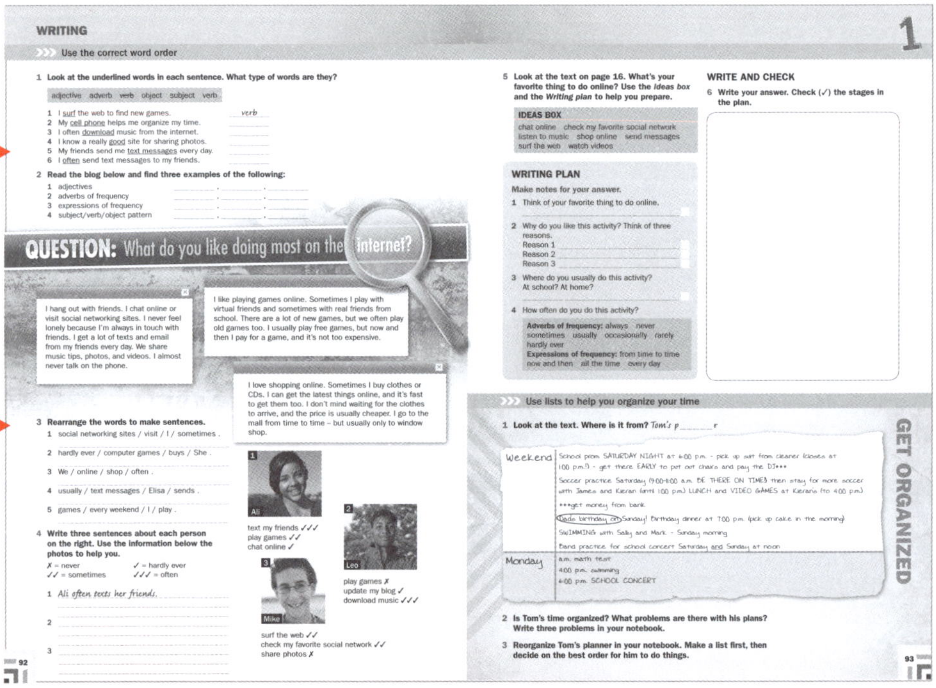

- The unit life skill is revisited, and students are challenged to apply the skill in a personalized new context.

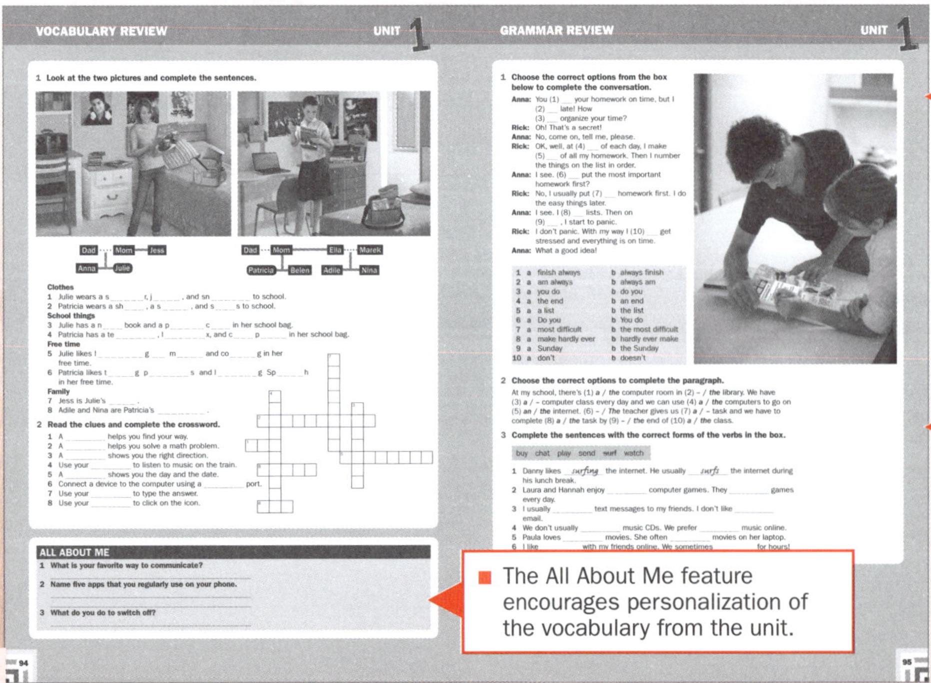

- Target vocabulary and grammar taken from any unit of the Student's Book covered to date are recontextualized and reviewed here, allowing students to monitor their own progress.
- The review pages offer cumulative assessment, with exercises combining two or more grammar points or vocabulary sets.
- The All About Me feature encourages personalization of the vocabulary from the unit.

MOVE BEYOND DIGITAL

The digital components of ***Move Beyond*** are easy to integrate into your regular classroom activities. The range of multimedia resources gives teachers an excellent opportunity to digitize their lessons and present the material in different ways, which varies the pace and dynamics in the classroom. Classwork, homework, and testing are all accommodated in the ***Move Beyond*** Teacher's Resource Center, where plenty of flexible additional materials for both online and offline use can be found.

Go to mee2.macmillaneducation.com to access

- *Move Beyond* Level 3 Presentation Kit, consisting of a digital Student's Book designed for classroom presentation
- *Move Beyond* Level 3 Teacher's Resource Center for extra materials, tests, videos, and downloadable audio

Teacher's Resource Center

The Teacher's Resource Center provides teachers with downloadable extra grammar and vocabulary worksheets, tips, and testing materials to support the course. It contains a whole range of additional ***Move Beyond*** materials to be used in the classroom or assigned for homework, as well as access to everything in the Student's Resource Center.

Full answer keys and scripts for all course components.

Extra Grammar and Vocabulary worksheets.

Further ideas and activities for exploring the ***Move Beyond*** videos.

Teacher's notes to accompany the worksheets.

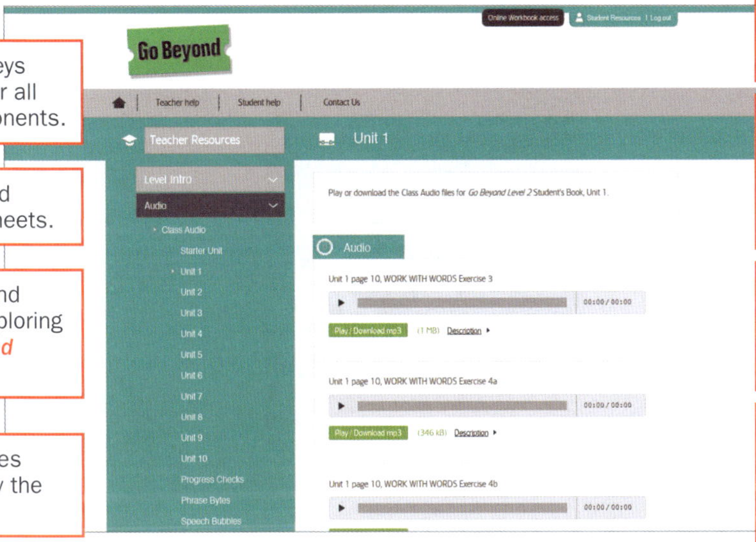

Tips and model answers to accompany the Student's Book and Workbook writing tasks.

A teacher-delivered speaking section to accompany every Student's Book Progress Check.

Static PDF tests for each unit and for the beginning, middle, and end of each level.

A link to special ***Move Beyond*** materials on www.onestopenglish.com, as well as access to other useful onestopenglish resources.

Presentation Kit

The Presentation Kit includes a projectable digital version of the ***Move Beyond*** Student's Book for teachers to use in class to promote "eyes-up" learning and student interaction. Easily downloadable to multiple devices from mee2.macmillaneducation.com, the Presentation Kit can also be used for lesson preparation at home.

Once downloaded, the Presentation Kit can be used offline. Audio recordings, videos, and answer keys are embedded in the pages for easy reference along with optional pop-up audio scripts and video subtitles, which are synched to the content. There are also fully interactive exercises to work through as a class.

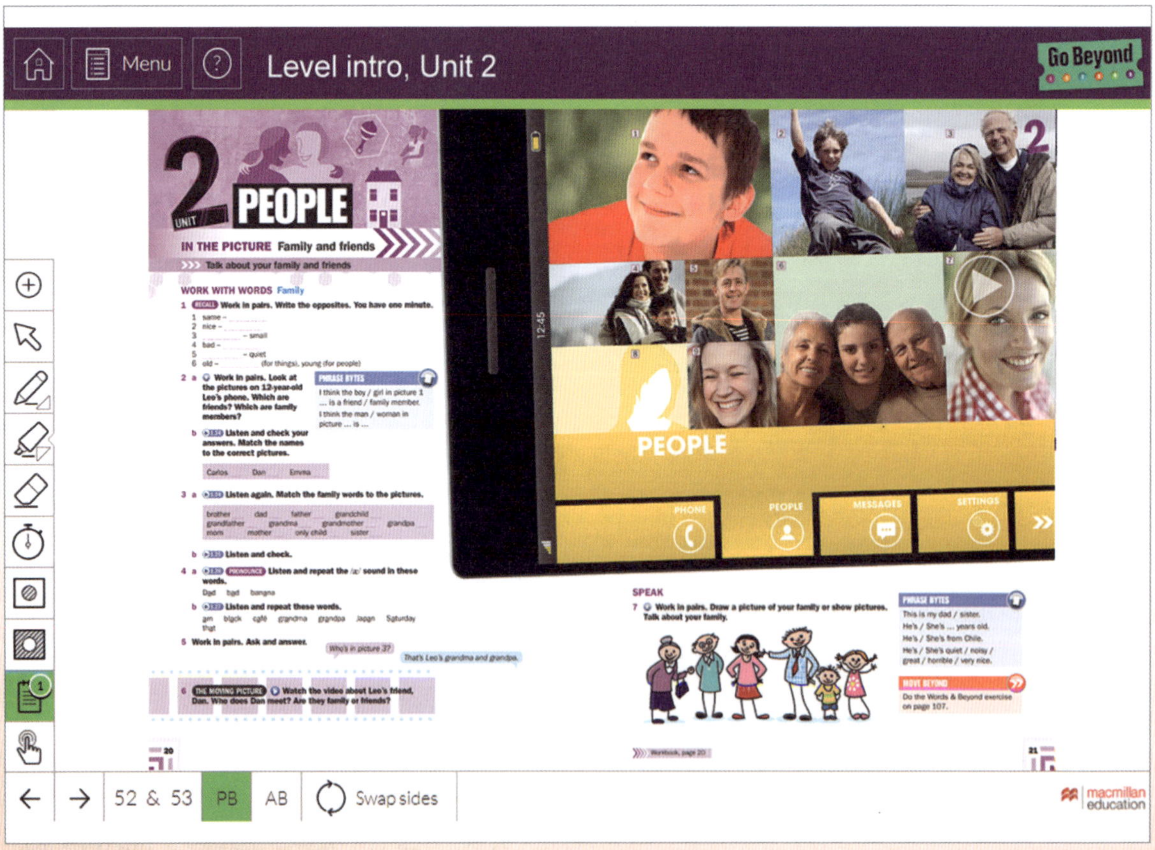

MOVE BEYOND DIGITAL

Move Beyond videos

There is a video for each *Move Beyond* unit, adding richness and variety to the material. The Moving Picture videos from the opening spreads bring global experiences into the classroom. The videos include documentary clips, vox pops, slideshows, digital animation, and YouTube-style videos. These engaging visuals support listening skills and act as conversation starters.

The *Move Beyond* videos are embedded in the Presentation Kit and supplied on a DVD-ROM at the back of the combined Student's Book/Workbook. Teachers can also access them at home via the Teacher's Resource Center.

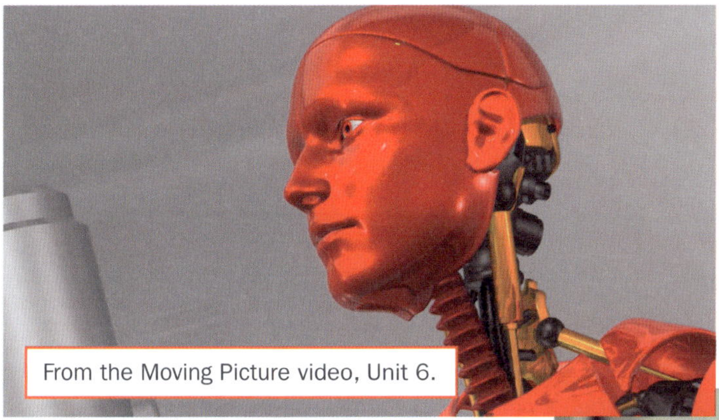

From the Moving Picture video, Unit 6.

From the Moving Picture video, Unit 5.

Video Tips

You can extend the activities or use the videos separately by using some of these video tips.

Before you watch

Students can predict what they'll see and hear in the video.

- Show students the title of the video or give them the topic and ask them to brainstorm vocabulary they think will come up.
- Show the video using the "Fast forward" option or show one or two stills from the video and ask students to predict what is happening or what people are saying.
- Show the first few seconds of the video and ask students to predict what will happen next.

While you watch

You can ask students to watch the videos normally or use just the picture or audio.

A Picture with no sound

- In pairs, one student watches and describes what he or she sees to a partner, who takes notes. They then watch together and discuss differences.
- Make a worksheet with screen shots from scenes in the video. Students write their own dialog or complete speech bubbles.
- Students write their own scripts for what they see. They then speak over the video, providing the narration or character voices. Finally, they compare their versions to the original.

B Sound with no picture

- Students listen to the sound only and speculate in pairs/groups about what they hear. They then watch to see if they were right.

C Picture and sound

- Students make notes as they watch and then compare notes with a partner or in groups.
- After showing the video a first time, give students cards with key words or phrases from the video. As students watch the video a second time, ask them to hold up their cards each time they hear the key word or phrase from their cards in the video.

After you watch

Use these activities in conjunction with the before/while you watch or as the main activity.

- Students create a fictional story, write a news story, or do a role-play based on the video or part of it.
- Students write an email or a text message to somebody in the video. They can also make a brochure, ad, fact file, or poster related to a topic or place in the video.
- Show students still photos of people from the video and ask them to make a brief biography for that person – name, age, nationality, family, likes and dislikes, hobbies, and favorite food.

TEACHING TIPS

To optimize your teaching experience with *Move Beyond*, we've put together some tips for the following key areas:

- Classroom management
- Teaching vocabulary and grammar
- Teaching skills
- Teaching pronunciation

Classroom management

Managing a classroom of teenagers is not always easy, and good classroom management, including organizing resources, creating an effective learning environment, monitoring student progress, and anticipating potential obstacles to learning, is crucial for keeping students on track. The following tips will help you maximize the time in the classroom and ensure a productive learning environment.

Set time limits

Realistic time limits challenge students and engage them in the task so that they are less likely to be disruptive. Use the as a guide for what proportion of the lesson you should spend on each task. Set the time limit after you have explained the task and checked that students understand the instructions. You can give regular updates on the time remaining for a task. For example, during a three-minute task you might give a *One minute to go* warning, then *Only thirty seconds left ...*, etc.

Encourage peer checking

Students appreciate the opportunity to look at a partner's answers to make sure they have the right idea. If students are allowed to compare their answers, they'll have more confidence in them and therefore will be more likely to volunteer them. It also gives students an opportunity to develop their ability to compare and explain in English why they chose their answers.

At this age, students are often frightened of making mistakes in front of their peers. Point out to students, whenever possible, that making mistakes is positive, reminding them that the most successful learners are usually the ones who are not afraid to experiment and make mistakes.

Vary selection techniques

Keep students alert by varying the ways you select them to answer questions. Alternate between selecting students to give answers and asking for volunteers in order to involve all students in the process of checking answers.

Another option is to select a student and let him or her decide which question to answer. This is good for less confident students, as it allows them to answer questions that they are more likely to have right. This student can then choose who will answer the next question. Alternatively, if you have closely monitored students while they were doing the exercise, "randomly" call on the students who have the correct answers. Both of these techniques are good for giving students confidence to speak and offer up their answers in class.

Correct errors effectively

It is important not to overcorrect, as this can make students lose confidence. However, undercorrecting leads to students developing bad language habits and decreases their ability to communicate in the long term. When students are carrying out pairwork exercises, the focus is on fluency, and it's better not to correct errors. However, monitor students and note important errors and good use of language to go over at the end of the exercise in a feedback session. Allow a few minutes of class time for error correction. Write the errors on the board without saying who made the mistake and elicit correct answers from the class.

Reward students

You can reward students for good answers or improvement with instant feedback, but it's also useful to create a system to be used throughout the term in which points are awarded for improvement, effort, or work in a particular skill or area. Award certificates or small prizes for students at the end of the term. Longer-term goals can help keep students motivated throughout the year.

Be aware of different learning styles

Different students have different ways of learning. Ensure that each student is catered to by varying approaches and activities to include a combination of visual (pictures, presentations, writing), auditory (listening, pair, and group conversation activities), and kinesthetic (moving, computer work) activities.

Be sensitive

Some students may not want their problems shared with the class. Use your discretion when discussing any personal topics in class and be prepared to have an alternative task ready if students are not willing to join the discussion.

Teaching vocabulary and grammar

The following tips give you some ideas for teaching vocabulary and grammar, as well as some reminders about commonly confused words and forms.

Remembering words

Encourage students to practice vocabulary by saying words in English when they go to various places. Recommend to students that they spend 10–15 minutes every day writing lists of vocabulary and saying these words aloud. The more they repeat this procedure, the more they will familiarize themselves with the words. Students can surround themselves with English by labeling their home with stickers or sticky notes. Ask students to think of their own methods for remembering vocabulary and to try it for a month. At the end of the month, ask them to give feedback to the class on whether their methods were successful.

Words in context

In ***Move Beyond*** students always meet new language within a context first so that they can see how the target language is used and in what situations. Encourage students to learn in this way outside the classroom too by choosing three students each month to be "Culture reporter," "Music reporter," and "News reporter." Ask them to spend one hour researching their areas on the internet and to report anything interesting they find back to the class.

Test before you teach

Starting a grammar lesson with a *test-before-you-teach* type activity helps you find out how much students already know. If students have problems with form and use in the initial stage, you may need to provide more guidance during the lesson. However, if students are familiar with form and use, you can move more quickly through the lesson.

Make students grammar experts

Each Student's Book contains a Grammar Database with a reference to all grammar points from that level. As a review activity, when you are coming to the end of the level, put students in groups of three or four and assign each group a grammar point from the database that they have studied. Tell them that they have 10 minutes to become "experts" on this grammar and that they should prepare a short presentation of this point with a couple of examples to demonstrate it. Give the groups 10–15 minutes to prepare their presentations. Then put students into new groups with each of the different grammar points represented. Students then peer-teach their grammar points to their groups.

Recall, recycle, review

The ***Move Beyond*** course is structured so that students have the opportunity to recall previously learned vocabulary, recycle new language throughout the unit, and review what they have learned.

Look for other ways to incorporate these three stages; for example, by using games to review language or having short conversations at the beginning of the lesson to recycle language in a different context.

A2+ Adjectives ending in *-ed* and *-ing*

Point out to students that adjectives ending in *-ed* describe how you feel. Adjectives ending in *-ing* usually describe the effect that something has on your ideas and feelings.

Like all adjectives, *-ing* and *-ed* adjectives can be used in front of a noun and can be modified by adverbs such as *very* and *really*. They can also be used in the comparative and superlative forms, for example, *... are always more exciting than other games.*

A2+ *Watch* or *see*?

When talking about movies, television, sports, plays, etc., we generally use *watch* to emphasize that the experience is in progress, whereas we use *see* to talk about a complete performance. For example:

I love watching television in the evenings.

We were watching a soccer game when you called.

Last night I saw a great show on TV.

Have you ever seen The Sound of Music?

A2+ *When* and *while*

While and *when* introduce information related to time. We use *when* to talk about something that interrupts a longer action or event: *John was cooking when the phone rang.*

We usually use *while* to indicate that during the time that an action was in progress, another event occurred. However, *when* can also be used in this case: *While John was cooking, the phone rang. / When John was cooking, the phone rang.*

A2+ *Funny* or *fun*?

Students often confuse these two words, so it is worth pointing out the difference:

funny is an adjective used to describe things or people that make us laugh;

fun is both a noun (e.g., *We had fun at the party*) and an adjective (e.g., *We had a fun time at the party).*

Suggest to students that if they are talking about something that makes them laugh, they should use *funny*. If they are talking about something that they enjoy, they should use *fun*.

A2+ Stative verbs

All verbs in English are classified as either stative verbs or action verbs. Stative verbs refer to the way things are, whereas action verbs refer to things we do. The most important difference between stative and action verbs is that action verbs can be used in progressive tenses and stative verbs are rarely used in progressive tenses. Generally, stative verbs fall into four groups: verbs describing thought or opinions (e.g., *know, understand)*, verbs showing emotions (e.g., *love, hate, want, need*), verbs showing possession (e.g., *have, belong*), and verbs showing senses (e.g., *hear, smell).*

A2+ Present progressive tense

The present progressive is especially common with the expressions *tonight, tomorrow, this weekend*, etc., and with these verbs: *go, come, meet, see, leave,* and *arrive*.

It's often used for talking about definite arrangements and plans such as appointments and meetings (e.g., *On October 23rd I'm seeing my doctor).* Try to incorporate this use into informal classroom conversation, asking students: *What are you doing this Saturday? Where are you going this evening?*

A2+ Countable and uncountable nouns

Countable nouns can be used in both the singular and the plural form (e.g., *one egg, four eggs*). Uncountable nouns, on the other hand, generally do not divide into separate units and cannot be easily counted. Many nouns can be both, depending on whether we're using them as units or as a mass; for example, *glass* (the material used for windows) is uncountable but *a glass* (something you drink from) is countable.

Like many other grammar points, you can review countable and uncountable nouns in the reading texts during the course. When students have finished reading, you can ask them to find as many examples as they can of both types of noun in the text.

A2+ Articles

Choosing the correct article (*a, an, the,* or zero article) can be difficult for learners of English at any stage. Remember always to teach new nouns with *a* or *an* so that the use becomes natural for students. The following activity can help students learn one of the differences between *a* and *the*. Place some real objects (e.g., books) around the room. Drill two simple sentences: *Could you pass me the book, please?* and *Could you pass me a book, please?* Whenever they say *the,* they must point at the specific object they want. When they use *a,* they lift both hands in a general "asking" gesture. The listener now gives them what they asked for (i.e., either a specific book or any book). This student then makes a new request.

A2+ Adjectival phrases

Students often want to know why certain prepositions are used with certain adjectives or verbs. Unfortunately there is no simple formula, so memorizing the dependent prepositions is often the only answer.

Some ideas that can help students memorize adjective + preposition combinations are:

- to use them in sentences that mean something personal to students (e.g., *My grandmother's scared of spiders).*
- to group adjectives according to the prepositions that go with them (e.g., *of* with *tired, scared,* and *full).*

Teaching skills

Writing

Make it a group activity

Try to incorporate group work into writing lessons so that it is not always a solitary activity. Put students into small groups to brainstorm ideas before they write. Allow students to work together on one piece of written work.

Ask students to write to or email you

Schedule a task once a month where students email or write to you with a response to a set question. This could be anything from *What is your favorite lesson from the unit so far? Why?* to *What are your goals in English?* Remember to indicate to them whether you expect a formal or informal email/letter. This is a very effective way to get feedback from your students and to get them into the routine of regular writing.

Dictation activities

Dictation activities are very useful for practicing listening and writing accuracy. Try to avoid just reading long chunks of text aloud and instead work on using shorter but more engaging dictation activities. This suggestion can work well and can incorporate recently studied vocabulary sets:

- Read a numbered list of descriptions of words aloud (e.g., *Number 1, the name of your favorite band; Number 2, the last person you saw*).
- Students should write down their own answers.
- When they've finished their lists, dictate a short story that you've written, but with blanks where students will write their own chosen words. For example, *I was walking through the park when I met [Number 1]. [Number 2] was singing with them.*
- Ask one or two students to read their versions aloud at the end.

Speaking

Keep topics interesting and relevant

The topics in ***Move Beyond*** are all designed to be relevant and engaging to teenagers. When you are doing any speaking task, make sure it will be something your class will want to talk about so that students will make an effort to try to communicate on the topic.

Be patient

Don't be tempted to interrupt or to start talking when students hesitate. Remember to give some time after asking students a question, as they need to assimilate the language and prepare their responses. Avoid repeating the question in different ways, as this will disrupt their train of thought.

Manage class discussions

In class discussions, it is common for the more confident students to dominate, but it is important for you to act as a facilitator and encourage everyone to speak. The following technique can be used to ensure that everyone speaks, and physical movement helps maintain interest.

- Put students in pairs and label them A or B. The As stand in a circle facing outward. The Bs stand in a bigger circle around them facing inward, each facing their partners.
- Read the first discussion question aloud and give students two minutes to discuss it with their partners.
- Clap your hands as a signal for the B students to move one place to the right, and either discuss the same question or the next one.
- After four or five turns, ask students to sit down again, and you can then choose one or two students to give their opinions.

Disappearing conversation

Write a short, six-line conversation on the board and ask your students to read it aloud and then to practice it in pairs. Start erasing one or two words at a time and ask students to read it aloud again. Soon they will be able to remember the whole conversation with nothing written on the board.

TEACHING TIPS

Listening

Encourage prediction

Predicting content is something that we all do in our first language before and while we are listening.

- **Predict the topic.** Where possible, draw students' attention to any images on the Student's Book page and ask them what they think the topic will be.
- **Predict the speakers.** Hand out printouts of the audio script for a chosen conversation in the Student's Book. Ask students to cover the speakers' names with a piece of paper, and then ask them to read the conversation and guess the age, gender, and relationship between the speakers. Write their ideas on the board and after you have listened to the audio, check whether any of their guesses were correct.
- **Predict the word.** While playing the audio track, press the pause button mid-sentence and ask students if they can predict the next word. Repeat this process throughout the track. At the end of the exercise, ask students if any of their guesses were correct and if so, why they chose that word. Remember not to comment on the accuracy of their guesses during the exercise – the goal isn't to get everything right, but to concentrate on the language and topic in order to make guessing possible.

Loop dictation

Loop dictation is a technique that you can use in reading lessons. Loop dictation gives students the chance to listen more intensively, and can be used to introduce a reading text.

- Select the first paragraph (or small section) of the reading text from the lesson. Make sure students have their books closed.
- Start reading aloud at a natural, but steady, speed and ask them to write down what they hear.
- When you get to the end, go straight back to the start and read again so you are repeating the text in a continuous "loop."
- When a student thinks he or she has a perfect version of the text, he or she calls out, "Stop!" Put students into groups of three or four to allow them to compare what they have. Then allow them to open their books and check against the original.

Make students active listeners

In most listening exercises, students take a passive "eavesdropping" role that doesn't really prepare them for all situations in which they will be expected to both listen and react. To give them some practice at reading and then responding, choose a conversation from the Student's Book or Workbook and read the first line aloud. Ask students to take on the other role (without looking at the audio script). Once they have heard your line, they should respond. Continue the process (either by using the next line of the conversation or by responding to what students have said). At the end, hand out copies of the audio script.

Reading

Jigsaw reading

For longer pieces of reading, put students in pairs and give them a section each to read. When they have finished reading, encourage students to tell each other what they have read and to ask each other questions. Then allow time for them to read the full piece.

Encourage prediction

As with listening, being able to predict what's coming can help understanding. Tell students they are going to read a particular type of text (e.g., a recipe, a letter of complaint, or some instructions on how to drive a car). Have these texts ready on handouts, but don't give them to students yet. Put students in pairs and give them five minutes to write down five words or phrases they think they will read in the text. Then hand out the texts and ask them to circle the words and phrases if they find them.

What's the context?

Knowing the context of a text can help students with the content and goal. Put students in pairs and give each pair a set of decontextualized words and sentences for them to read. Give them five minutes to answer the following questions:

- Where does the word/sentence/text come from?
- Who might be reading it and when?
- What does it mean?

Some ideas to use are:

- Danger! This animal can bite!
- Click *Start* and *Run*.
- No eating in the waiting room.
- Turn left at the first traffic light and turn right at the second corner.

Teaching pronunciation

Be aware of how sounds are made

Pronunciation can often be overlooked in the classroom, but it is a key part of students' ability to communicate effectively, and in a more passive sense, to listen and understand language. When approaching pronunciation tasks, make sure that students are aware of all the factors involved in making sounds (the position of the tongue, lips, etc.) and that you can explain how to make them. Remember that the primary goal is not for students to sound like native speakers but for them to produce the sounds in a way that allows them to communicate effectively.

Vary drilling techniques

Drilling can be a useful technique if employed in the right way. Make sure you vary the type of drilling you do with your class so that it does not become monotonous and meaningless repetition. Choral drilling (the whole class repeating a word or phrase together after you) works well when students are saying new language for the first time, and you can then move to individuals. Back-chaining (starting at the end of the phrase or word and building up a syllable or chunk at a time) works particularly well with longer sentences. You can alter your delivery (e.g., to a "whisper drill") if your class is becoming a bit noisy.

TEACHING TIPS

Stressed and unstressed articles

Articles and prepositions are often unstressed when we speak. This means they are produced more rapidly and with a glide. Drill the stressed (strong) and unstressed (weak) forms:

of /əv/ (weak), /ɒv/ (strong)

a /ə/ (weak), /eɪ/ (strong)

an /ən/ (weak), /æn/ (strong)

Content words are the important words that carry the meaning or sense in a phrase and are therefore usually stressed (these are usually nouns, main verbs, and adjectives).

Sentence stress

Function words are not usually stressed in English. When these words are unstressed, a weak form of the word is used:

you /jə/ (weak) /juː/ (strong)

the /ðə/ (weak) /ðiː/ (strong)

will /wəl/ (weak) /wɪl/ (strong)

Raising awareness of sentence stress will not only help improve students' pronunciation, but will help their listening skills as they will become used to listening for the content words and to hearing the weak forms of function words.

Stressed and unstressed form of *was*

Counting the number of words in a sentence and sentence dictations are useful activities that can help raise awareness of weak forms. Point out to students that the pronunciation of *was* changes according to its position in the sentence. At the beginning or end of a sentence it is stressed. In the middle of a sentence it is often unstressed:

Was the owl holding something? Yes, it was. /wɒz/

It was flying. /wəz/

A2+ Simple past

In the simple past, the regular verb ending *-ed* is pronounced /d/ after all voiced consonant sounds and /t/ after all voiceless consonant sounds. Remind students that we do not pronounce the preceding *e* in either of these cases – the extra syllable is only pronounced on verbs that end in a *t* or *d*.

Point out to students that the difference between the /d/ and /t/ is very small, and it is much more important to remember to pronounce /ɪd/ after verbs that end in *t* and *d*. In fact, many teachers do not insist on the distinction between the /t/ and /d/ endings on past tense regular verbs (e.g., *opened* vs. *walked*), preferring to focus simply on whether or not there is an extra syllable (e.g., *started*, *ended*, *visited*).

The important thing is to make sure that students differentiate between the simple present and simple past by clearly pronouncing the /t/, /d/, or /ɪd/ ending.

A2+ Adjectives ending in *-ed*

Remind students that they follow the same pronunciation rules as the *-ed* endings in the simple past:

/d/ after a voiced sound (e.g., *surprised)*

/t/ after an unvoiced sound (e.g., *relaxed)*

/ɪd/ after *t* or *d* (e.g., *excited)*

Drill the *-ed* adjectives in Unit 10, page 107 chorally to practice the pronunciation.

A2+ Spelling *g* sounds → /g/, /dʒ/, /ʒ/

In the list of workplace vocabulary in Unit 7, page 76, three different sounds for the letter *g* are represented.

- In *travel agency*, the letter *g* is pronounced as /dʒ/.
- In *garage*, the first *g* is pronounced as /g/.
- In *garage*, the second *g* is pronounced either as /ʒ/ or /dʒ/. (This is because the word *garage* comes from French, where the second *g* would originally have been pronounced as /ʒ/. Many English speakers now anglicize the sound and say /dʒ/.)

A general rule is:

- when *g* is followed by *e*, *i*, or *y*, it is pronounced /dʒ/.
- when it is followed by *a*, *o*, *u*, *l*, or *r*, it is pronounced /g/.

However, there are many exceptions to this rule, such as *get*, *give*, etc.

A2+ Consonant clusters

Consonant sounds that occur together are known as consonant clusters. These can be difficult for students, particularly if the consonants are not normally pronounced together in their own language(s). If your students are having particular difficulty with any of the clusters in the words, try isolating the cluster and ask them to repeat the two sounds a number of times without a pause (e.g., /brbrbrbr/, or /stststst/). You could also try back-chaining (i.e., building up the sounds in the word from the end to the beginning, e.g., *bridge*: /dʒ/, /ɪdʒ/, /rɪdʒ/, /brɪdʒ/).

A2+ /tʃ/ sound

The /tʃ/ sound is made by raising the middle of the tongue to the hard palate behind the teeth and blowing air through forcefully to create a small explosion. The most common spelling for the /tʃ/ sound is *ch*. However, this sound is also found in words with *-ture*, as in *nature*, *picture*, and *furniture*. You may want to contrast the /tʃ/ sound with the /ʃ/ sound, as in *share*. If your students are having difficulty with /tʃ/ sound, ask them to repeat the minimal pairs *share/chair* or *wash/watch*. Tell them that /tʃ/ is an abrupt sound, whereas /ʃ/ can continue as long as they have enough breath!

GAMES

Used judiciously, games can be a very useful tool in the classroom. Not only can they inject energy and a change of tempo, they can also be used to practice and consolidate target language. The games below can be adapted for use with different target language.

The Book Quiz

The book quiz is a good way of starting the course and familiarizing students with the Student's Book, but it can also be used as a way of reviewing topics later in the term. Have 10 questions about the book ready (e.g., *How many units are there? What's the topic of Unit 5? On what page can you find a list of irregular verbs?*). Read the questions aloud, and the student who is quickest at finding the answer wins.

Hot Seat

Divide the class into three or four teams. Place three or four chairs separately, each facing the class with the board or a screen behind them. Each team elects one person to sit in the hot seat. Each team has two minutes to describe as much vocabulary as they can for their team member in the hot seat to guess the word.

Explain that teams can't say the word, act out the word, draw the word, spell the word, or point to the word.

Write the first word on the board or screen. If the first person in the hot seat guesses, another student comes to the front, and so on. If the word is too difficult for the person in the hot seat, they can "pass" to the next person.

Example: *riding a bicycle*. Possible clues: *It's an activity. You do it in your free time. There are two wheels. You use your legs.*

Broken Telephone

Divide the class into groups of about 10 students, from the front to the back of the classroom.

Give one student in each group a sentence to memorize (e.g., *Dave's cousin is coming to stay at 10 o'clock on Friday morning).*

Each student whispers the sentence to the next student, and so on, until it reaches the last person in the group.

The last person in the group then says the sentence out loud. The first person says whether the original sentence has changed, and if so, how.

Kim's Game

- Show students about 10 everyday objects (or objects related to the lesson vocabulary) one by one (e.g., a pen, sticky notes, a cell phone, some keys, a watch, a hairbrush, some tissue, a wallet, an apple). Check that they know the name of each one.
- Place them on the table and cover them with a cloth.
- Encourage students to work in pairs to remember what's there and where the objects are (e.g., *The pen is next to the cell phone*, etc).
- To make sure students speak in English, write the sentence prompt: *There's a* ________ *and a* ________ .

Snowman

To elicit a word or phrase or to give extra practice at spelling, write short lines for each letter of the word or phrase on the board and invite students to guess letters. For each incorrect guess, draw a part of a snowman: one circle for the head, one for the body, then two arms, three buttons, a hat, two eyes, and a smile.

Mystery Word

This game can be used to introduce students to some of the techniques they will be using in Unit 1, where they look at the subskill of understanding new words when reading.

- On the board, write a nonsense word like *flib*.
- Tell students that *flib* is a mystery word and that to guess the word they will need some more information.
- Now write *a flib* and ask students what they now know about the word (i.e., that it is a noun). Prompt them by underlining the article.
- Next add: *We use a flib to eat ...* Elicit ideas for the meaning of *flib*. Prompt students by asking: *What do we use to eat?* and miming someone eating with utensils. Write students' suggestions on the board.
- Finally write: *We use a flib to eat soup.* Ideally, students will come up with *spoon*, or possibly *bowl*. Either could be correct.
- Remind students how important it is to think about the meaning of the words that come before and after the mystery word, as well as to recognize what *type* of word the mystery word is.

If you have time, play the mystery word game again with *flib* as a verb; for example, *flib / I flib / I flib English ... / I flib English because it is a useful language in the world today*.

Three in a Row

This can be used to review vocabulary or grammar.

- Divide the class into two teams and draw a 3x3 grid on the board.
- In each cell write words from a vocabulary set or verbs in the base form.
- One team chooses a cell and has to form a correct sentence using that word. If the word is a verb, the sentence must also use the target tense(s) (e.g., simple past or past progressive).
- If their sentence is correct, they "take" the cell and it's the other team's turn.
- The goal is to get three cells in a row. The game can be adapted for use with many of the language items, and a larger grid can be used to make it last longer and improve the opportunities for tactical game play.

Twenty Questions

This is a good game to practice question formation, as well as vocabulary.

- Ask one student to think of an object, a person, or a place.
- The rest of the class can ask 20 questions, but the student can answer only *yes* or *no*.
- After 20 questions, the class has to guess what the object, person, or place is.

Categories

Group students in teams of four or five and ask them to write the names of three or four recently studied vocabulary sets, each at the top of a separate column (e.g., *technology, rooms in a house, classroom objects*). Choose a letter of the alphabet and give students two minutes to come up with as many words beginning with that letter as they can that are connected to the categories and write them in the correct column. After two minutes, choose another letter. When students have tried with three letters, count up the number of correctly spelled words; the team with the most points wins.

USING THE *MOVE BEYOND* TEACHER'S EDITION

This Teacher's Edition is a valuable and practical resource. With its clear and comprehensive teaching notes, audio scripts and answer keys, background notes, and extra features, it will help you plan and deliver impactful, well-paced, and memorable lessons.

The unit topic, content, and lesson objectives of each unit are clearly presented.

The target language, functions, and stages of each lesson are outlined, with suggested timings for each stage shown visually to help you pace your lesson. The darker gray shading shows the part of the lesson already completed, and the lighter gray shows the amount of time allocated for each stage.

The Get Started feature provides an activity to start the lesson and is an opportunity to recycle language and prepare students for the lesson. These warm-ups don't require any additional preparation or materials.

Activities that recycle language are labeled with the recycle icon.

Clear and concise procedural notes maximize the Student's Book material.

Alternative procedure suggestions are provided, offering a different approach to teaching the Student's Book content. These alternatives appeal to different learning styles and abilities.

Useful and interesting background information on specific lesson topics is provided to help with the presentation of the content.

UNIT 4 WHAT'S COOKING?

IN THE PICTURE Inside the kitchen

Talk about food and cooking

Page 40–41

STAGE	TIME	FOCUS
GET STARTED		Practice the pronunciation of /uː/ in *food* (/fuːd/) and /ʊ/ in *cook* (/kʊk/) and introduce the theme of the unit.
WORK WITH WORDS		Recycle food vocabulary and learn ne[...] Watch a video about a summer camp [...]
SPEAK		Talk about food you like and what you [...]

Get started

Write the following two sentences with blanks on the board and ask students to think of the words to fill in the blanks (the target words are *food* and *cook*).

That's my favorite restaurant. The ___ is always delicious.
You need to ___ potatoes for 20 minutes.

Drill the *oo* in *food* (/fuːd/) and tell students that the /uː/ sound is very common in English. Point out that the major characteristic of this sound is that your lips form a small circle.

Drill the *oo* in *cook* (/kʊk/) by asking students to create the sound by starting with /uː/ and then relaxing the lips to a /ʊ/. Drill both sounds, first chorally and then individually, using other suitable words such as the following: *tooth* (/tuːθ/), *took* (/tʊk/), *tooth* (/tuːθ/), *took* (/tʊk/).

Play *Pronunciation Maze*. Draw this pronunciation maze on the board and ask students to find a way across the maze, starting from *food* and moving through words in the /uː/ route across, up, or down until they get to *zoo*. Explain that the line must connect one word with another without other words between them, and that they will not necessarily use all of the words with the /uː/ sound.

hook	*foot*	*took*	*football*
food	*school*	*looked*	*soon*
good	*tooth*	*book*	*stood*
cool	*room*	*too*	*look*
wood	*notebook*	*choose*	*cook*
spoon	*hood*	*kangaroo*	*zoo*

ANSWERS
food, school, tooth, room, too, choose, kangaroo, zoo

Draw students' attention to the title of the unit and ask [...]em what they think the unit is going to be about (*food, dri[...] and health*). Point out that *What's cooki[...]* can mean "What's happening?" or "What's going on?" [...]n slang.

WORK WITH WORDS

1 RECALL

- Refer students to the example words in the table and elicit another example for each heading.
- Divide the class into pairs to brainstorm and add more words. Set a three-minute time limit for this.
- Write the list headings on the board and invite students to call out more words for you to write up.
- Highlight the pronunciation of *steak* (/steɪk/), as many students find this word difficult to pronounce. Drill the words, first chorally, and then individually.
- Ask students to do the **Work with Words** task on page 72.

Alternative procedure

You could make this into a competition to see which pair can think of the most correctly spelled words in three minutes. After three minutes, ask pairs to exchange lists.

Elicit food words from the class and write them on the board. Inform students that they can give one point for every correctly spelled word and two points for a correctly spelled word that no one else has thought of. Invite students to total up their points at the end of the exercise to see which pair has won.

MOVE BEYOND FOR TEACHERS

Tomato – vegetable or fruit?

Tomatoes are often called vegetables; however, a tomato is technically the fruit of the tomato plant.

2 44

- Refer students to the photos and explain that they are going to listen to someone giving instructions in the kitchen. Ask students to predict what they think the instructions could be for each photo.

76

USING THE *MOVE BEYOND* TEACHER'S EDITION

Answer keys and audio scripts are embedded within the teaching notes.

- Encourage students to listen for any food words from Exercise 1 and use these to help them identify the correct photo. Play the track and ask them to write the letters for the photos (a–e) in the order they hear them.
- Let students compare their answers in pairs before you check them as a class.

ANSWERS / AUDIO SCRIPT 44

1 c 2 a 3 d 4 b 5 e

OK. So first you beat the eggs in a large bowl like this. After that, you chop an onion – carefully. Don't forget to do it on a cutting board. Then you heat some oil in a frying pan and fry the chicken. Here's some lemon juice. You pour the lemon juice into a saucepan and stir slowly. Now, with a knife, you cut some bread. I love the smell of fresh bread!

3 45

- Refer students to the words for kitchen equipment and ask them to find each item in one of the photos. Draw students' attention to the example before they start.
- Check answers as a class by choosing different students to point to the items.
- Play the track for students to listen and repeat.

ANSWERS / AUDIO SCRIPT 45

2 d 3 c 4 a; c; e 5 a; e

See Student's Book, page 40, for audio script.

Fast finishers

Ask fast finishers to find the silent letters in these words in Exercise 2 (*bowl*, *board*, *knife*).

4 46

- Play the track for students to listen and repeat the words.

AUDIO SCRIPT

See Student's Book, page 40.

Activity suggestions for fast finishers are provided throughout the lessons.

5 47

- Refer students back to the words ... explain that these are the answer ...
- After students have filled in the blanks, play the track for them to listen and check.

ANSWERS / AUDIO SCRIPT 47

2 chop 3 cutting board 4 frying pan 5 fry 6 pour 7 saucepan 8 knife

See Student's Book, page 40, for audio script.

6a

- Divide the class into pairs to match the verbs in Exercise 4 to some of the words they wrote in Exercise 1. Draw students' attention to the examples before they start.
- Encourage students to make a list of their collocations in their notebooks to study later.

6b

- In the same pairs, ask students to act out some of the actions. You could ask a pair of more confident students to demonstrate this activity first for the class.

Alternative procedure

Divide the class into two teams. A volunteer from each team comes to the front of the class and acts out cooking instructions for the team to guess. If the team guesses correctly, the team wins a point and a volunteer from the other team comes to the front. Set a time limit (e.g., two minutes). The team with the most points at the end of the time wins the game.

7 THE MOVING PICTURE

- Elicit the meaning of the acronym *NYC* (*New York City*). Explain to students that they are going to watch a video about a summer camp for teenagers.
- Play the video and encourage students to write down things they like and don't like about Passport NYC.
- Let students compare their answers in pairs and discuss whether they would like to go to Passport NYC and why or why not.
- In a class discussion, invite different students to report what their partner said.

VIDEO SCRIPT

Narrator:	Are you a foodie? Do you love food? Join us at Passport NYC – the summer camp for teenage foodies. Spend the summer in New York City and learn to cook with some of the city's top chefs! At Passport NYC, teens from all over the world come to New York City to live, have fun, and learn about cooking with professionals.
Chef:	You finish cooking in the curry sauce. OK? But right now what I've done is I've forced the sugars out of them ... brown them a little bit ... Everything hands on, that's the whole process. We don't want them to sit back and watch me cook. I know how to cook. We want them to be in the forefront and experience the unknown. To get really a sense of what it would be to work professionally in the kitchen, not just learning how to cook for home.
Zoe:	Other campers are from everywhere. There's some from Mexico, and one of my roommates is from Taiwan, and D.C., and Jersey.
Aaron:	It's a really, really, really good way to meet people that you really wouldn't normally hang out with that have the same interests as you and you start to make a whole new other group of friends.
Narrator:	Come to New York City, learn to cook, make friends, and have fun.

Complete scripts for the Moving Picture videos are embedded in the lesson notes.

- ... students to the advertisement on page 41. Divide the class into pairs to answer the questions. Allow two minutes.
- Elicit different students' answers in a class discussion.

Alternative procedure

Try a mix of pair work and group work. Question 1 is more straightforward and suited to pair work. Questions 2 and 3 could be discussed in small groups. Alternating groupings gives students a chance to work with different students and varies the rhythm of work.

Extra activity

Recycle the simple present. Divide the class into groups to write about a typical day's activities at the Passport NYC summer camp. In a less confident class, brainstorm activities (e.g., *get up*, *have an English class*, *learn how to cook a new dish*, *clean the kitchen*, *have lunch*, *have a workshop with a famous chef*, *visit the Statue of Liberty*). Encourage students to start: *On a typical day at Passport NYC, we ... .*

The optional extra activities provide ideas for extending the lesson and offering additional practice.

MOVE BEYOND

Ask students to do the **Move Beyond** task on page 72.

Homework

Ask students to write a diary entry for a day at Passport NYC. Encourage them to describe what they learned to cook, what they ate, and which famous chef they met.

Task-based homework is provided at the end of every lesson and is related to the topic or skill of the lesson.

77

Other features

The Teacher's Edition also contains:

Procedural notes for the Unit Reviews and Progress Checks
Full and detailed notes are given for the Unit Reviews and Progress Checks in the Student's Book.

Workbook answer keys and audio scripts
At the back of the Teacher's Edition, answer keys and audio scripts are given for the corresponding Workbook.

Teaching Tips
Pages 24–29 of the Teacher's Edition provide useful tips on classroom management; teaching vocabulary, grammar, skills, and pronunciation; and using games in the classroom.

A DAY IN DYLAN'S LIFE

STAGE	TIME	FOCUS
GET STARTED		Play a game to help students and teachers learn names quickly.
BEFORE SCHOOL: THINK AND READ		Talk about activities that you do before school. Read the comic strip and compare your activities with the activities in the story.
RECALL		Recycle vocabulary to talk about your family, clothes, and everyday objects, and grammar structures *have* and *there is/there are*.
AFTER SCHOOL: THINK AND READ		Talk about activities that you do after school. Read the comic strip and identify a boy's activities.
RECALL		Recycle classroom phrases, likes and dislikes, and question words. Read about Dylan's life and write a description of your own life.

Get started

Play a game of *Quick-Fire Ball* to help students and teachers learn names quickly. Begin by saying your name: *My name's ... . What's your name?* and tossing a ball or scrunched up piece of paper to a student. That student responds by saying his or her name (e.g., *My name's Sara Johnson. What's your name?*) and so on.

BEFORE SCHOOL

Page 4

THINK AND READ

1

- Divide the board into two columns and label the column on the left *Before* and the column on the right *After*. Students will have a visual representation in their notebooks of before- and after-school activities, and they will be able to compare and contrast them easily.
- Ask students to close their books and think of three activities they do before school. Encourage them to share their answers and write them under the heading *Before*.

SUGGESTED ANSWERS

wake up, get up, brush my teeth, take a shower, wash my hands/face, have breakfast, get dressed, pack my bag, comb/brush my hair, watch TV

2 01

- Ask students to read the comic strip. Don't play the audio at this point.
- Ask students if the activities they thought of in Exercise 1 are in the story.
- Play the track and ask students to listen as they read the story again.

Extra activity

Ask some simple comprehension questions about the comic strip: *What time does Dylan wake up?* (seven o'clock in the morning); *What time does he get up?* (7:10–7:20); *How many sisters does he have?* (two); *How many bathrooms are there in Dylan's house?* (one); *What does he wear to school?* (black pants, a white shirt, a green sweatshirt, and black shoes); *Who does he have breakfast with?* (his dad); *What does he do at breakfast time?* (he watches TV); *How does he go to school?* (by bus); *Who does he meet on the bus?* (his friend); *What time does he get to school?* (8:30).

Divide the class into pairs to find as many differences as they can between what Dylan does before school and what they do.

AUDIO SCRIPT 01

See Student's Book, pages 6–7.

RECALL

1

- Refer students to the family tree and ask them to write the missing words for Dylan's family members.
- Let students compare their answers in pairs. Check answers as a class.

ANSWERS

1 grandparents 2 grandma (grandmother)
3 grandpa (grandfather) 4 uncle 5 dad (father)
6 mom (mother) 7 sister

Fast finishers

Fast finishers can write a list of other family members and share them with the class when everyone has finished the exercise (e.g., *brother*, *cousin*, *grandchildren*, *nephew*, *niece*).

2a 02

- Go over the example sentence with the class. Then ask students to complete the remaining sentences about Dylan.
- Play the track for students to listen and check their answers.
- Play the track again and encourage students to repeat the sentences, paying particular attention to the contracted forms.

ANSWERS / AUDIO SCRIPT 02

1 *Dylan has a mom and a dad.*
2 He has two sisters. He doesn't have any brothers.
3 Dylan's dad has a brother. He doesn't have a sister.
4 Dylan and his sisters don't have any cousins.
5 But they have four grandparents.

2b

- Divide the class into pairs to ask and answer questions about their own families. Remind them to use the words in Exercise 1.
- Before they start, invite two confident volunteers to demonstrate by reading the model exchange aloud.
- Circulate and monitor to give help as necessary.

3a

- Refer students back to the comic and ask them to find and underline eight words for clothes (e.g., *pants*).
- Ask them to add four more words to their list and to compare them in pairs and then in groups of four, each time adding any new items to the list.

ANSWERS
pants, jeans, shirt, sweatshirt, shoes, sneakers, skirt, dress
Other possible words for clothes: coat, hat, jacket, sweater, shorts, T-shirt, ...

3b

- Encourage students to say what their favorite clothes are. They could do this as a class or in groups.

Alternative procedure
Divide the class into pairs to describe their favorite clothes. Ask students to take turns listening to each other and drawing the clothes their partner describes. When they have finished, choose different students to tell the class about their favorite clothes.

4 (03)

- As a way of testing students' knowledge before reviewing or teaching these objects, play *Kim's Game* (see Games, page 29) with suitable items you can find around the classroom or in your own bag.
- Ask students to match the columns to form the names of the objects.
- Play the track for students to listen and check. Finally, elicit whether the objects are spelled as one word or two words.

ANSWERS / AUDIO SCRIPT (03)
1 *notebook* 2 lunchbox 3 class schedule 4 textbook
5 pencil case 6 house key

5a

- Ask students to write sentences using *there is/isn't* or *there are/aren't*. Elicit or point out that they need to look at the check mark or X to see whether the sentence should be affirmative or negative.
- Let students compare their answers in pairs before you check them as a class.

ANSWERS
2 there is a blue pencil case 3 there isn't a class schedule
4 there is a lunchbox 5 there aren't a lot of textbooks
6 there isn't a house key

5b

- Divide the class into pairs to take turns asking and answering questions about what there is in their school bags.
- Before they start, refer students to the model conversation and invite a confident pair of students to model the exchange first.
- Circulate and monitor to give help as necessary.

6

- Divide the class into pairs to tell each other about their morning routines.
- Before they start, draw students' attention to the model in the speech bubble.
- Monitor and note good use of language and errors to go over in a feedback session at the end of the exercise. (See Teaching Tips, *Correct errors effectively*, page 24)

AFTER SCHOOL *Page 6*

THINK AND READ

1

- Have students close their books. Write the heading *After* on the right-hand side of the board next to the list of *Before* activities from earlier or rewrite the list if necessary.
- Ask students to think of three activities they do after school. Encourage them to share their different activities as you write them under the *After* heading. Students now have a visual representation to copy into their notebooks, allowing them to compare and contrast before- and after-school activities easily.
- Refer students to the list in the book and ask them to check the things they usually do after school.

2 (04)

- Ask students to listen and read the comic strip and find out which of the things mentioned in Exercise 1 Dylan does today.
- Check by choosing a student to answer the question.

ANSWER / AUDIO SCRIPT (04)
Dylan meets people, goes to a club, and does homework.
See Student's Book, pages 8–9, for audio script.

RECALL

1 (05)

- Refer students back to the comic and ask them to find classroom phrases (*Close your books! For homework, write ...*).
- Go over the example sentence with the class and ask students to put the remaining classroom phrases in the correct order.
- Play the track for students to listen and check their answers.
- Play the track again for students to listen and repeat.

ANSWERS / AUDIO SCRIPT (05)
1 *Open your books to page 24.*
2 Can you repeat that, please?
3 I don't understand the question.
4 Can I go to the bathroom, please?
5 Can I borrow a pen, please?
6 How do you say "pizarra" in English?

2a (06)

- Read the example sentence aloud and ask students to write sentences for the remaining activities. Remind students that they need to look at the check mark or X to see whether the sentence should be affirmative or negative.
- Play the track for students to listen and check their answers.

ANSWERS / AUDIO SCRIPT (06)
1 *He likes cooking.*
2 He likes listening to music.
3 He likes reading.
4 He likes swimming.
5 He doesn't like acting.
6 He doesn't like speaking Spanish.

2b

- Divide the class into pairs to take turns telling each other which activities in Exercise 2a they like and dislike. Draw students' attention to the examples in the speech bubbles before they start.
- Encourage students to extend the conversation and tell their partner more activities they like or don't like.
- Circulate and monitor as they work.

3a 07

- Ask students to complete the conversation with the question words in the box. Go over the example before they start.
- When they have finished, play the track for students to listen and check their answers.
- Ask students: *Why does Dylan say he likes drama if he doesn't like acting?* Choose a student to answer the question.

ANSWERS / AUDIO SCRIPT 07

He doesn't tell the truth because he likes the girl.

Anna:	What time is it?
Dylan:	It's 4:15. Why do you want to know?
Anna:	I want to go to the drama club. When does it start?
Dylan:	At 4:30.
Anna:	Where does the club meet? Do you know?
Dylan:	In the auditorium.
Anna:	How long does it last?
Dylan:	Forty-five minutes.
Anna:	Who's the teacher?
Dylan:	Miss Harris. She's my class teacher.
Anna:	Do you like drama?
Dylan:	Um ... yes, I love it.

3b

- Divide the class into pairs to ask and answer questions about another school club in the comic strip (e.g., the music, cooking, swimming, Spanish, or book clubs).
- Draw students' attention to the model conversation. Point out that students may have to invent some of the information themselves.
- Monitor and note good use of language and errors to go over in a feedback session at the end of the exercise.

4a

- Ask students to read Dylan's homework and find the six false facts.
- Let students compare their answers in pairs before you check them as a class.

ANSWERS

2 He doesn't always get up at 7:10.
3 He has breakfast with his dad.
4 He doesn't wear jeans and sneakers to school.
5 His teacher's name is Miss Harris.
6 He doesn't always tell the truth.

4b

- Ask students to write a similar text about their own lives and include three false facts.
- Circulate and monitor as they work and offer support as needed.
- Divide the class into pairs to exchange their work and read each other's texts to find the false facts.
- In a class feedback session, invite different students to share a false fact from their partner's description and correct the false information.

Homework

Ask students to write a short text (at least 10 sentences) describing what they do before and after school. They should include one false sentence in their texts. At the beginning of the next class, divide the class into pairs to read their texts aloud to each other to guess which sentence is false.

1 SWITCH ON

UNIT

IN THE PICTURE An app for everything

Talk about communication and technology *Pages 8–9*

STAGE	TIME	FOCUS
GET STARTED		Brainstorm ways of communicating.
WORK WITH WORDS		Recycle vocabulary of technological devices. Introduce vocabulary related to apps.
SPEAK		Rank apps according to their usefulness. Discuss ideas for a new app. Watch a video of some teenagers talking about apps and discuss what they say.

Get started

Write the word *communication* on the board and elicit or provide a simple definition (e.g., *the ways we share information or tell other people about our ideas, feelings, opinions*).

Divide the class into pairs and give them two minutes to brainstorm different ways we communicate. If necessary, prompt them to think about these categories: *speaking*, *writing*, *body language*, *sounds*, *images*.

Elicit some examples and write a list on the board (e.g., ***Speaking:*** *face-to face, by telephone, by video*; ***Writing:*** *emails, text messages [SMS], instant messages, letters, stories, newspaper reports, articles*; ***Body language:*** *facial expressions, gestures*; ***Sounds:*** *songs, music*; ***Images:*** *emoticons, picture messages [MMS], art, photos*).

Encourage students to discuss which of these methods of communication they have used so far today.

WORK WITH WORDS

1 RECALL

- Divide the class into pairs to look at the pictures. Set a time limit of two minutes for them to make a list in their notebooks of the devices they can see, as well as any other things related to communication and technology that they already know. This activates any existing knowledge of the topic in preparation for the unit. (See Teaching Tips, *Recall, recycle, review*, page 25.)
- Check answers as a class and invite students to read any extra items they added to their lists aloud for you to write them on the board.
- Remind or explain to students that the word *device(s)* (/dɪˈvaɪs(ɪz)/) is used to describe all of the technological items they have listed (e.g., *A camera is a device for taking photos*).
- Ask students to do the **Work with Words** task on page 69.

ANSWERS

tablet, (desktop) computer, MP3 player, camera, laptop, game console

MOVE BEYOND FOR TEACHERS

Apps

App is short for *application*. (Don't mention this fact to students because in Exercise 6 they will be quizzed about this.)

Apps are computer programs usually used on cell phones or tablets that are designed to be practical or entertaining. A map app, for example, might allow you to check your location or give you directions to a particular address. Young people who are still in school have designed some very successful apps. Your students may find it motivating to learn about such cases. You can find examples via a quick search on the internet.

2

- Ask students to match the icons on page 9 to the kinds of apps listed in the box. Set a time limit of two minutes.
- As students finish, let them compare their answers in pairs. Don't confirm any answers at this point.

3 ▶08

- Play the track for students to check their answers.
- Play the track again for students to listen and repeat.

ANSWERS / AUDIO SCRIPT ▶08

1 maps 2 games 3 notes 4 messages 5 calculator 6 calendar 7 compass 8 social networking 9 web browser 10 mail 11 app store 12 videos

4a ▶09 PRONOUNCE

- Ask students to listen and underline the /æ/ sound (m<u>a</u>ps).

4b ▶10

- Play the track for students to listen and underline the /æ/ sound in each word.
- Invite individual students to come to the board and write the words, underlining the /æ/ sound.

- Ask the rest of the class if they agree and, if not, elicit the correct answers.
- Play the track again for students to repeat the words. (See Teaching tips, *Vary drilling techniques*, page 27, for suggestions on drilling words.)

ANSWERS / AUDIO SCRIPT 10

app store   calculator   calendar   camera   laptop   tablet

5

- Refer students to the list of apps in Exercise 2 and to the list 1–8.
- Before they start, go over the example answer with the class.
- Elicit the difference between *location* and *destination* (location *is the place where you are, and* destination *is the place where you are going*).
- Ask students to match the apps to the uses in the list and then check answers as a class.

ANSWERS

2 compass; maps   3 mail; messages; social networking
4 social networking; messages   5 calculator   6 maps
7 calendar, notes   8 app store

6

- Ask students to do the *Mini App Quiz* on their own and then compare their answers in pairs.
- Choose students to read the answers aloud to check as a class.

ANSWERS

1 A application   2 C a program   3 C 2008

SPEAK

7

- Divide the class into pairs and ask them to decide which of the two tasks they would prefer to do.
- Refer students to the language in the PHRASE BYTES box and suggest that they use these phrases to start their discussions.
- Set a time limit of five minutes, but be prepared to extend this if students need more time to discuss their ideas.
- When they have finished, choose a pair to tell the class about the apps they chose from Exercise 2 and why. Invite the rest of the class to say whether they agree or disagree.
- Finally, invite two or three pairs to present their ideas for a new app. Note: If you are going to ask students to prepare a presentation for homework, you may wish to omit this step at this point.

8 THE MOVING PICTURE

- Tell students they are going to watch a video of some teenagers talking about apps. Play the video and ask students to watch and make a note of the apps the teenagers mention and which ones they say are their favorites.
- Check answers as a class. Encourage students to say whether they like the apps mentioned and to say other apps that they like.

ANSWERS / VIDEO SCRIPT

See underlined text in video script for answers.

Girl 1: Yeah, so, what apps do you guys have?
Boy 1: I have a lot, you know.
Girl 2: Yeah, I have tons. I use apps way too much. I have, like, photography ones, social networking ones ...
Boy 2: I have a lot of music apps. I love my music apps.
Girl 2: ... and a lot of games.
Boy 1: Yeah.
Boy 2: Yeah. What apps do you guys use the most?
Boy 1: Um ... well, I like the social networking apps.
Girl 2/Boy 2: ... same ...
Girl 2: If I didn't have social networking apps, I don't know how I'd cope.
Boy 2: Yeah ... kinda ... kind of keeps you connected to everyone else.
Girls: Yeah.
Girl 1: I love that. I think it's a great way to connect with people.
Girl 2: Yeah, but ... what's your favorite??
Girl 1: I love Twitter. I think that's ...
Boy 1: I'd have to say it's Instagram.
Boy 2: Yeah, Instagram, definitely.
Girl 2: Uh ... Tumblr!
Boy 1: Tumblr?
Girl 2: Tumblr's the one.
Boy 1: Yeah.
Girl 2: It's the best.

MOVE BEYOND

Ask students to do the **Move Beyond** task on page 69.

Extra activity

Read the following exercise aloud to students (or dictate the sentences) and ask them to make notes on one or more suitable kinds of apps.

What apps do these people need? (Suggested answers are in parentheses.)

1 *John likes to keep in touch with his friends.* (social networking, email, messages)
2 *Sarah often forgets when she has to meet people. She isn't very organized.* (calendar, notes)
3 *Felix uses the internet a lot to find out information.* (web browser)
4 *Troy loves math.* (calculator)
5 *Helen organizes the drama club at her school. She needs to send information to the members of the club.* (email, messages)
6 *Billie likes trying new apps.* (app store)
7 *Nestor gets lost all the time. He can't remember the names of streets.* (maps, compass)

Homework

Task 2 of Exercise 7 can be extended into a project. Have students work in groups to prepare a presentation for the app they have invented and make a poster or a PowerPoint presentation. At the beginning of the next class, ask students to present their apps. The rest of the class can vote on which app they would invest in.

If students have worked on Task 1 in Exercise 7, they can prepare a presentation to support their choices.

READING Switch off

Understand new words Page 10

STAGE	TIME	FOCUS
GET STARTED		Play a game to guess the meaning of a mystery word. Introduce some of the reading subskill techniques that are practiced in the lesson.
SPEAK AND READ		Read a magazine article and do a survey about the need to switch off. Practice understanding new words (reading subskill).
REACT		Discuss the survey results and say whether you agree or disagree. Talk about the difficulty of switching off. Rank free-time activities and compare rankings with those of a classmate.

Get started

Play a game of *Mystery Word* (see Games, page 29), which introduces students to some of the techniques they will be using in this lesson for practicing the subskill of understanding new words when reading.

SPEAK AND READ

1

- Ask students to read the sentences and decide if they are true for them.
- Divide the class into pairs to explain why the sentences are or aren't true for them; for example, *Well, number one isn't true for me. I don't have lots of free time because every weekday except Wednesday I have an activity after school. I also have a lot of homework, and on weekends I have to help my dad in his store.*

2 11

- Find out how often students read magazines and elicit some examples of the kinds of magazines they like reading. Tell students they are going to read the first part of a magazine article.
- Refer students to the photos that accompany the article and elicit what the people are doing and how they might be feeling.
- Ask students to read the first paragraph of the extract. Don't play the audio at this point. It is an extra feature, and suggestions for using it in class are included at the end of the lesson.
- Reassure students by telling them not to worry if they don't understand every word. Ask them to underline any words they don't know as they read.

3a

- Ask students how many words they underlined. Tell them they are going to look at some techniques that can help them understand new words without looking them up in a dictionary.
- Focus students on the HOW TO box and read the first tip aloud, quickly reviewing the four parts of speech mentioned and eliciting a simple definition of each one; for example, *a verb is a word to describe an action*; *a noun is the name of a person, place, or thing*; *an adjective gives us more information about a noun*; *an adverb gives us more information about a verb or about frequency*. Ask students to give you examples of these parts of speech from the text.
- Read the second tip aloud and ask students to give you some examples of words that are similar in English and their language.
- Read the third tip aloud and remind students that it is important to take into account the general topic of the text, as well as the immediate context of the unfamiliar word(s).

3b

- Refer students back to the words they underlined in the article. Ask them to work individually to write a possible definition for each word on a separate page of their notebooks or a piece of paper. Ask them not to write the word next to their definition (as this will affect the next exercise).
- You may need to give students plenty of positive encouragement for this task, reminding them that it doesn't matter if they're wrong and that they will get better as they practice the technique more. Encourage them to be imaginative and creative.

Alternative procedure: more confident classes

Challenge more confident students to write definitions and point out some of the more difficult words or expressions for them to work with (e.g., *relax*, *hardly ever*, *during*, *turn off*, *from time to time*, *full*). Tell them that although they may understand the meaning, you'd like them to focus on using their English to write clear definitions.

4

- Divide the class into pairs and have them exchange their definitions.
- Ask them to read their partners' definitions and try to find the correct words in the text.
- Circulate and monitor, making a note of any particularly good definitions.
- In a class feedback session at the end of the exercise, choose students to read the best definitions aloud.

5

- Refer students to the survey and ask them to answer it individually and calculate their scores. Set a time limit of four minutes for this.
- When they have calculated their score, ask students to read the corresponding explanation.

Extra activity

Divide the class into pairs to do the survey again, but this time they should predict what their partners' answers will be by checking the answers in a different color. Then have them take turns telling their partners about their predictions. Their partners should respond, saying whether the predictions are right or wrong. For example:

A: *I think you watch TV once a day or more.*

B: *No. I often watch TV, but not every day. Some days I don't have time. I think you sometimes read and send email.*

A: *Wrong. I rarely use email. I prefer to send texts or chat on Facebook.*

REACT

6

- First, ask students to read the questions and make notes about their answers. Set a time limit of three minutes.
- Divide the class into pairs and ask students to discuss their opinions using the phrases in the **PHRASE BYTES** box.
- Monitor as students are doing the exercise and make a note of any language you wish to highlight at the end.
- Finish by giving language feedback and inviting several students to share their answers with the class.

MOVE BEYOND

Ask students to put the survey activities in order of preference and then to compare and explain their choices in pairs.

Extra activity

Ask students to close their books and give them a list of the verbs used in the *Switch Off* survey questions (i.e., *watch*, *listen*, *play*, *call*, *send*, *read and send*, *use*, *chat*, *go*, *watch*). Ask them to reconstruct the survey items. You could draw images on the board to prompt them (e.g., a TV, musical notes, a video game console, two friends, a cell phone showing a text message).

Recorded reading text ▶11

The audio track could be used for less confident students to listen to while reading the text for a second time. For more confident students, use the track for Exercise 4. Encourage students to close their books and listen for the word that matches their partner's definition.

Homework

Prepare a short text for students, or suggest one from a suitable website, that relates to the topic of switching off and relaxing away from the internet, cell phones, etc. Ask students to read the text and write possible definitions for any unfamiliar words using the techniques they have practiced in class. You could also ask them to write a short summary of the text in two or three sentences.

GRAMMAR Simple present, adverbs, and expressions of frequency

Talk about how often you do things

Page 11

STAGE	TIME	FOCUS
GET STARTED		Recycle the simple present by doing a puzzle to discover a hidden word.
READ		Read a short conversation. Answer a main idea question.
STUDY		Refer to examples from the reading text to help you complete the grammar rules and examples. Expand knowledge of frequency adverbs.
PRACTICE		Practice using the simple present and expressions of frequency in controlled and free exercises.
SPEAK		Conduct a survey of other students about how they contact their friends. Consolidate the use of the simple present third person singular by explaining the survey results to a classmate.

Get started

This word puzzle activity is designed to remind students about some of the basics of the simple present. Draw the grid on the board without the words and ask students to copy it.

Ask students to use the clues to complete the answers and find the hidden word. Explain that an apostrophe (') takes one box. Once they have discovered the hidden word (*device*), ask them to give you some examples of technological devices (e.g., *camera*, *laptop*, *tablet*).

Clues

1 The negative form of *does*.
2 My friends in other countries ________ me emails all the time.
3 My sister ________ in Ireland, so I don't see her very often.
4 The negative form of *is*.
5 My friend Veronica and I ________ online every night using social networking apps.
6 ________ your teacher give you a lot of homework?

1			D	O	E	S	N	'	T
2		S	E	N	D				
3	L	I	V	E	S				
4			I	S	N	'	T		
5			C	H	A	T			
6	D	O	E	S					

READ Grammar in context

1

- Ask students to tell you about any blogs they read.
- Tell them they are going to read a conversation between two students who use a class blog. Ask them if they think a class blog is a good idea and why or why not.
- Ask students to read the conversation and answer the question. Then check the answer as a class.

ANSWER

Because Carla doesn't see his messages on the class blog.

STUDY

2

- Ask students to read the grammar explanations about the simple present and circle the correct options to complete the rules and examples.
- Let students compare their answers in pairs. Then read through the rules with the class, choosing different students to give answers.

ANSWERS
don't doesn't Do; do

Extra activity
If you think students would benefit from a review of the simple present form, refer them to the **Grammar Database** on page 64 or go through it with them.

For less confident classes, you could do some additional practice in class. For example, if students are unsure when to use *don't* and when to use *doesn't*, do a quick substitution drill with them. Drill the sentence: *I don't have time.* Write on the board or say a series of different subjects one by one and indicate that students should repeat the sentence starting with the new subject (e.g., *you*, *my father*, *we*, *my cousins*, *Mr. Jones*, *Grandma*).

If students are unsure about word order in questions, write an example question on the board: *How often do you use the class blog?* Elicit the subject (*you*), the verb (*use*), and the auxiliary (*do*) and write each part of speech below the corresponding word. Repeat this procedure with a Yes/No question to show that the word order is the same whether or not a question word is used. Ask students to give you some more examples of questions in the simple present following the pattern given in the explanation.

3

- Refer students back to the conversation in Exercise 1 and draw their attention to the words in bold. Tell them that these are adverbs and expressions of frequency.
- Ask students to read the explanations and to circle the correct options to complete the rules.
- Check answers by choosing different students to read the explanations and examples aloud.

ANSWERS
before after end

- Refer students to the chart and point out that some of the adverbs have a similar meaning (e.g., *often*, *regularly*).

Extra activity
Have students close their books. Write the adverbs on cards and draw a line on the board and label the left end *0%* and the right end *100%*. Distribute the cards among your students and invite them to place the cards on the board in the correct place on the line. Remind them that some of the adverbs have similar meanings. Once the cards have been attached to the line, ask the class to decide together if they are all in the correct place.

PRACTICE

4

- To lead into the exercise, find out if your students have cell phones with cameras. Ask how often they take pictures or videos with their cameras.
- Tell students they are going to read an interview between a woman doing a survey about cell phones and a boy named Jude.
- Ask them to read the interview and complete it with the simple present form of the verbs.
- Check answers as a class and then divide the class into pairs to practice the conversation.

ANSWERS
2 does 3 do you use 4 look 5 don't take 6 use

5a

- Ask students to rewrite the sentences putting the adverbs and expressions in the correct position. Remind them to look at the explanations in Exercise 3 if they are unsure.
- Let students compare their answers in pairs before you choose students to read their answers aloud to the class.

ANSWERS
2 I can't play video games every day.
3 I occasionally listen to music when I do my homework.
4 From time to time I watch videos on the internet. / I watch videos on the internet from time to time.
5 My cell phone is rarely turned on.
6 Now and then I send text messages to friends. / I send text messages to friends now and then.
Note that in #2, the time expression has to go at the end because the sentence is negative.

5b

- Ask students to look back at their sentences in Exercise 5a and change them as necessary to make them true for them.
- Before they start, write an example on the board that shows the kinds of changes that may have to be made; for example, *I often check my email. / I check my email from time to time. / I sometimes check my email.*
- Set a time limit of five minutes for them to change the sentences and write their personalized versions in their notebooks. Monitor and offer help as necessary.
- Have students compare their sentences in pairs, giving reasons for their answers.

6

- Ask students to work individually to write four questions with *How often* in order to create a survey about ways to contact friends. Point out that they should use the prompts in the box.
- Circulate and monitor to check that students' questions are correct.

ANSWERS
How often do you call your friends?
How often do you chat online with your friends?
How often do you send emails to your friends?
How often do you send text messages to your friends?

Fast finishers
Encourage fast finishers to add other similar questions to their surveys.

SPEAK

7

- Divide the class into pairs to interview each other using their surveys. Set a time limit of five minutes for this. Point out that they should make a note of their partner's answers.
- Ask students to get together with another pair to tell their new partners the results of their survey. Remind students that they will be using the third person singular, so they will need to add *-s*, *-es*, or *-ies*.

Homework

To personalize the grammar point, refer students back to the sentences in Exercise 5a and ask them to rewrite them to make true sentences about their own friends or family; for example, *My friend Joanna checks her email every evening. My dad never plays video games. My grandma's cell phone is hardly ever turned on.*

LISTENING AND VOCABULARY Raspberry Pi

Listen for the main ideas *Page 12*

STAGE	TIME	FOCUS
GET STARTED		Identify four pairs of homophones including *pi* and *pie*.
WORK WITH WORDS		Talk about studying computers. Match computer parts to a picture.
LISTEN		Listen to a news report to understand the main ideas (listening subskill). Listen again and practice a test-style multiple-choice task.
REACT		React to the listening text. Talk about how students use computers and whether it is important to learn to write code.

MOVE BEYOND FOR TEACHERS

Raspberry Pi

The Raspberry Pi is a tiny computer the size of a credit card developed in the UK with the goal of sparking students' interest in computers and teaching computer science in schools. For more information, you can visit the Raspberry Pi website: www.raspberrypi.org. The name is a play on the words *pi* and *pie*, which are homophones (i.e., words of different meaning and spelling that are pronounced the same).

Get started

In order to understand some of the humor in the listening text in this lesson, students will have to be aware of the meanings of the homophones *pie* and *pi*.

Write these two sentences with blanks on the board:

Spiders have ______________ *legs.*
The children ______________ *their sandwiches quickly because they were hungry.*

Elicit words to fill in the blanks (*eight*, *ate*). Ask students if there is any difference in pronunciation between the two words that filled in the blanks. (*No, both words are pronounced* /eɪt/.)

Tell students that in English there are some pairs of words that have exactly the same pronunciation but different spellings and different meanings.

Write the following words on the board: *pie*, *won*, *they're*, *one*, *new*, *their*, *knew*, *pi*. Clarify the meanings of any words students do not know. (Students may not know *pi*, which is part of the name of the computer that they are going to hear about in this lesson. You could explain that *pi* [π] is the name of a Greek letter and also a mathematical number.) Ask students to match the words that have the same pronunciation.

ANSWERS

pie/pi won/one their/they're new/knew

WORK WITH WORDS

1

- Divide the class into pairs to answer and discuss the questions.
- In a class feedback session, take a class vote to see if the majority of the class likes or doesn't like studying computers.

Alternative procedure

Books closed. Dictate questions 1 and 2 for students to discuss in pairs.

2

- Refer students to the picture and ask them to match the computer parts in the box to the different items.
- Let them compare their answers in pairs, but don't confirm the answers at this point.

3 12

- Play the track for students to listen and check their answers.
- Play the track again for students to listen and repeat.

ANSWERS / AUDIO SCRIPT 12

1 microphone 2 headphones 3 speaker 4 screen
5 monitor 6 printer 7 webcam 8 USB port 9 mouse
10 keyboard

4

- Ask students to categorize the computer parts according to their uses.
- As they finish, let them compare their answers in pairs before you choose different students to read their answers aloud.

ANSWERS

2 speaker; headphones 3 screen; monitor; webcam
4 USB port

LISTEN

5a

- Tell students that they are going to hear a news report from a school website twice. Point out that the first time they hear it, they shouldn't worry too much about specific information but should just listen for the main ideas.
- Refer students to the HOW TO box and go through the tips with them.

5b 13

- Give students a minute to read the three summary options before you play the track.
- Ask them to listen and choose the option that best summarizes the report.
- Do a quick poll by asking students to raise their hands if they think the answer is 1, 2, or 3. Then confirm the correct answer.

ANSWER / AUDIO SCRIPT 13

3 A school is using a small computer to teach students how computers work.

Tom: Welcome to Newton School TV! You can watch video reports from different schools in Newton. My name's Tom Smith, and I study at Newton Middle School. Today I'm in a computer class in my school, and I'm here to find out about the Raspberry Pi. What exactly is the Raspberry Pi? It sounds like something you eat.
Sally: Well, we just call it the Pi, and it's a computer.
Tom: Is this it? It's very small.
Sally: That's right. It's a very simple computer. But it works really well!
Tom: So tell me about it.
Sally: Well, you can connect it to a monitor or a TV, and it has USB ports to connect a keyboard and mouse.
Tom: Can we turn it on now?
Sally: Yes, of course.
Tom: Can it connect to the internet?
Sally: Yes. There's a port for a fast internet connection.
Tom: OK. So what do you use the Pi for?
Sally: We use it to learn how computers work.
Jan: And sometimes we use it to write code.
Tom: Code?
Jan: The instructions for a computer. With code, we can create our own games and programs.
Tom: That's amazing. I have no idea how computers work.
Jan: The Pi may be small, but it can do a lot of things! And it's from the UK. It's a British invention.
Tom: One final question. Does it make lunch?
Jan: Excuse me?
Tom: Talking about the Raspberry Pi is making me really hungry! Lunchtime! That's why I'm hungry!

6

- Ask students to reflect on which tips from the HOW TO box helped them do Exercise 5b and to check them.

7 13

Exam-type task

- Give students a minute to read the multiple-choice questions before you play the track again.
- Let them compare their answers in pairs before you check answers as a class.

ANSWERS

1 B 2 B 3 A 4 B

REACT

8

- Divide the class into pairs to answer the questions using the PHRASE BYTES box to help them.

Alternative procedures

If you are looking for a more creative way to set up this speaking activity and your students enjoy role-play activities, you could try these ideas:

For question 1: One student plays the role of an older person who doesn't know much about computers, and the other has to tell the "older" person about computers and what they are used for. The "older" person should pretend to know nothing about computers and ask as many questions as possible. The "younger" person should try to convince his or her partner that computers are useful and fun.

For question 2: Together students brainstorm as many reasons as they can think of for both sides of the argument (i.e., whether learning to write code is important or not). Each student then takes one side and tries to convince the other of his or her position.

MOVE BEYOND

Ask students to do the **Move Beyond** task on page 69.

Extra activity

Play a game of *Hot Seat* (see Games, page 29) using the computer parts vocabulary from Exercise 2.

Homework

Ask students to read the audio script of track 13 and to make a list of all the computer-related vocabulary. Encourage them to add any further words or expressions from the **Words & Beyond** exercises, page 69, to their list. Explain that they should memorize the words and their meanings for a quick vocabulary test in the next class.

GRAMMAR Articles: *a/an*, *the*, and zero article

Use *a/an*, *the*, and zero article to refer to things

Page 13

STAGE	TIME	FOCUS
GET STARTED		Play a game of *Three in a Row*. Identify errors in the use of articles.
READ		Read a short description for gist.
STUDY		Find examples in the reading text and match them to the grammar explanations.
PRACTICE		Practice using articles in controlled exercises.
SPEAK		Speak for 30 seconds on a range of topics. Focus on fluency.

Get started

Play a game of *Three in a Row* (see Games, page 29) to test students' knowledge of articles. This will help you see how much extra help they might need with the grammar input of today's lesson.

Next to the grid, write the list of sentences (see below). To be able to add their symbols to the grid, students have to say whether the sentence is correct. If it isn't, they have to give the correct version.

Divide the class into two teams and start by tossing a coin to see which team goes first.

A *My father is teacher.* (✗ My father is a teacher.)
B *We went to the beach on the weekend.* (✓)
C *I read an interesting article on internet.* (✗ … on the internet.)
D *There is a old church in the center of the city.* (✗ There is an old church …)
E *My brother really loves the dogs.* (✗ My brother really loves dogs.)
F *Harriet is from United States of America.* (✗ … the United States of America.)
G *President of the USA in 2012 was Barack Obama.* (✗ The president …)
H *Every day I have the breakfast at 8:00.* (✗ … I have ~~the~~ breakfast …)
I *We live in big house.* (✗ We live in a big house.)

MOVE BEYOND FOR TEACHERS

Tossing a coin

In English-speaking countries, as in many cultures, tossing a coin is a common way to decide who will go first in a game. The two sides of the coin are called *heads* and *tails*. *Heads* refers to the head of the leader or statesman on one side of the coin, and *tails* is traditionally used for the other side, probably because the tail is seen as the opposite of the head.

READ Grammar in context

MOVE BEYOND FOR TEACHERS

Silicon Valley

Silicon Valley is an area near San Francisco in California. It is the center of technological innovation in the USA and is called Silicon Valley because many of the original technology companies in the area were silicon chip manufacturers or developers.

Waldorf Schools follow an educational philosophy based on the ideas of Rudolf Steiner and aim to nurture a range of capacities in children, including the physical, emotional, intellectual, aesthetic, moral, and spiritual capacities.

1

- Find out what your students know about Silicon Valley and tell them they are going to read about a school there.
- Ask students to find out what is unusual about the school by reading the description. Set a time limit of one minute and then choose a student to answer the question.
- Ask students if they can think of any advantages of attending a school where there is no technology.

ANSWER

The school is unusual because they don't use technology, just books and blackboards, and yet it is located in Silicon Valley, where many technology companies are based.

STUDY

2

- Refer students to the explanations of the use of articles and read through them with the class.
- Ask students to work individually to match the examples in the text to the explanations.
- Let them compare their answers in pairs before you check them as a class.

ANSWERS

a job: 9 a specific thing: 8 superlatives and dates: 4
plural place names: 3 things in general: 7

Extra activity

You may wish to give students more examples as you check through the explanations and examples from the text.

a/an +:
- one example of a thing (e.g., *This is* ***a*** *page from the Student's Book*). Contrast with a specific page (see below).
- a job (e.g., *My brother is* ***a*** *doctor*).

the +:
- a specific thing (e.g., *This is* ***the*** *page from the Student's Book that we looked at in the last class*).
- the only example of a thing (e.g., ***the*** *sun*, ***the*** *moon*, ***the*** *president of France*).
- superlatives and dates (e.g., *Today is Monday,* ***the*** *third of March*).
- something mentioned before (e.g., *My mother works in an office.* ***The*** *office is downtown*).
- plural place names (e.g., ***the*** *Philippines*, ***the*** *Cayman Islands*, ***the*** *Netherlands*, ***the*** *Himalayas*).

no article +:
- things in general (e.g., ***Dogs*** *are wonderful pets*).
- meals, days, and singular place names (e.g., *What do you eat for* ***breakfast****?*).

(See Teaching Tips, *Articles*, page 26.)

PRACTICE

3

- Ask students to complete the sentences with *the* or no article (–).
- When checking answers as a class, ask students to say why *the* is used or not used, referring to the explanations in the box.

ANSWERS
2 The (a specific thing) 3 (-); (-) (things in general)
4 The (the only example of a thing); the (superlative); (-) (things in general); the (the only example of a thing)

Fast finishers
Ask fast finishers to work in pairs to exchange opinions about statements 3 and 4 in Exercise 3. Alternatively, ask students to write a few lines saying what they think.

4

- Ask students to work individually to circle the correct options.
- Monitor as they are doing the task, and when most students have finished, tell them they should have three examples of *a* and three of *the*. Give them a minute to reconsider their answers if necessary before you confirm answers.

ANSWERS
1 a (one example of a thing) 2 the (a specific thing, i.e., Ray's kitchen) 3 a (one example of a thing) 4 a (one example of a thing) 5 the (superlative) 6 the (a specific thing, i.e., Ray's house)

5

- Give students one minute to read the text about Ellen. Tell them not to worry about the blanks as they read.
- After one minute, have them cover the text and elicit from them as much information about Ellen as possible. Prompt with questions such as: *Where does Ellen study? Why does she love computer classes? When is her computer class?*
- Ask students to complete the text with articles where necessary.
- Let them compare answers in pairs before you check them as a class.

ANSWERS
2 (-) 3 (-) 4 (-) 5 the 6 a 7 (-) 8 the
9 (-) 10 (-) 11 The 12 an

SPEAK

6

- Divide the class into pairs to take turns choosing a topic and speaking for 30 seconds without stopping.
- Stress that the goal is to speak as fluently as possible but that they should also think about using articles correctly where necessary.

Extra activity
Remind students that articles are most often pronounced in their weak form with the *schwa* sound /ə/. Contrast the strong and weak forms by writing the phonetic symbols on the board and modeling the pronunciation: *a* /eɪ/ (strong), /ə/ (weak); *an* /æn/ (strong), /ən/ (weak); *the* /ðiː/ (strong), /ðə/ (weak). (See Teaching Tips, *Sentence stress*, page 28.)

Divide the class into pairs to read the conversation in Exercise 4. Pay attention to their pronunciation of the articles.

Homework

Ask students to write a text like Ellen's, talking about their favorite subject at school. Encourage them to pay particular attention to how they use articles in their text. Set a word limit of 80–100 words. In the next class, choose a few students to read their texts aloud.

LANGUAGE &BEYOND *GET ORGANIZED*

Use lists to help you organize your time *Page 14*

STAGE	TIME	FOCUS
GET STARTED		Talk about how you remember the things you have to do.
READ		Read the notes on Jasmin's bulletin board and place them in a planner.
DO		Work with another student to decide on priorities for Jasmin.
REFLECT		Discuss the challenges of organizing time and how being organized or disorganized makes you feel.
EXTEND		Make a list and prioritize it. Compare lists with other students and discuss your priorities and how they were decided.

LIFE SKILLS

USING LISTS TO HELP YOU ORGANIZE YOUR TIME

Teenagers are generally coming to terms with greater independence and increasing responsibilities in their lives and need to learn how to manage their time. Introducing teenagers to time management techniques can really empower them and boost their confidence. Making lists and prioritizing tasks are two fundamental principles of effective time management. Making lists can help students feel less stressed and more in control, as they do not have to worry about forgetting things. The actual act of making a list can also help them clarify exactly what needs to be done over a certain period of time. An important follow-up step is prioritizing what is important and deciding what can be achieved in a given amount of time. Checking off tasks on a list as they are done helps students feel good about what they have achieved and reminds them what still needs to be completed.

Get started

Ask students if they keep a planner so that they don't forget things they have to do each week. Elicit from students some other ways of remembering what they have to do (e.g., *writing lists; setting cell phone alerts; and writing notes on their hands, sticky notes, bulletin boards*).

Ask if anyone has ever forgotten to do something important.

READ

1

- Divide the class into pairs. Ask them to look at Jasmin's bulletin board for 20 seconds and then close their books.
- Ask them to remember as many things about Jasmin as they can. Before they start, prompt them with questions such as: *What does she like doing? What is she studying? Who are her friends?* Set a one-minute time limit.
- Invite different pairs to say one piece of information to see how much they remember.
- Ask students to transfer the relevant information from Jasmin's bulletin board into her planner.

ANSWERS

Thursday: study math, French, and chemistry; 7 p.m.: movie, *The Abyss*
Friday: math, French, and chemistry exams
4 p.m.: guitar lesson
6 p.m. or before: Maggie's house for sleepover (take sleeping bag)
Saturday: 10 a.m.: sister's basketball final
1 p.m.: Colin's party

2

- Refer students to Jasmin's planner and elicit students' thoughts on the questions as a class.

DO

3

- Divide the class into pairs to make suggestions as to how Jasmin can organize her time. Set a time limit of five minutes and refer students to the **PHRASE BYTES** box for ideas for how to start their discussion.
- Elicit some responses as a class and invite students to say whether they agree or disagree with the comments made.

REFLECT

4

- Ask students if it was easy or difficult to organize Jasmin's time and why. If students have difficulty answering, ask some follow-up questions such as: *Which things do you think Jasmin really wanted to do? Which did she have to do? How do you decide between things you have to do and things you really want to do? How would Jasmin feel if she went to the movies on Thursday evening instead of preparing for her exams and her guitar lesson? How do you feel when you are unprepared for exams or classes? How do you feel when you've prepared well for something?*
- Divide the class into pairs to discuss questions 2 and 3. Set a time limit of four minutes for this.
- Choose a student to read the **REFLECTION POINT** aloud and invite students to participate in a class discussion, prompting with: *Why is it important to put items in order on a list? Why does writing a list and deciding which things are more important help you feel less stressed?*
- Ask them to discuss how lists could be useful in the following: *studying, job, household chores, keeping in touch with friends, shopping, personal goals, future plans.*

EXTEND

5

- Ask students to work individually to make a list of the things they need to do over the next three days and then to prioritize what they have to do from most to least important. Set a time limit of five minutes for this.

6

- Divide the class into small groups to share their lists and explain how they decided on the best order to do things.

Homework

Ask students to write a short reflection on the lesson to address the following questions: *What did you learn in today's lesson? Was what we talked about useful for you? Why or why not?*

Suggest a word limit of 100 words. Have students compare answers and share their thoughts in the next class.

SPEAKING Say what you think

Ask for and give opinions *Page 15*

STAGE	TIME	FOCUS
GET STARTED		Describe what is happening in the stills from internet videos on page 15.
SPEAK		Talk about internet videos and predict what will happen next in the videos pictured.
LISTEN		Listen to four teenagers giving their opinions about an internet video. Study and practice expressions for asking and giving opinions (speaking subskill).
ACT		Ask and give opinions on topics related to technology.

Get started

Ask students how often they watch videos on the internet and what kinds of videos they watch. Ask them what sites they use to watch videos.

Refer students to the stills from some internet videos on page 15, and invite them to say who (or what) they see and what is happening. Write some key vocabulary on the board (e.g., *sky, ocean, flying suit, standing up, singing, microphones, playing Wii tennis, living room, jump, trampoline, cat, dog, paw*).

SPEAK

1

- Divide the class into pairs to discuss the questions. Set a time limit of five minutes for this.
- As you monitor their discussions, listen for creative ideas as to what happens next in each video and make a note so that you can choose these students to share their ideas at the end of the five minutes.

Alternative procedure

If you have internet access in your classroom, show the class a funny video. Check that it's appropriate before the lesson. Pause the video from time to time to elicit from students what is going on. Stop the video just before something goes wrong or something surprising happens. Ask them to make predictions about what happens next in the video. Finally, play the ending for them to see if their predictions were correct.

Extra activity

Ask students to think of a funny video they have seen and give them five minutes to prepare an explanation of what happens. Encourage them to think about the language they will need and to ask you about any words they don't know. The simple present is often used to relate what happens in movies or books, and it would be appropriate for students to use it here to describe the video they have chosen.

LISTEN

2 ▶14

- Have students close their books. Play the track for them to listen and find out what the friends think about the video they are watching.
- Be prepared to help students with some of the vocabulary; for example, *original* (new, interesting, something no one has thought of or seen before), *cruel* (causing pain or suffering), *just* (only).

ANSWERS / AUDIO SCRIPT ▶14

The friends think the video is funny. Laura doesn't think it's very original. Tina thinks it's a little mean.

Adam: Hey, guys. Watch this! ... So, what do you think about it?
Laura: I think it's OK. I don't think it's very original, but it's funny.
Adam: What do you think, Tina?
Tina: I don't know. I think it's kind of funny, but it's also a little mean.
Adam: Mean?
Tina: Yes. Do you think the dog's happy?
Adam: No, maybe not.
Ben: Hey, what are you doing with my tablet?
Laura: We're watching that video.
Ben: So what do you think about it? Just funny, or really, really funny?

3 ▶14

- Ask students to open their books and fill in the blanks in the conversation with *think* or *know*.
- Play the track a second time for students to check their answers.

ANSWERS

1, 2, 3, 4, 6, 7, 8 think   5 know

4

- Ask students to transform the statement into a negative one. Encourage them to try to do it without looking back at the conversation.
- Once they have written their answers, they can check whether it's correct by looking for the phrase in the conversation.

ANSWER

I don't think it's very original.

5 ▶15

- Ask students to listen and repeat the expressions from the conversation.

AUDIO SCRIPT ▶15

1 What do you think about it?
2 I think it's OK.
3 I don't think it's very original.
4 What do you think?
5 I don't know.
6 Do you think the dog's happy?

ACT

6 ▶16

- Divide the class into groups of three or four to discuss their opinions about different topics related to technology.
- Encourage them to ask for and give reasons for their opinions and to use the language in the PHRASEBOOK box.
- Refer students to the phrases in the PHRASEBOOK box. Play the track for them to listen and repeat.

Alternative procedure: less confident classes

If you have students who are shy or reluctant to express their own opinions, you could write some role cards and make the activity a role-play (e.g., four different characters discussing social networking sites: a teenager, a teacher, a senior citizen, and a marketing expert). The role cards should give information about the character's attitude and the opinions the character should contribute.

Homework

Ask students to write five questions to find out their classmates' opinions. Give them some examples if necessary (e.g., *Do people spend too much time on the internet?*). Students are free to choose the topics for their questions.

Choose the best questions to post on a class blog or website or put them up in the classroom and encourage students to write their opinions about them before or after classes or during breaks. These opinion forums will also be useful for fast finishers during class.

WRITING Could you live without your cell phone?

Use the correct word order Page 16

STAGE	TIME	FOCUS
GET STARTED		Talk about the advantages and disadvantages of cell phones. Say whether you could live without your cell phone.
READ		Read a question on a website and compare opinions. Read tips on using the correct word order (writing subskill). Find examples of each tip in the texts.
PRACTICE		Practice putting words in the correct order.
DISCUSS		Give reasons to have or not to have a cell phone.
WRITE		Write reasons to have or not to have a cell phone.
SHARE		Debate the pros and cons of cell phones. Talk about other devices.

Get started

In pairs or small groups, have the class brainstorm at least three positive and three negative things about cell phones. Ask how many could live without their cell phones.

READ

1

- Refer students to the answers from a website forum.
- Ask students to read them and tell a partner which answer is closer to their own view and explain why.

2a

- Write the following jumbled sentence on the board: *call I my friend best usually every day.*
- Ask students if this sentence makes sense in English and elicit that the problem is the word order.
- Ask students to help you reconstruct the sentence correctly on the board: *I usually call my best friend every day.*
- With students' help, label the following elements of the sentence: subject (*I*), verb (*call*), object (*my best friend*), adverb of frequency (*usually*), expression of frequency (*every day*), superlative adjective (*best*).
- Read through the HOW TO box with students, using the sentence on the board as an example.

2b

- Ask students to find two more examples of each tip in the website answers.
- Let them compare answers in pairs before checking answers as a class.

> **ANSWERS**
> **Sentences starting with SVO:** I have a really old phone; I don't need another one; I (hardly ever) use it; People (sometimes) call me; I do everything; I use it; I (rarely) call friends; I (never) have time; I send text messages
> **Adverbs of frequency before the main verb:** I hardly ever use it; People sometimes call me; I rarely call friends; I never have time
> **Expressions of frequency after SVO:** I use it every day; I send text messages about 20 times a day
> **Adjectives before nouns:** old phone; the most important thing

PRACTICE

3

- Ask students to put the words in the correct order.
- Encourage them to check their answers against the tips in the HOW TO box before you choose different students to read their sentences aloud and check answers as a class.

> **ANSWERS**
> 2 I rarely send text messages.
> 3 I call my best friends every night.
> 4 I'm using a new app for browsing the web right now.
> 5 I hardly ever watch videos on my cell phone.

DISCUSS

4

- Ask students to work in pairs or small groups and talk about reasons to have or not to have a cell phone.
- Write useful language on the board to help them. For example:
  It's a good / bad idea to have a cell phone because … .
  I always / never use my cell phone to … .

WRITE

5

- Explain to students that they are now going to write five reasons to have or not to have a cell phone.
- Write two sample reasons on the board:
  I call my parents if I miss my bus in the afternoon.
  I sometimes send photos of my fat cat to my friends.
- Ask students which of the reasons is more important and explain that they should organize their reasons by putting the most important ones first.
- Remind students to use correct word order and refer them to the HOW TO box. Ask them to point out SVO patterns in the sentences on the board.

SHARE

6

- Divide the class into small groups. Check that there are students with different opinions in each group.
- Explain that they should try to persuade the students with a different point of view to agree with them.
- Have a class discussion about other devices that students feel they can or can't live without. Encourage them to give reasons.

> **Homework**
> Ask students to write their answer to another question (e.g., *Could you live without the internet? Could you live without television?*). Set a word limit of 100 words. Remind them to focus on using the correct word order.

Introduction

Unit Reviews bring together all the grammar and vocabulary seen in the unit. Students can refer to the **Grammar Database** and **Words & Beyond** pages first and then do the exercises. Alternatively, they can try the exercises first and then study the reference material if necessary. Unit Reviews can be used in the classroom or for self-study at home. Procedural notes are provided here for their use in the classroom.

As in a test, in the Unit Reviews students can clearly see how many points they can score for each exercise. When they have finished, encourage students to exchange books with a partner and check each other's work, totaling up the score.

VOCABULARY Applications (Apps)

1

- Refer students to the title and pictures. Elicit why they think the pictures are titled *The first apps* (*they show how people did certain things before computers and apps were invented*).
- Ask students to write in the missing letters to complete the names of the apps.
- Invite students to come to the board and write their answers. Ask the rest of the class if they agree and make any necessary corrections.

ANSWERS
1 games 2 maps 3 notes 4 messages 5 mail
6 videos 7 calendar 8 calculator 9 social networking
10 app store

Computer parts

2

- Ask students to look at the picture and label the computer parts correctly.
- Check answers as a class by choosing different students to say the answers.

ANSWERS
1 headphones 2 webcam 3 screen 4 speaker
5 printer 6 keyboard 7 mouse 8 monitor

GRAMMAR Simple present, adverbs, and expressions of frequency

3

- Ask students to read quickly through the conversation between an employee at the Computer Museum and a caller requesting information.
- Ask them to choose the correct options to complete the conversation.
- Let students compare their answers in pairs before you check answers as a class. When eliciting answers, encourage students to justify their choices.
- Finally, ask students to practice the completed conversation in pairs.

ANSWERS
1 Do you 2 we're always 3 do 4 pay
5 doesn't 6 normally has
7 from time to time we get 8 run

Articles: *a/an*, *the*, and zero article

4

- Tell students that they are going to read about a social networking site called WeAreFriends. Encourage them to read through the text quickly before they start to answer.
- Ask students to complete the description with *a/an*, *the*, or no article (–).
- Check answers as a class by choosing different students to read the description aloud sentence by sentence and eliciting why they chose each answer.

ANSWERS
1 the 2 a 3 (-) 4 the 5 the 6 a 7 a
8 (-)

Extra Resources

Go to the Teacher's Resource Center at mee2.macmillaneducation.com for:

- downloadable audio and audio scripts for the Student's Book and Workbook;
- videos and video scripts;
- extra vocabulary at two levels of difficulty;
- extra grammar at two levels of difficulty;
- CLIL lessons, with full teacher's notes;
- life skills lessons, with full teacher's notes;
- Speaking Database materials;
- the Move Beyond Level 3 wordlist;
- tips for using the Grammar Database
- and more!

Go to Workbook pages 84–95 for further practice material.

2 HOME AND AWAY

IN THE PICTURE Three apartments

Talk about homes and household chores *Pages 18–19*

STAGE	TIME	FOCUS
GET STARTED		Introduce the theme of the unit. Brainstorm chores around the house.
WORK WITH WORDS		Review and learn vocabulary for household objects and chores. Watch a video and listen for specific information. Pronounce words that have silent letters.
SPEAK		Use vocabulary from the lesson to ask and answer questions about chores.

Get started

Ask students: *What do you think this unit is going to be about?* (what people do inside their homes and what they do when they are away, i.e., somewhere different).

Elicit what *home* and *away* mean in a sports context (*home is the place where a sports team is based; when it plays at a place where the opposing team is based, it is playing away*).

Encourage students to think of household chores, and write them on the board (e.g., *do the laundry*, *make your bed*, *clean your room*, *feed the pet*, *walk the dog*, *do the dishes*, *set the table*, *sweep the floor*, *vacuum*). Use this as an opportunity to pre-teach target vocabulary if necessary. Elicit from students which household chores they like and don't like doing and why.

WORK WITH WORDS

1 RECALL

- Divide the class into pairs. Refer students to the picture of the three apartments. Set a three-minute time limit for them to list as many words as they can under the headings.
- If some students finish earlier than others, ask them to compare their lists with another pair.
- Invite students to write their answers on the board. Alternatively, check answers as a class, encouraging students to read any extra items they added to their lists aloud.
- Ask students to do the **Work with Words** task on page 70.
- Highlight that the stress is on the first syllable in *living room*, *washing machine*, and *dining room*, and practice the pronunciation of any vocabulary items as necessary.

2 ▶17

- Refer students back to the picture and ask them to read sentences 1–6 to find the names of the people to write in the picture. Point out the example given: *d Ethan*.
- Divide the class into pairs to compare their answers.
- Play the track for students to check their answers.

ANSWERS / AUDIO SCRIPT ▶17

a Josh b Alyssa c Nick *d Ethan* e Tyler f Linda

1 d Ethan is making his bed.
2 f Linda is loading the dishwasher.
3 b Alyssa is setting the table.
4 c Nick is vacuuming his room.
5 e Tyler is doing the laundry.
6 a Josh is mopping the floor.

3 ▶18

- Check that students know the meaning of all the household chores in the box.
- Play the track for students to listen and write what the people in the picture are doing one hour later. Elicit the tense being used (present progressive) and how this is formed (correct form of *be* + verb + *-ing*).
- Encourage students to work in pairs to compare their answers. Do not confirm answers at this point.

ANSWERS / AUDIO SCRIPT ▶18

1
Josh: Do you want any help with the dishes, Alyssa?
Alyssa: No, Josh. You finish clearing the table.
2
Nick: Where are you going, Ethan?
Ethan: I'm taking out the trash. Back in a minute, Nick.
Nick: Wait for me. I'm sorting the recycling.
3
Tyler: Linda! I can't hear the radio!
Linda: I can't hear you, Tyler. What did you say?
Tyler: Nothing, Linda.

4 ▶19

- Play the track for students to listen and check their answers to Exercise 3.
- Check that students have spelled *taking* correctly and, if necessary, remind them that when words end in one consonant and *e*, we delete the *e* and add *-ing*.
- Play the track again for students to listen and repeat.

ANSWERS / AUDIO SCRIPT ▶19

1 Josh is *clearing the table*.
2 Alyssa is washing the dishes.
3 Nick is sorting the recycling.
4 Ethan is taking out the trash.
5 Tyler is doing the ironing.
6 Linda is vacuuming.

5 THE MOVING PICTURE ▶

- Explain to students that they are going to watch a video of two teenagers doing household chores. Play the video and ask students to watch and make notes of what Tyler is doing.

ANSWERS / VIDEO SCRIPT

Nick: What are you doing, Tyler?
Tyler: I'm vacuuming.
Nick: What are you doing, Tyler?
Tyler: I'm mopping the kitchen floor.
Nick: What are you doing now, Tyler?
Tyler: I'm sorting the recycling.
Nick: What are you doing, Tyler?
Tyler: I'm taking out the trash.
Nick: What are you doing now, Tyler?
Tyler: I'm washing the dishes.
Nick: What are you doing, Tyler?
Tyler: I'm making my bed.

Extra activity

Play the video again with the sound turned down. Pause after each activity and ask students to try to remember the exact words for the conversation in each frame.

6

- Divide the class into pairs. Ask students to take turns acting out one of the chores from Exercise 2 or 3 for their partners to guess.
- Invite a more confident pair of students to demonstrate the activity for the class before they start.

Alternative procedure

Divide the class into two teams to race against each other. Write down the chores from Exercises 2 and 3 on pieces of paper and give one piece of paper to a volunteer from each team. The volunteer then acts out the activity without speaking and the volunteer's team guesses what it is.

When a team guesses correctly, another volunteer comes up for a piece of paper and acts out the next activity. The first team to say all the household chores wins.

7a ▶20 PRONOUNCE

- Play the track for students to listen to the word and underline the silent letter.

ANSWER / AUDIO SCRIPT ▶20

The *e* is silent.
make

7b ▶21

- Explain to students that two of the words have more than one silent letter.
- Play the track for students to listen and underline the silent letters in the words.
- Play the track again, eliciting the answers for students to check. Encourage them to repeat the words.
- Point out that the *e* in *knife* and the second *e* in *Wednesday* are silent too.
- Encourage students to think of other words with silent letters (e.g., *raspberry*, *vehicle*, *isle*, *know*, *often*).

ANSWERS / AUDIO SCRIPT ▶21

hour island knife listen load Wednesday

Extra activity

Dictate these groups of words for students to write in their notebooks:

1 listen castle last

2 know knee king

3 hour happy honest

Elicit which word in each group does not have a silent letter. Then ask students to underline the silent letter and circle its "talking partner" (i.e., the vowel or consonant that comes next to the silent letter, which is pronounced).

SPEAK

Extra activity

Elicit the adverbs of frequency from Unit 1 and write them on the board in random order (*never*, *sometimes*, *always*, *usually*, *normally*, *often*, *hardly ever*, etc.). Ask students to put them in order from the most to the least frequent.

8

- Divide the class into pairs to take turns asking and answering the questions using the options given. Circulate and monitor to make sure students are forming the questions correctly in question 3.
- Choose individual students to report their partner's answers to the class.

Extra activity

Ask students to estimate how much time they spend on each activity in a typical week. Invite students to come to the board and write the total amount of time they spend on household chores to see how they compare with the class average.

MOVE BEYOND

Ask students to do the **Move Beyond** task on page 70.

Homework

Ask students to write a description of their house or apartment. Remind them to use the vocabulary from the lesson and recycle the structures *be*, *have*, and *there is / there are*. Ask them to include one false sentence.

At the beginning of the next class, invite students to read their descriptions in small groups or pairs for the other students to guess which piece of information is false.

READING Living together

Understand the main ideas

Page 20

STAGE	TIME	FOCUS
GET STARTED		Recycle language from the previous lesson and discuss the advantages and disadvantages of family life.
SPEAK AND READ		Read a text quickly to understand the main ideas (reading subskill). Read the text again to find specific information.
REACT		Compare your family to the family in the text and express personal opinions on the topic of living together.

Get started

Ask students to close their books and make a list of advantages and disadvantages of living together in their family home.

Elicit ideas from different students and write them on the board (e.g., *Advantages: company, support, comfort*; *Disadvantages: lack of space, housework, sharing a bedroom, noise*).

Use this opportunity to pre-teach some of the target vocabulary from this lesson and recycle vocabulary to talk about household chores from the previous lesson.

SPEAK AND READ

1

- Divide the class into pairs to discuss the answers to the questions.
- Choose two or three students to report back to the class about where their partners live and the people they live with.

2a

- Encourage students to think of any tips they know for understanding the main ideas in a text. Elicit ideas and discuss as a class.
- Ask students to read the HOW TO box and see if they thought of the same tips.
- Ask them to cover the box and elicit the four tips. With the class, discuss how these tips can help them understand the main ideas in a text.

2b 22

- Ask students to read the article quickly and choose the best description, A, B, or C. Don't play the audio at this point. It is an extra feature, and suggestions for using it in class are included at the end of the lesson.
- Conduct a quick class survey by asking students to raise their hands to indicate whether they think the answer is A, B, or C. (This avoids putting the pressure on any one student.)
- Ask students what information helped them answer the question. (The text describes only one apartment, so A is incorrect. The style of the text is wrong for an official report – it would be more formal and factual – so C is incorrect. Ethan is giving his opinion on his family life, so B is the correct answer.)

ANSWER

B A teenage boy's view of life with his family.

Alternative procedure: less confident classes

Some of the words in the text may be difficult for less confident students. In this case, write words from the text and definitions in a random order on the board. Ask students to match the words with the correct definition.

An informal word for children – kids

Members of your family, especially those who do not live with you – relatives

Speak to each other in an angry way because you disagree – argue

Happening frequently or existing in large amounts or numbers – common

3

- Ask students to read the article again and check the information included.
- Set a two-minute time limit to encourage students to speed read, or scan, the text.
- As you check answers with the class, ask students to identify the paragraphs in which the information is found.

ANSWERS

Description of a family ✓ (paragraphs 1 and 3)
Facts about families in New York ✓ (paragraph 2)
Information about family life in China ✗
Interview with a parent ✗
The opinions of a teenage family member ✓ (paragraphs 3 and 4)

4

- Ask students to check the tips in the HOW TO box that helped them decide on both the general description and the information included in the text.
- Elicit from the class which tips they used and encourage students to check them.

MOVE BEYOND FOR TEACHERS

Economy and the family

The economic downturn has accelerated the trend toward several generations living under the same roof. As of 2010, 4.4 million homes in the USA held three generations or more under one roof, a 15 percent increase from 3.8 million households two years earlier.

In traditional Chinese culture, the family is the basic unit of society, while individuals are only one part of the family. In the past, extended families typically had four generations living under one roof. Although modern Chinese families often include only two generations living together, the tradition of four generations living together still remains.

5

Exam-type task

- Ask students to read the article again, this time in more detail, and decide if each statement is correct or incorrect.
- Check answers as a class. Ask students to justify their answers by identifying where they found the correct answers in the text or by correcting the information if a statement is incorrect.

ANSWERS

1 C (*In New York, it's common for several generations of a family to live in the same home.*)
2 I (*We have a lot of relatives in New York ... ; My dad is originally from China ...*)
3 I (*It's a fun place.*)
4 I (*There isn't a lot of space here ...*)
5 C (*Nick never cleans the bedroom.*)
6 I (*Mom and I argue a lot.*)

Fast finishers

Write some comprehension questions on the board for fast finishers to answer; for example, *How many kids live in the apartment?* (three) *How often does Ethan see his relatives?* (every day) *Who does Ethan argue with?* (his dad, his grandfather, and his mom).

MOVE BEYOND

Divide the class into pairs. Refer students back to the pictures on pages 18–19 and ask them to take turns describing what is happening in one of the other apartments.

Alternative procedure: more confident classes

Divide the class into pairs. Ask each student to choose one of the three apartments on pages 18–19. Students then take turns asking each other questions to find out which apartment their partners have chosen. This is a good opportunity for students to recycle vocabulary from the Starter unit by talking about different family members using the grammatical structure *Is there / Are there ... ?*

REACT

6

- Divide the class into pairs to discuss the questions about their reactions to the text.
- In a class discussion, invite different students to share their answers, encouraging them to say why their home is similar to or different from the Wang home.
- Ask students whether they argue with the people they live with and, if they do, how they solve the issues. Remember this could be a sensitive topic for some students, so try to keep the discussion light.

Recorded reading text 22

The audio can be used with Exercise 3. Ask students to cover the text and then play the audio track. Ask them to raise their hands when they hear each piece of information. Alternatively, the audio track could be used with Exercise 5. Ask students to cover the text and choose "C" or "I" based just on the listening. Then allow them to read the text again to check their answers.

Homework

Dictate these questions for students to write in their notebooks:

1 Is there anything funny or different about your family?

2 Does someone in your family keep a family tree? How far back can you trace your family history?

Ask students to answer the questions for homework and draw a family tree for at least three generations in their family. At the beginning of the next class, you could ask students to describe their families to a partner.

GRAMMAR Present progressive and simple present

Talk about things happening now, and about habits and routines *Page 21*

STAGE	TIME	FOCUS
GET STARTED		Recycle the simple present and introduce the topic of the lesson and the present progressive.
READ AND LISTEN		Read and listen for specific information.
STUDY		Refer to examples from a phone conversation to help you complete rules about the simple present, the present progressive, and stative verbs.
PRACTICE		Complete a conversation with the present progressive.
SPEAK		Discuss your daily schedule with a partner.

Get started

Ask students: *What activities do you do on a regular basis?* (e.g., *go to school, play soccer on Tuesday nights, have a guitar lesson*). Write their answers on the board.

Use this opportunity to recycle vocabulary and the simple present for routines and habits from Unit 1.

Ask students to write two sentences about a family member's routines and habits and two sentences to describe what a family member is doing now.

Circulate and monitor as students work to see how well they cope with this task and how much they already know. (See Teaching Tips, *Correct errors effectively*, page 24.)

READ AND LISTEN Grammar in context

1 ▶23

- Play the track for students to read and listen to the phone conversation. Ask them to make a note of why Beth is calling Jake.
- Check the answer as a class and ask students: *What do you think the relationship is between the speakers?* (They are school friends.)
- Divide the class into pairs to practice the conversation. Then have them switch roles and read it again. To make this more fun, and more like a real telephone conversation, ask students to sit back-to-back.

> **ANSWER / AUDIO SCRIPT** ▶23
> Beth is calling Jake because she needs his help with some math.
> See Student's Book, page 23, for audio script.

STUDY

2

- Ask students to underline the verbs in the simple present in Exercise 1. Elicit examples from the class.
- On the board, write the verbs *like*, *know*, *understand*, and *need* and elicit a sentence with each one. Write the sentences on the board, making sure that they are all in the simple present.
- Ask students what the sentences have in common, pointing to the verbs if necessary. Elicit that they are all in the simple present and that these verbs are not used with a progressive tense. Explain that they are stative verbs. (See Teaching Tips, *Stative verbs*, page 25.)
- Now ask students to underline the verbs in the present progressive in Exercise 1. Elicit examples from the class.
- Ask students to complete the explanations by considering the underlined examples from Exercise 1.
- Let students compare their answers with a partner before you check them as a class.

> **ANSWERS**
> simple present simple present simple present present progressive

PRACTICE

3

- Refer students to the conversation between Rob and Jake and go over the example sentence with the class.
- Ask them to complete the rest of the conversation with verbs in the present progressive form, using contracted forms wherever possible.
- Let students compare their answers in pairs before you check them as a class.

> **ANSWERS**
> 2 'm looking 3 's playing 4 're not/aren't practicing
> 5 's shopping 6 's studying

Alternative procedure: less confident classes

If students are unsure of the form of the present progressive, draw the following table on the board and fill in a few examples. Give students a couple of minutes to complete the table. Then ask different students to come up and fill in the table on the board. You may want to point out that there are two correct negative forms (e.g., *you aren't / you're not; he isn't / he's not*).

Affirmative sentences	*Negative sentences*
I'm playing.	*I'm not playing.*
He/She/It's playing.	*He/She/It isn't playing.*
We/You/They're playing.	*We/You/They aren't playing.*
Questions	***Short forms***
Am I playing?	*Yes, I am. / No, I'm not.*
Is he/she/it playing?	*Yes, he/she/it is.* *No, he/she/it isn't.*
Are we/you/they playing?	*Yes, we/you/they are.* *No, we/you/they aren't.*

4

- Refer students to the picture and invite them to predict what they think the text is going to be about (*a large family*).
- Ask them to read the text and choose the correct verb options. Draw students' attention to the example answer before they start.
- Let students compare answers before you check them as a class.

> **ANSWERS**
> 2 needs 3 usually take 4 is washing 5 are vacuuming
> 6 cleaning 7 spend 8 come 9 always has
> 10 is eating

5

- Ask students to read through the first two options. Elicit the correct option and the reason why (*simple present because* like *is a stative verb*).
- Ask students to check the correct options for the rest of the conversation. Tell them to underline the stative verb in their chosen options.
- Check answers and discuss any questions students may have.

> **ANSWERS**
> 2 a; understand 3 b; need 4 a; know 5 b; hate

SPEAK

6

- Choose two confident students to model the conversation first, or if necessary, begin by asking a student the questions.
- Divide the class into pairs to take turns saying a day and a time and asking what their partners usually do on that day and time.
- Highlight that this is a two-part conversation: first students imagine what they are doing at a particular time, and then they say whether this action is typical of their daily routine.

Homework

Ask students to describe a typical scene in their home at 8:30 p.m. They should write what their family members are doing at this time using the present progressive tense and vocabulary from the unit so far.

LISTENING AND VOCABULARY Soap opera

Understand a situation Page 22

STAGE	TIME	FOCUS
GET STARTED		Introduce the idea of soap operas.
SPEAK AND LISTEN		Discuss soap operas. Listen for specific information and talk about how to understand a situation when you listen (listening subskill).
REACT		Compare and discuss different endings for a soap opera.
WORK WITH WORDS		Identify free-time activities. Talk about your weekend free-time activities.

Get started

Write *soap opera* on the board and ask students if they know what it is (*a television series about the imaginary lives of a group of people*). Tell students that a soap opera is often simply called *a soap*.

Divide the class into pairs to think of kinds of people who often appear in soap operas (e.g., *a criminal, boyfriends and girlfriends*) and typical settings (e.g., *a family business, a hotel, the workplace*).

Do a "live listening" (see below) and talk about your favorite soap opera or a soap opera that you know. Ask some simple comprehension questions afterward to check understanding; for example, *Where is the soap opera set? What is it about? Is it popular?*

MODEL LIVE LISTENING

I like Home and Away, *an Australian soap opera that has the same name as this unit! The soap takes place in the fictional town of Summer Bay, on the Australian coast, and a lot of action takes place on the beach, like in many Australian towns. The people in the story come from four different families, and episodes are about the relationships among these people and things that happen to them. Many of the main characters are still the same after 20 years. There are shows for 46 weeks a year.*

SPEAK AND LISTEN

1

- Divide the class into pairs to discuss the questions about soap operas.
- Discuss their answers and ideas as a class.

2a

- Refer students to the HOW TO box and ask a volunteer to read the tips aloud for the class.
- Ask students: *How do you know if people who are having a conversation in your language know each other well?* (informal language, friendly intonation, laughter, etc.).

2b 24

- Draw students' attention to the first few lines of the excerpt from a soap opera to help situate them at the beginning of the listening.
- Ask students to predict why they think Sal isn't happy and what the relationship among the three people might be.
- Play the track for students to listen and answer the questions. Remind them that they are only listening for general information at this stage.
- Let students compare their answers in pairs to build confidence. When checking answers as a class, ask students which sound helped them decide where the soap opera takes place (*the school bell*).

ANSWERS / AUDIO SCRIPT 24

1 They are friends at school. They play together in a band.
2 They're outside the school.
3 The singer is leaving the group.

Keira: Hiya, Sal.
Sal: Hi!
Jack: What's up? You don't look very happy.
Sal: Nothing.
Jack: We're trying to arrange a practice on Saturday, but it's really hard. I'm going ice skating in the morning ...
Keira: ... and I'm meeting Lizzie and Sharon in the afternoon.
Jack: But you're only going shopping with them.
Keira: So?
Jack: So why can't you go shopping in the morning?
Keira: Why can't you go ice skating in the afternoon?
Jack: Because I have a class. I can't change it. Anyway, what about you, Sal? What are you doing on Saturday?
Sal: We need to talk.
Keira: What about?
Sal: I'm leaving the group.
Keira: What? Sal, you can't. We're playing at the school concert in two weeks. You're the singer!
Jack: Why do you want to leave?
Sal: You really don't know?
Jack: No, I don't.
Sal: Here's Tom. Ask *him*.
Keira: Sal, don't go. Sal, wait!
Tom: Hi, guys. What's up?
Keira: It's Sal. She's leaving the group.
Tom: I know.
Keira: You know? Why didn't you tell us?
Tom: It's kind of complicated. We're not speaking anymore.
Keira: You're kidding! Since when?
Tom: Since yesterday.
Keira: But we're playing in two weeks. And she's the singer. We can't play without her.
Jack: Here comes Mr. Gibbons.
Keira: Hello, Mr. Gibbons.
Mr. Gibbons: Hello, Keira, Jack, Tom. What are you all doing here?
Keira: We're talking about the concert.
Mr. Gibbons: Oh! I have some good news. The local radio station is coming to record it.
Jack: Oh, no!
Mr. Gibbons: What's wrong?
Tom: There's a problem.

3

- Ask students to look back at the HOW TO box and to check the tips that helped them in Exercise 2b.
- Discuss students' ideas as a class.

4 ▶24

- Play the track again for students to listen and match the sentence halves. Go over the example answer with the class before they start.
- Let students compare their answers in pairs before you elicit the answers from different students.

ANSWERS
2 Keira is hanging out with Lizzie and Sharon in the afternoon.
3 Mr. Gibbons has some good news.
4 Tom isn't speaking to Sal.
5 Sal is leaving the group.
6 The group is playing in two weeks.

Alternative procedure: less confident classes

In a less confident class, ask students some follow-up comprehension questions to make sure they have fully understood the listening. For example: *What do they want to do on Saturday morning?* (They want to practice together for the concert in two weeks.) *Why can't Jack go ice skating on Saturday afternoon?* (He has a class.) *Why is Sal leaving the group?* (She isn't speaking to Tom anymore.) *Why is she so important in the group?* (She's the singer, and they can't play without her.) *What good news does Mr. Gibbons have?* (A local radio station is coming to record the concert.)

Extra activity

Point out to students that watching soap operas is a great way to develop their English, as these programs are full of "everyday English."

Write the definitions of some typical English expressions on the board. Then play the track again for students to match the definitions to the expressions they hear:

An expression to say you don't believe something because it is so surprising. (You're kidding!)

An expression used for asking what's wrong / an informal way of saying "How are you?" (What's up?)

An expression used for saying "Be careful." (Watch out.)

Ask students to write a couple of sentences for each of these expressions to show they understand what they mean and how to use them.

REACT

5

- Divide the class into pairs to discuss what they think will happen next and at the concert in two weeks' time.
- Elicit and discuss students' ideas as a class.

WORK WITH WORDS

6a

- Refer students to the pictures a–j and ask them to match these to the list of free-time activities.
- Let students compare their answers before checking them as a class.

ANSWERS
a collect cards b read magazines c go ice skating
d use social networking sites e play an instrument
f watch online videos g go to acting class h visit exhibitions
i hang out with friends j do judo

6b

- Encourage students to think of other free-time activities using the verbs in Exercise 6a and write them in their notebooks.

Extra activity

Play a game of *Hot Seat* (see Games, page 29) using free-time activities. If this is the first time the class has played, do an example with them first.

7

- Divide the class into pairs to talk about the free-time activities they usually do on weekends. Read the examples and give one of your own before they start.
- Invite a few students to explain to the class what their partner's weekend activities are.

Alternative procedure: more confident classes

Tell students that they are going to circulate, as if at a party, and that they must have a conversation with at least three different people about their free-time activities. If space is limited, divide the class into pairs and tell them to turn around and join the pair of students behind them to make a group of four. You could put some quiet music on in the background to create a relaxed atmosphere.

Before they start the activity, elicit the most common question words and write them on the board: *Why*, *Where*, *How*, *What*, *Who*, *When*. Tell students that they must try to make each conversation last for as long as possible by asking at least three follow-up questions using the question words. Model this activity with a pair of more confident students first.

Model exchange:

A: On Saturdays, I usually go shopping.

B: Where do you go shopping?

A: I usually go to the Gold Star shopping mall.

B: Who do you go with?

A: I usually go with my sister.

B: How do you get there?

A: By bus.

MOVE BEYOND

Ask students to do the **Move Beyond** task on page 70.

Homework

Ask students to write a formal email to a friend to describe their typical weekend free-time activities. Ask them to write 80–100 words and to include one false sentence. At the beginning of the next class, students can read their texts aloud for a partner to guess the false piece of information.

GRAMMAR Present progressive for future arrangements

Talk about arrangements in the future Page 23

STAGE	TIME	FOCUS
GET STARTED		Define and discuss arrangements in the future.
READ AND LISTEN		Read and listen for specific information.
STUDY		Complete examples of the present progressive for future arrangements.
PRACTICE		Recognize and produce target language in written exercises.
SPEAK		Produce target language in a speaking task to discuss future arrangements.

Get started

Write the word *arrangement* on the board and elicit its meaning (*definite plans for a future event*). Then write the following verbs and time expressions: *go*, *come*, *meet*, *see*, *stay*, *tonight*, *tomorrow*, and *this weekend*.

Divide the class into pairs to tell each other about two future arrangements they have planned using the verbs and time expressions on the board. As a guide, write these example sentences on the board and elicit words to fill in the blanks:

I ________ (meet) my ________ next ________.
My friend ________ (come) to ________ on ________.
I ________ (see) my ________ on ________ night.

Monitor as students speak, noting some examples of their sentences. Then write some of their sentences on the board and ask students to say whether the tense they used was correct or incorrect.

Introduce the present progressive for talking about future arrangements and tell students that today they will learn how to use this tense. (See Teaching Tips, *Present progressive tense*, page 25.)

READ AND LISTEN Grammar in context

1 25

- Refer students to the photo on page 25 and ask them to describe it.
- Play the track for students to read and listen in order to answer the question about what Mario and Fiona are doing on the weekend. Suggest that they underline the relevant words in the conversation.
- Elicit answers from the class and ask them to read aloud the lines from the text that tell them the answer.

ANSWERS / AUDIO SCRIPT 25

Mario is playing soccer. (*We're playing away in Newton.*)
Fiona is helping her dad clean the house. (*I'm helping Dad clean the house this weekend.*)
See Student's Book, page 23, for audio script.

STUDY

2

- Ask students to circle the time expressions in the conversation in Exercise 1 (*on the weekend*, *on Saturday*, *this weekend*, *next week*, *at the end of the month*).
- Read the grammar rules aloud and ask students to complete the examples. Check answers as a class.

ANSWERS

is playing on the weekend

PRACTICE

3

- Draw students' attention to the example sentence and ask them to write the rest of the questions using the prompts.
- Monitor and offer help if necessary.
- Give students time to compare their answers in pairs before you check them as a class. To do this, choose different students to give the answers.

ANSWERS

2 Where is the team playing?
3 Who is Fiona helping on Saturday?
4 Why are they cleaning the house?
5 When is Fiona's cousin leaving?

Extra activity

The acronym QASV (Question, Auxiliary, Subject, Verb) is often taught to help students formulate questions with the words in the correct order. Ask students to make up a mnemonic from the letters that is easier for them to remember (e.g., Quit Apps [that] Show Viruses).

4

- Ask students to answer the questions from Exercise 3.
- Then let them compare their answers in pairs before you check them as a class.

ANSWERS

1 He's playing on Saturday. 2 It's playing in Newton.
3 She's helping her dad.
4 They're cleaning the house because her cousin is coming to stay.
5 She's leaving at the end of the month.

5

- Refer students to Mario's planner for next week. Ask them to write sentences about his plans. Go over the example sentence before they start.
- Give students time to compare their answers before you check them as a class.

ANSWERS

On Wednesday he's going to the movies at 7:15 p.m./quarter past seven.
On Thursday he's going to an acting class at 6:20 p.m./twenty past six.
On Friday he's meeting Fiona and her cousin in the afternoon.
On Saturday he's doing judo.

6

- Ask students to put the time expressions in the correct order starting with the most recent.
- Invite different volunteers to write them on the board to check the answers.

ANSWERS

2 this afternoon 3 at 7 p.m. 4 tonight 5 tomorrow
6 this weekend 7 next week 8 in two weeks 9 next year

7

- Encourage students to think about their own arrangements and complete the sentences.
- Divide the class into small groups to share their information. Circulate to check their use of the present progressive. (See Teaching Tips, *Correct errors effectively*, page 24.)

Alternative procedure: more confident classes

Ask students to write sentences about three true arrangements and one false one. Divide the class into pairs to take turns reading their sentences aloud to each other and guessing the false one.

SPEAK

8

- Divide the class into pairs and ask Student A to look at the plans on page 75 of the Student's Book and Student B to look at the plans on page 76.
- Explain that they are trying to arrange to go to a movie and need to find a suitable time. Draw students' attention to the example conversation and ask a more confident pair of students to model the conversation for the rest of the class.
- Circulate and monitor as they work, making notes on anything you would like to give feedback on at the end of the exercise.

Homework

Ask students to imagine and write a famous person's arrangements for their blog, using the same sentence prompts as in Exercise 7. They should include enough clues for other students to guess who the person is. At the beginning of the next class, students can read their arrangements aloud in small groups for others to guess who the famous person is.

You could read these sentences aloud as an example:
This evening I'm practicing with my team. On the weekend I'm playing a soccer game against Madrid. Next month I'm traveling to play with my national team in Argentina. In the summer I'm spending time with my family and my little son.
Answer = Lionel Messi

LANGUAGE & BEYOND GET THINKING

Identify the cause of a problem

Page 24

STAGE	TIME	FOCUS
GET STARTED		Introduce the idea of understanding a problem and finding a solution by using a problem-solving model.
SPEAK AND READ		Look at a problem and discuss different points of view.
DO		Suggest solutions to a problem.
REFLECT		Talk about the importance of recognizing different points of view.
EXTEND		Think of and discuss solutions to a different problem.

LIFE SKILLS

UNDERSTANDING A PROBLEM

The best way to deal with conflict is to negotiate with the other person involved. One of the most effective ideas is the "win-win" approach. This approach is about both people being satisfied with the outcome. Point out to students that negotiating skills are important in many jobs and also in their personal life.

To reach a win-win outcome, you have to find out what you both want and where there are areas that you can both agree on. This means listening to each other and developing empathy. Remind students that it is important to stay calm in any negotiation.

Ask students how listening and empathy can help them solve the problems they talked about at the beginning of the lesson and how they can apply these problem-solving techniques in their own lives.

Get started

Recycle the life skill that students studied in Unit 1. Divide the class into pairs to write a list of any problems that they are having right now at school (e.g., *too much homework, too many exams, not enough lockers, not enough study time*).
Elicit items from students' lists and write them on the board. Encourage students to choose their own most important problem.

Write the six steps of a "Problem-Solving Model" on the board:
1 *Define the problem.*
2 *Set the goal.*
3 *Think about your options.*
4 *Take an action.*
5 *Check that it works.*
6 *Change it until the goal is reached.*

Encourage students, in the same pairs, to help each other solve their problems by talking through each step of the Problem-Solving Model. If appropriate, invite some more-confident students to talk about their partner's problem and say whether they talked about strategies for each step.

SPEAK AND READ

1

- Refer students to the pictures and ask them to identify the problem. Elicit possible causes of the problem as a class.

2

- Divide the class into pairs and ask Student A to read Lauren's point of view and Student B to read Grace's point of view.

Fast finishers

Write the following definitions on the board and ask students to find words in the texts to match them:

To behave in a particular way because you want someone to believe that something is true when it isn't. (pretend)

When people are treated equally and in a reasonable way. (fair)

3

- Ask students, in the same pairs, to take turns explaining the point of view they have just read, in their own words, to their partner.

DO

4

- Divide the class into small groups to answer the questions. Set a time limit of five minutes.
- Ask a spokesperson from each group to say how the group answered the questions.

ANSWERS

1 Both of them.
2 No, they don't understand each other's problem.
3 They both think the other person / the situation is unfair.

5

- In the same groups, ask students to think of and discuss possible solutions to the problems. Draw attention to the prompts to give students ideas about what they can say.

REFLECT

6

- Ask students to discuss the questions as a class.
- Invite a volunteer to read the REFLECTION POINT aloud to see if the class agrees with it.

EXTEND

7

- Invite a volunteer to read what Ethan says aloud. Then divide the class into different groups to discuss Ethan's problem. Set a suitable time limit for this.
- Ask the groups to choose a spokesperson to share their ideas with the class.

Homework

Ask students to write a short letter for the Problem Page of a teenage magazine about a problem they are having. At the beginning of the next class, ask students to exchange their problems and use the Problem-Solving Model to help them think of a solution to the problem.

SPEAKING On the phone

Check that you understand on the phone Page 25

STAGE	TIME	FOCUS
GET STARTED		Play a game of *Broken Telephone* to introduce the idea of communicating clearly.
SPEAK		Talk about your family phone.
LISTEN		Listen for general and specific information in a telephone conversation. Learn how to check that you understand on the phone (speaking subskill).
ACT		Role-play leaving a message on the phone.

Get started

Play a game of *Broken Telephone* (see Games, page 29) to introduce the idea of communication breakdown and the importance of good pronunciation when talking on the phone. Explain to students that today they will learn some expressions that English speakers use when they don't hear something clearly.

SPEAK

1

- Divide the class into pairs to discuss the questions.
- Invite different pairs to share their answers with the class.

Alternative procedure

You could leave this exercise until the end of the class to finish off with a class discussion and survey about family phones. (In this case, ask students to raise their hands and ask a student to count and write the numbers on the board.)

LISTEN

2 26

- Have students close their books and play the first track for them to find out who Matt wants to speak to and why. Explain that they will hear only Kate's side of the conversation.
- Let them compare answers before checking as a class.

ANSWERS / AUDIO SCRIPT 26

Matt is calling Keith. He wants to tell Keith to meet him outside the Treetop coffee shop at eight o'clock.

Kate: Hello?
Kate: Hi, Matt. Keith isn't here right now.
Kate: Yes. Hold on. Let me get a pen ... OK. I'm ready.
Kate: Sorry? Can you say that again? It's a bad connection.
Kate: How do you spell that?
Kate: Outside the Treetop coffee shop. At eight o'clock ... Sorry. You're breaking up. I can't hear you. Could you repeat that?
Kate: 555-348-7792. OK.
Kate: Bye.

3a

- Invite a volunteer to read the tips in the HOW TO box aloud. Ask the class if they think it is good advice.
- Point out that even native speakers ask each other to repeat and confirm information. This is especially important if you are taking a message for someone else.

3b 27

- Ask students to try to complete the common phrases that were used in the conversation. They could work individually or in pairs. Before they start, refer them to the example answer.
- Play the track for students to listen and check their answers.
- Play the track again for students to listen and repeat.

ANSWERS / AUDIO SCRIPT 27

1 *Sorry? Can you say that again?*
2 It's a bad connection.
3 How do you spell that?
4 Sorry. You're breaking up.
5 I can't hear you.
6 Could you repeat that?

4

- Ask students to complete the conversation in Exercise 2 with the sentences given. You may want to let them do this in pairs.
- Read the part of Kate aloud and invite different students to read the part of Matt. Each time ask the rest of the class if they agree, but don't confirm the answers.

5 28

- Now play the complete conversation for students to listen and check their answers.
- Divide the class into pairs and ask them to read the conversation aloud. They could sit back-to-back to do this.

ANSWERS / AUDIO SCRIPT 28

1 c 2 a 3 g 4 f 5 b 6 d 7 e

Kate: Hello?
Matt: Hi. It's Matt. Can I speak to Keith?
Kate: Hi, Matt. Keith isn't here right now.
Matt: Can I leave a message?
Kate: Yes. Hold on. Let me get a pen ... OK. I'm ready.
Matt: Tell him we're ...
Kate: Sorry? Can you say that again? It's a bad connection.
Matt: I'm calling from the train. I said we're all meeting at eight outside the Treetop coffee shop.
Kate: How do you spell that?
Matt: T-r-e-e-t-o-p.
Kate: Outside the Treetop coffee shop. At eight o'clock ... Sorry. You're breaking up. I can't hear you. Could you repeat that?
Matt: If there's a problem, he can call me at 555-348-7792.
Kate: 555-348-7792. OK.
Matt: Thanks, Kate. Bye.
Kate: Bye.

6

- Ask students to work individually to write Kate's note for Keith.
- Let students compare their notes in pairs. Then check them as a class by inviting several students to read their note aloud.

MODEL ANSWER

Keith, Matt called. You're all meeting at 8:00 outside the Treetop coffee shop. You can call him at 555-348-7792 if there's a problem.

ACT

7 29

- Divide the class into groups of four and then have students form pairs within their groups.
- Ask each pair to prepare a message to leave in a phone conversation. Remind them to use phrases from Exercise 3b and the PHRASEBOOK box.
- Play the track for students to listen and repeat the phrases from the PHRASEBOOK box.
- When they have written their messages, ask students to take turns calling a student in the other pair, asking to speak to someone who isn't there, and leaving a message for that person.
- Point out that when they have finished, they should check that the information in the message is complete and correct.
- Circulate and monitor as they work, making notes of anything you would like to give feedback on at the end of the activity.
- Ask one or two confident pairs to perform their conversations in front of the class to end the exercise.

Homework

Ask students to write a short article for a teen magazine about the advantages and disadvantages of the different kinds of phones in Exercise 1. Brainstorm some ideas to help students start writing (*expensive/cheap, noisy/private, portable/not portable*, etc.).

To help less confident students, write some sentence prompts on the board:

The good/bad thing about (a landline, a cell phone, an internet phone) is ... .

WRITING My status update

Use *and*, *also*, and *too*

Page 26

STAGE	TIME	FOCUS
GET STARTED		Introduce the idea of a status update.
SPEAK AND READ		Talk about photos. Read updates and match them to the photos. Explore the use of *and*, *also*, and *too* to link similar ideas (writing subskill).
PRACTICE		Produce target language in a written exercise.
DISCUSS		Plan a dream vacation.
WRITE		Write a status update about your dream vacation.
SHARE		Describe your dream vacation to classmates. Decide which vacation you would like to take and which one you would not like to take.

Get started

Play a game of *Snowman* (see Games, page 29) to introduce one of the lesson's key vocabulary items: *status update* (6 + 6 letters).

Elicit the meaning of *status update* (*a short, text-based entry telling your friends what you are doing and feeling*) and ask students where they think they can find status updates (*on social networking sites*).

SPEAK AND READ

1

- Refer students to the photos and ask them to describe them in pairs.
- Direct students' attention to the PHRASE BYTES box.

SUGGESTED ANSWERS
This is a photo of a boat ride.
This is a big tower, but I don't know what's in it.
This is an old building. Maybe it's a museum or historic site.
I think this is a government building or a museum.
This is an orca (killer whale).

2

- Ask students to read the updates and identify the place that is not mentioned.
- When checking answers as a class, ask which photo is not mentioned and elicit the reasons for their answers.

ANSWERS
Update 1 mentions whales and an aquarium, and there is a whale in photo e.
Update 2 mentions a boat on the river (photo a) and the Tower of the Americas (photo b).
Update 3 mentions a big hotel, and photo d looks like a hotel.
Photo c (the Alamo) is not mentioned. The Alamo is an old building, and the updates don't mention old buildings.

3a

- Invite a volunteer to read the tips in the HOW TO box aloud.

3b

- Refer students back to the status updates in Exercise 2 to find examples of *and*, *too*, and *also*.
- Choose different students around the class to say the answers.

ANSWERS
We're also having pizza tonight.
...and we're sitting in a boat on the river.
You can watch a video too.

PRACTICE

4

- Ask students to write the sentences with the words in parentheses. Draw their attention to the example sentence.
- Let students compare their answers in pairs before you check them as a class.

ANSWERS
2 I like traveling. I like staying at home too.
3 It's raining and the bus is late.
4 I love reading. Ana also loves books.
5 This evening I'm meeting friends and we're going to the movies.
6 New York is an amazing city. San Antonio is an interesting place too.

DISCUSS

5

- Write *dream vacation* on the board and check meaning by asking: *Is it a good thing?* (Yes!) *Is it really going to happen?* (Probably not.)
- Tell students about your dream vacation, saying where you'd like to go and what you'd like to do.
- Ask them to work in pairs and decide on a dream vacation destination. Encourage them to talk about the fun activities they would like to do.

Alternative procedure: less confident classes
Ask students to close their eyes. Take them on a short, guided visualization in preparation for talking and writing about their dream vacation; for example, *I want you to imagine it's the first day of summer vacation. How do you feel? Excited? Relaxed? Imagine you are going somewhere amazing with your family or with your friends. Where are you going? How are you getting there? Now imagine you are there. What's it like? Is it hot? Cold? What are you doing? etc.*

WRITE

6

- Tell students that they are going to write a status update about their dream vacation.
- Go over the first instruction in the box. Explain that this refers to the content they should include in their status update. Ask students to point out examples from the status updates about San Antonio. For example: Describe where you are. (*I'm with my family in San Antonio. We're staying in a big hotel near downtown.*) Describe what you're doing. (*It's day two of our weekend in San Antonio and we're sitting in a boat on a river.*)
- Remind students to use the present progressive when they write about activities happening now and in the near future. Point out that when we update our status on social networking sites, we often use the present progressive to write or talk about the activity that is taking place or arrangements for the future. Refer students to status update 2 and ask them which activity is happening in the photo (i.e., *We're sitting in a boat*), and which is arranged for the near future (i.e., *Dad is taking me up the Tower of the Americas this afternoon*).
- Encourage students to connect their ideas with *and*, *to*, and *also* as they did in Exercise 4. Refer them to examples from the San Antonio status updates if necessary.
- Set a time limit of 15 minutes. Monitor and remind students of the content and language they should be including as you check their work.

SHARE

7

- Organize students into small groups of no more than five.
- Ask them to take turns reading their status updates and describing their dream vacations.
- Ask them to discuss as a group which of the vacations they would all like to take, giving reasons for their preferences. Encourage them to choose one of the vacations that everyone in the group would enjoy.
- Ask each group to report back to the class on the vacation they have chosen and why they would like it. Ask if there were any vacations mentioned that they would *not* like to take and why.

Homework

Ask students to find three photos of tourist attractions in a city they've visited or would like to visit. Encourage them to write a status update for each photo to explain to a friend what they are doing at that moment, as they'd do on a social networking site. Ask students to cut out their photos and status updates. At the beginning of the next class, ask students to work in pairs to exchange their status updates and photos for their partners to match back together.

VOCABULARY Homes and household chores

1

- Refer students to the picture and elicit what household chores they think Harry can do.
- Ask them to complete the missing words in the text using the first letter as a clue.
- Check answers as a class by choosing different students to give the answers.

ANSWERS
1 make 2 clean 3 vacuum 4 mop
5 laundry 6 ironing 7 set 8 clear 9 wash
10 dishwasher 11 recycling 12 trash

Free-time activities

2

- Refer students to the verbs in the box and ask them to use them to complete the free-time activities listed.
- Let students compare their answers in pairs before checking them as a class.

ANSWERS
1 visit 2 go 3 do 4 play 5 read 6 go
7 hang out 8 use 9 watch 10 collect

GRAMMAR Present progressive and simple present

3

- Refer students to the postcard format and elicit when people usually send postcards (*when on vacation*).
- Ask students to complete the postcard by using the prompts in parentheses. Point out that they need to decide whether each verb should be in the simple present or present progressive according to the context.
- Check answers as a class by asking different students to read a sentence aloud.

ANSWERS
1 I'm writing 2 sun is shining 3 I'm sitting
4 She loves 5 She comes 6 Dad's shopping
7 isn't playing 8 Are you doing

Present progressive for future arrangements

4

- Encourage students to read through the phone conversation quickly to get the gist of it.
- Ask them to put Harry's words in the correct order to complete the conversation.
- Check answers as a class by asking a confident pair of students to read the conversation aloud.

ANSWERS
1 Hello. It's Harry.
2 When are you coming home?
3 I am going back to the factory tonight.
4 They are fixing some problems.
5 Another robot is starting work tomorrow.
6 He's arriving at 9 a.m. His name is Harry too.

Extra Resources

Go to the Teacher's Resource Center at mee2.macmillaneducation.com for:

- the Speaking section of the Progress Check 1&2;
- a downloadable project linked to Units 1–2;
- downloadable audio and audio scripts for the Student's Book and Workbook;
- videos and video scripts;
- extra vocabulary at two levels of difficulty;
- extra grammar at two levels of difficulty;
- culture lessons, with full teacher's notes;
- a life skills lesson, with full teacher's notes;
- Speaking Database materials;
- the Beyond A2+ wordlist;
- tips for using the Grammar Database;
- and more!

Go to Workbook pages 96–107 for further practice material.

PROGRESS CHECK 1&2

Preparing for the Progress Check

The Progress Check can be done either as review of the units or as a formal test. For the first one, it is a good idea to have students prepare thoroughly so that they get into the habit of regularly reviewing what they have learned. Reassure the class that the Progress Check contains only material that they have covered in the previous two units.

Ask students what they would advise a friend who was about to take a test. Students should be able to come up with tips such as *Try to relax. Read the instructions carefully. Don't worry about unknown words.* Write these on the board before asking the class to vote on the most important tip.

Vocabulary review

- Draw a table on the board with the following headings: *Applications (Apps), Computer parts, Homes and household chores, Free-time activities.*
- Invite students to come to the board and write vocabulary items under each heading; as they do this, check that everyone remembers the items. The list does not need to be complete.
- With several items in each column, refer students to the Unit Reviews on pages 17 and 27. Encourage them to call out any items that they missed. Students can then go through the Progress Check and see how many of the items they can find.

Grammar review

- Remind students that they studied a number of grammar points on pages 11, 13, 21, and 23. Start a "race," in which students tell you the main grammar points from each unit. (Unit 1 – Simple present, adverbs, and expressions of frequency; Articles: *a/an, the,* and zero article; Unit 2 – Present progressive and simple present; Present progressive for future arrangements). Write these on the board, asking for examples as students call them out.

Optional warm-up activities

READ Exercise 1

- Ask students to look at Exercise 1 in the Progress Check and ask the following questions: *What kind of questions are they?* (four-option multiple choice); *Where do you find the answers?* (in the text).
- Ask students to tell you what they understand *without* reading the main text. If necessary, tell them to look at the information above the main text. Elicit the following:
  The app is very popular (it has five stars).
  The app is for sale (there is a button saying Buy now*).*
  The app is called Family Solutions *(suggesting that it helps with family problems).*
- Point out how much useful information students have discovered before they even start reading the text.

LISTEN Exercise 2

- Refer students back to the listening activities and the HOW TO boxes on pages 12 and 22. Ask several students to tell you which tips they thought were the most useful.
- Inform students that they can (and should) find out a lot of useful information even before they start listening. Illustrate this to them by discussing the following questions about the first item:
  What are they selling? (a computer)
  What are the numbers? (prices)
  What is going to happen? (either a customer talking to a store clerk about buying a computer, or someone advertising a computer)
- Divide the class into pairs or small groups and ask them to discuss the other items in a similar way. After a minute or two, ask questions about items 2–5.

WRITE Exercise 3

- Write the following on the board:
  A I don't go to the movies very often.
  B I .... *to the movies.*
- Tell students to think about what they need to write to make the sentences grammatically correct. Point out that the blank should not have more than three words. Ask them to tell you what is missing in the second sentence (*the verb and the expression of frequency*).
- Point out that the blank can be filled with another negative (i.e., *I <u>don't often go</u> to the movies*). However, that would technically be four words because *don't* counts as two words (*do not*). So ask students to think of another expression of frequency that fits but does not change the meaning. Elicit the following possible answers and write them on the board: *I <u>rarely go</u> to the movies. / I <u>hardly ever go</u> to the movies. / I <u>occasionally go</u> to the movies.*

The activity above will help students answer the first two questions in Exercise 3. Give help with the other two questions (e.g., Question 3: elicit that the noun *teacher* needs a different verb and an article; Question 4: elicit that the verb should be in the present progressive tense).

WRITE Exercise 4

- Refer students back to the work they did on correct word order on page 16 and the use of *and, also,* and *too* on page 26. Make sure students understand the importance of these grammar points in their own writing.
- Ask students to write their names and one or two of their own free-time activities on a piece of paper. Collect the pieces of paper and ask different students: *How often do you (play soccer)? / When do you (watch videos)?*

Doing the Progress Check

READ

1

- If you have decided not to do the full warm-up, remind students of the reading texts and the HOW TO boxes that they have studied (on pages 10 and 20), as well as the information they learned about apps (from pages 18 and 9). Stress that they do not need to understand every word of the text in order to answer the questions.
- Go through the **Test-Taking Tips** with the class and make sure they understand that this is the best way to approach multiple-choice questions.
- Allow 10–15 minutes for this section.

ANSWERS
1 C 2 C 3 B 4 A 5 C

LISTEN

2 ▶30

- If you have decided not to do the full warm-up, encourage students to spend a minute or two looking at the pictures and predicting what they might hear. Explain that they have to check one of the pictures according to what they hear.
- Go over the **Test-Taking Tips** for the listening task. Refer students back to the work they did on pages 12, 22, and 25.
- Point out that they will hear everything twice.

ANSWERS / AUDIO SCRIPT ▶30
1 B 2 C 3 C 4 A 5 B
1
How much is the computer?
Announcer: This week only! This super computer with monitor, keyboard, and printer usually costs $499. But you can save $200 – yes, $200! – and pay only $299. That's right, $299. Only at Computerland.

2
Where is Danny?
Girl: Hi, Danny, can you hear me? I'm ...
Boy: Can you say that again?
Girl: I'm at the bus stop. I'm waiting for the bus.
Boy: OK. I'm at the movie theater. I'm waiting for you!

3
Where are the speakers, and what are they talking about?
Reporter: Excuse me ... Can I ask you some questions?
Teen: Uh ... What about?
Reporter: Cell phones. How many text messages do you send every day?
Teen: Uhmm ... well ... about 40, 50 maybe. Oh, sorry, I have to go, I have a message.

4
What are the girls doing tomorrow afternoon?
Girl 1: Do you want to go shopping tomorrow afternoon?
Girl 2: I hate shopping on Saturdays. It's always busy. What about ice skating?
Girl 1: Um ... yeah, OK. I'm going to judo in the morning, but the class is over at 11:30.

5
Which instrument does the boy want to play?
Boy: I want to learn how to play an instrument, but I don't know which one. I don't want to play the guitar ... What do you think?
Girl: Well, my brother plays the piano and my sister plays the drums. I think the piano sounds much nicer!
Boy: Hm, playing the drums is a good idea. I think the piano's a little boring.

WRITE

3

- Read through the **Test-Taking Tips** for this task. Make sure students understand that they can write one, two, or three words in the blanks but no more.
- Explain that this kind of task is often grammar-based. Mention the main grammar points they have studied in Units 1 and 2 (i.e., Unit 1 – Simple present, adverbs, and expressions of frequency; Articles: *a/an*, *the*, and zero article; Unit 2 – Present progressive and simple present; Present progressive for future arrangements).
- Stress that the meaning of the second sentence has to match that of the first sentence.
- Explain that spelling is important in this kind of task. In a real test, they would lose points for spelling mistakes.

ANSWERS
1 I hardly ever read books. 2 I always watch online videos after school. 3 My mom is a math teacher. 4 I'm meeting my friend tomorrow.

4

- Since this is the first test of students' writing, spend a few minutes going through the task with them, eliciting whom they have to write to and what their message must include (the three bullet points) in order for them to get full credit.
- Refer students back to the writing activities and the HOW TO boxes on pages 16 and 26. Ask what they learned from these tasks. Stress the importance of correct word order. Remind them to include sentences with *and*, *also*, and *too*.
- Finally, remind students of the word limit and the importance of checking their own spelling, grammar, etc.

MODEL ANSWER
Hi, Angelo.
I listen to music every day. I sometimes listen online, but I usually chat. I can also play the guitar. I have lessons on Tuesdays and Thursdays. What activities do you do? How often do you do them?

After the Progress Check

Optional game

This game follows up on the theme from the writing section and will help lighten the atmosphere after the test.

- Ask students to look back at the free-time activities on page 22.
- Write the following question on the board: *What are you doing tomorrow?*
- Elicit different answers from individual students (tell them that it does not have to be true). Then ask them what they are doing after that. (*So tomorrow you're doing judo. And then?*) Elicit from a few students sentences like: *Tomorrow I'm doing judo. Then I'm going to an acting class.*
- Tell students they are going to play a memory game and they have to try to remember what was said before.
- Begin by asking Student A: *What are you doing tomorrow?* (Elicit something like: *Tomorrow I'm doing judo. Then I'm going to an acting class.*)
- Ask Student A to ask Student B the same question. Student B then repeats the activities and adds one more; for example, *Tomorrow I'm doing judo. Then I'm going to an acting class. Then I'm going ice skating.*
- Student B then asks Student C, who repeats the three activities before adding a fourth.
- Keep going around the class until someone makes a mistake or can't think of a new activity. If the chain is broken, have that student start again and continue until all the members of the class have had a turn.

Feedback and extension

After the test has been graded, provide feedback to the class as a whole and individually as much as possible. Ask students which parts they found the most difficult and how they think they could improve their grades for next time.

READ

- Review the questions one at a time and encourage students to say which answers are wrong. Where there were mistakes, find out whether the problems were in understanding the text or the questions.
- The more reading in English students can do, the better. A lot of the online material they see will be in English. Explain that they can improve their reading by reading articles, messages, pop-ups, and instructions. Warn students that many comments, however, are not written in good English.

LISTEN

- Handing out photocopies of the audio script is a good way to provide feedback. Deal with any mistakes in this way. Seeing the conversations written down helps students recognize if they have misheard something. It will also help them become aware of distractors.

WRITE

- Students who struggled with Exercise 3 need to focus on the grammar points they have studied. Write one or two example sentences on the board and then divide students into groups of four to come up with more examples of their own. If necessary, give more examples for homework.
- For students who had difficulty with Exercise 4, do a similar task asking students to create a message saying what everyone is doing now. Ask a variety of questions about different people; for example, *What are you / What is Anna / What are your parents doing now?*
- Correct any mistakes and then write on the board: *Hi, Angelo*. Build up a written text on the board. You could write this yourself, based on suggestions, or have individual students come to the board and write a sentence each.

3 UNIT WILD WORLD

IN THE PICTURE The natural world

Talk about landscapes and natural features *Pages 30–31*

STAGE	TIME	FOCUS
GET STARTED		Recycle vocabulary and brainstorm natural features to introduce the theme of the unit.
WORK WITH WORDS		Match natural features to photos. Answer general knowledge questions about specific places in the world. Watch a video and listen for specific geographical information.
SPEAK		Use the vocabulary from the lesson to describe a natural feature.

Get started

Play a game of *Three in a Row* (see Games, page 29). Draw a grid on the board and label the squares A–I. Tell students to follow the instructions in order to win each corresponding square. Write the following on the board:

A *Name two different types of weather.* (windy, sunny, rainy, snowy, etc.)
B *What is blue, gray, or black and has clouds?* (the sky)
C *Name two animals you can find in the countryside.* (rabbit, mouse, fox, etc.)
D *What is the name of a space next to a house where you grow flowers and vegetables?* (a garden)
E *Name two insects you can find in the countryside.* (ants, bees, butterflies, caterpillars, etc.)
F *What are the names of the points on a compass: N, S, E, W?* (North, South, East, and West)
G *Can you name a flower in English?* (rose, daffodil, tulip, etc.)
H *Do we say "Mother" or "Father" Nature?* (Mother)
I *Name two natural features you can see on a beach.* (sand, sea/ocean, rocks, etc.)

WORK WITH WORDS

1 RECALL

- Divide the class into pairs to complete the words with the missing vowels. Explain that they can use the photos to help them. Set a one-minute time limit for this.
- As you check answers as a class, elicit the silent letter in *island* and highlight the pronunciation of *mountain* (/ˈmaʊntɪn/), as many students find this word difficult to pronounce. Chorally drill these words.
- Ask students to do the **Work with Words** task on page 71.

ANSWERS
2 island 3 mountain 4 river 5 ocean 6 tree

2 ▶31

- Refer students back to photos a–f and ask them to find examples of geographical features 1–6 in the photos. Point out the example answer before they start.
- Play the track for students to listen and check.
- Play the track again for students to listen and repeat.

ANSWERS / AUDIO SCRIPT ▶31
1 coast c 2 desert d 3 forest a 4 ice sheet b
5 lake e 6 savannah f
See Student's Book, page 32, for audio script.

3

- Ask students to use the words in Exercise 2 to complete the sentences. Encourage them to read the example sentence before they start.
- Ask students to compare their answers in pairs but don't confirm the answers yet.

4

- Go over the example sentence with students before they start. Then ask them to read the remaining clues and write the names of the places from Exercise 3.
- Ask students to compare their answers in pairs but don't confirm the answers yet.

Fast finishers
Write the following countries on the board for students to match the famous places with their geographical location: *the USA* (Crater Lake), *Tanzania* (the Serengeti), *Australia* (Ninety Mile Beach), *North Africa* (the Sahara), *Russia and Canada* (the Taiga), *the South Pole* (Antarctica).

5 THE MOVING PICTURE

- Explain to students that they are going to watch a video about landscapes and natural features. Encourage them to listen and check their answers to Exercises 3 and 4.
- Check answers as a class if students have any doubts about them. Explain that in sentence 3, the Sahara is referred to as the second largest desert because Antarctica, which is larger, is also considered a desert.

ANSWERS / VIDEO SCRIPT

Exercise 3
2 coast 3 desert 4 savannah 5 Lake; lake
6 ice sheet
Exercise 4
2 Crater Lake 3 Antarctica 4 Sahara
5 The Serengeti 6 The Taiga

Come with me on a journey around the world.
The Taiga is the largest forest in the world. It has a third of all the trees in the world.
Ninety Mile Beach is on the southeastern coast of Australia. From end to end, it's 151 kilometers long.
The Sahara is the second largest desert in the world. The name means "the great desert."
The Serengeti savannah is in Africa. It inspired the movie *The Lion King*.
Crater Lake is the deepest lake in the USA. The island on the west side of the lake is called Wizard Island.
A giant ice sheet covers Antarctica. It has the lowest temperature on Earth.

6 32

- Ask students to look at the picture and match the words to the letters.
- Play the track for students to listen and check their answers.
- Play the track again for students to listen and repeat.

ANSWERS / AUDIO SCRIPT 32

countryside (c) field (e) flower (d) grass (b)
hill (f) stream (a)

7 33

- Ask students to look again at the picture in Exercise 6 before completing the description.
- Let students compare their answers in pairs before you play the track for them to listen and check their answers.

ANSWERS / AUDIO SCRIPT 33

2 field 3 grass 4 stream 5 flowers 6 hill
See Student's Book, page 33, for audio script.

SPEAK

8

- Divide the class into pairs to take turns describing a natural feature in their country or a place near their homes.
- Explain that students should listen to their partners and draw a picture of the place they describe. Draw students' attention to the PHRASE BYTES box and encourage them to use similar phrases in their descriptions.

Alternative procedure: less confident classes
It might be useful to give students three minutes of quiet preparation time to prepare their answers in note form before they do this as a spoken activity.

MOVE BEYOND

Ask students to do the **Move Beyond** task on page 71.

Homework

Ask students to write a description of a natural feature in their country or a place near their homes for a student magazine using vocabulary from the lesson. Encourage them to illustrate it with a drawing or a printed photo from the internet. Display the descriptions and pictures in the classroom.

READING An environmental superstar

Find specific information *Page 32*

STAGE	TIME	FOCUS
GET STARTED		Introduce the topic of the lesson and discuss being green and protecting the environment.
SPEAK		Discuss giving presentations and speaking in public.
READ		Read the magazine profile of a teenage eco-campaigner and discuss tips on how to find specific information in a text (reading subskill).
REACT		React to the text. Express personal opinions on the topic.

Get started

Show the class pictures or write words on the board to represent different environmental issues (e.g., *a dripping tap, a car with a lot of people in it, a bicycle, a solar panel*). Encourage students to say whether each issue is good or bad for the environment and give reasons.

Divide the class into small groups to think of three or four ways to be environmentally friendly (e.g., *buy food locally and in season, use reusable containers, take public transportation, recycle*).

Refer students to the title of the lesson, *An environmental superstar*. Ask: *Do you know the names of any famous people who are fighting to protect the planet?* (e.g., Al Gore, Brad Pitt, Hayden Panettiere, Tobey Maguire).

SPEAK

1

- Divide the class into pairs to ask and answer the questions.
- Remind students that the PHRASE BYTES box can help them structure their answers.

- Choose two or three students to report back to the class about the last presentation their partners gave.

READ

2

- Refer students to the photo and the title of the article and ask them to read the questions.
- Divide the class into pairs to discuss the questions and try to guess the answers.

> **Alternative procedure: less confident classes**
> To encourage students to keep the conversation in English, recycle the phrases for discussing ideas that students saw in Unit 1 by writing them on the board: *What do you think?*, *I think … , I don't think … , I agree.*

3a

- Refer students to the tips in the HOW TO box on how to scan a text to find specific information. These tips encourage students to search only for the information they need. Explain to students that in order to do this they must know what they are looking for.
- After they have read the tips, ask them to cover the box and explain the tips in their own words.

3b ▶34

- Ask students to scan the profile of Felix Finkbeiner to find the answers to the questions in Exercise 2. Remind them not to read every word. Don't play the audio at this point. It is an extra feature, and a suggestion for using it in class is included at the end of the lesson.
- Check answers as a class by choosing different students to answer or by using the audio.

ANSWERS

1 He's 13. 2 He's at the United Nations in New York.
3 He's making a speech. 4 He wants people to plant trees.

4

- Encourage students to reflect and say which tips in the HOW TO box they used, give examples of the tips, and check them.

5

- Draw students' attention to the example, pointing out that this is the event that happened first.
- Ask them to read (not scan) the article completely this time. When they finish, have them number the events in order.
- You may want to have them compare their answers in pairs before checking them as a class.

ANSWERS

2 Felix gave a presentation to his class.
3 Felix started a tree-planting campaign.
4 Students created a website for Felix's campaign.
5 People from other countries joined his campaign.
6 Felix spoke at the United Nations.

REACT

6

- Divide the class into pairs to discuss what they think about Felix's campaign and to say whether they want to join it.
- Circulate and monitor as they work, making a note of anything you would like to give feedback on at the end of the exercise.

> **Fast finishers**
> Write some of the more complicated words in the text on the board (*speech*, *message*, *climate change*, *success*, *join*, *leader*, *goal*). Fast finishers can write definitions using their dictionaries and then read them aloud when everyone has finished. The rest of the class can match them to the words on the board.

MOVE BEYOND

Refer students back to the article. Ask them to find the verbs that come before the words in the list. You could ask more confident students to try to think of the verbs first and then check their answers by finding them in the article.

ANSWERS

make a speech *do* a project *win* the Nobel Prize
give the same presentation *start/join* a campaign
plant 50,000 trees

> **Recorded reading text** ▶34
> The audio can be used to check the answers to Exercise 3b. Pause the track at appropriate places and ask students to confirm their answers.

Homework

Ask students to look again at the title of the text, *Do you have the Felix Factor?* Ask students to answer the question, then write about someone they know who has "the Felix Factor." This could be someone famous, a family member, or a friend.

GRAMMAR Simple past

Describe completed events in the past *Page 33*

STAGE	TIME	FOCUS
GET STARTED		Introduce the lesson and check whether students are confident using the simple past.
READ		Read about another eco-campaigner.
STUDY		Use a text to complete rules and examples about the simple past, and review how to form questions and negative sentences.
PRACTICE		Produce target language in written exercises.
SPEAK		Use the simple past to interview a partner about his or her early school years.

Get started

Recycle the simple past. Monitor closely at this stage to establish whether students have consolidated their knowledge of this tense.

Dictate the verbs *finish*, *answer*, *correct*, and *depend* for students to write in their notebooks. Ask students to work individually to write the simple past affirmative, negative, and question form for each of the verbs with the subject *he*. Make sure students understand that the past form is the same for all persons (i.e., *I*, *you*, *he*, *she*, *it*, *we*, *they*).

Check answers as a class and elicit the pronunciation of the regular past tense endings of the verbs, /ɪd/, /t/, or /d/.

ANSWERS

finish /t/:	He finished	He didn't finish	Did he finish?
answer /d/:	He answered	He didn't answer	Did he answer?
correct /ɪd/:	He corrected	He didn't correct	Did he correct?
depend /ɪd/:	He depended	He didn't depend	Did he depend?

READ Grammar in context

1

- Draw students' attention to the photo and ask who they think it is.
- Ask students to read the conversation and say why Severn is famous.

ANSWER

She's famous because she gave a speech at the United Nations' Earth Summit in 1992 when she was 12.

STUDY

2

- Start by asking students to underline the simple past verbs in Exercise 1 (*talked*, *was*, *didn't see*, *saw*, *told*, *did she look*, *didn't*, *wasn't*).
- Ask students to complete the explanations and examples.
- Let students compare answers in pairs before you elicit answers from different students around the class.
- Refer students to the list of irregular verbs on page 140 of the Student's Book and remind them that these are used very frequently in English and that they have to learn them.

ANSWERS

-ed saw didn't Did; didn't Was; was

PRACTICE

3

- Ask students to complete the sentences with the simple past form of the verbs. Go over the example sentence before they start.
- Let students compare their answers in pairs before you check them as a class.

ANSWERS

2 was 3 became 4 started 5 were; traveled
6 bought; made

4a 35 PRONOUNCE

- Focus students' attention on the five past forms. Play the track for students to listen and underline the /ɔ/ sound.

ANSWERS / AUDIO SCRIPT 35

saw thought talked taught bought

4b 36

- Play the track for students to listen and repeat. Point out that the spellings are different but the sound is the same.

AUDIO SCRIPT 36

saw thought talked taught bought

Extra activity

Divide the class into pairs to brainstorm as many words as they can that have the same sound (e.g., *door*, *floor*, *horse*, *more*, *or*, *score*, *short*, *board*, *four*; *talk*, *walk*, *ball*, *call*, *saw*, *autumn*, *daughter*). Set a time limit of three minutes for this.

5

- Ask students to go back to the text on page 32 to find a reference to Wangari Maathai in the article about Felix Finkbeiner.
- Ask students to skim the text on page 33 to get the general idea of what it is about.
- Go over the example with the class and ask them to write the simple past of the remaining verbs to complete the biography.
- Let students compare their answers in pairs before you choose different students around the class to say the answers.

ANSWERS

2 was 3 was 4 finished 5 went 6 studied 7 got
8 began 9 won 10 died

Fast finishers

Ask fast finishers to categorize the regular simple past verbs according to their pronunciation: *started* (/ɪd/), *finished* (/t/), and *studied* (/d/).

6

- Draw students' attention to the example sentence.
- Ask students to work individually to correct the remaining sentences about Wangari Maathai.
- Check answers as a class.

ANSWERS

2 There weren't a lot of high schools for girls in Kenya.
3 She didn't study history at a university. She studied biology.
4 She didn't start the Green Tree Movement. She started the Green Belt Movement.
5 She didn't win the Nobel Prize for Literature. She won the Nobel Peace Prize.

MOVE BEYOND FOR TEACHERS

Wangari Maathai

When Wangari Maathai was awarded the 2004 Nobel Peace Prize for her "contribution to sustainable development, democracy and peace," she became the first African woman, and the first environmentalist, to win the prize. In her lifetime, she stood up courageously against the former oppressive regime in Kenya, and she served as an inspiration for many, especially women, in the fight for democratic rights and gender equality.

7

- Read the example sentence. Ask students to use the prompts given to write questions in the simple past.
- Let students compare their answers in pairs before you elicit answers from different students around the class.

ANSWERS
2 How old were you when you started there?
3 Did you like your first school?
4 When did you start middle school?
5 Who was your first new friend in middle school?

SPEAK

8

- Divide the class into pairs. Ask students to take turns interviewing their partners about their early school years using the questions in Exercise 7.
- Ask two confident students to model the first question before students do this in pairs.

Extra activity
Ask students to find other verbs in the simple past in the article on page 32. When they have finished, encourage them to compare their answers in pairs. Then ask students to group the regular verbs they found under the three headings: /ɪd/, /t/, and /d/.

ANSWERS
Irregular: was, made, spoke, did, saw, won, thought, gave, began
Regular: /ɪd/ started, decided, planted, wanted; /t/ asked, reached; /d/ called, joined, traveled

Homework

Ask students to write a short story that includes as many simple past verbs as possible from the lesson. Encourage them to include at least three regular and three irregular verbs, and at least one example of *was* and *were*. At the beginning of the next class, divide the class into pairs to read their stories to each other. As students listen, they should write a list of the simple past verbs they hear. When they have finished, ask them to compare their stories and lists. You could then ask students to try to retell their partners' stories using the past tense verbs on their lists as cues.

LISTENING AND VOCABULARY Wonderful wildlife photos

Take notes

Page 34

STAGE	TIME	FOCUS
GET STARTED		Introduce the topic of taking personal photographs.
SPEAK AND LISTEN		Discuss taking photos. Listen and take notes about three different wildlife stories (listening subskill).
REACT		Compare and discuss reactions to the photos.
WORK WITH WORDS		Identify and categorize wildlife.

Get started

To introduce the topic, tell students about the kinds of photographs you take and where you keep them. Use the model given below or your own information. If possible, show students some of your photos. Invite students to ask you some questions (e.g., *How often do you take photos? What do you take photos of? What do you do with your photos?*).

MODEL LIVE LISTENING:
I take photos every day. I had a camera, but I often forgot to put it in my bag. I have a cell phone that takes good photos, so I use that now instead. I usually take photos of what I'm doing and people around me. I like to upload my photos onto my laptop in the evening.

SPEAK AND LISTEN

1

- Divide the class into pairs to talk about how often they take photos and what they take photos of.
- Invite different students to share their information with the class.

2

- Refer students to the three photos and encourage them to say where they think each of the animals is. Remind them of vocabulary on pages 30–31.

3a

- Ask students to read the tips in the HOW TO box about how to take notes.

3b 37

- Refer students to the question words in the instructions and suggest that they use these as a guide for taking notes as they listen.
- Tell students they will hear the track twice. Play the track once for students to listen and take notes about the three photos in Exercise 2.
- Play the track again and ask them to complete their notes.
- Encourage students to compare their notes in pairs before you elicit examples of notes from different students around the class.

AUDIO SCRIPT 37

Last year, I was in Florida with my family. One day, we were walking through some long grass near a river when I saw a snake. The snake was eating a really fat frog! It was holding the frog's head in its mouth – but the frog wasn't moving. It was terrible! As we were walking away, I looked back – the snake was still lying there, but I couldn't see the frog.

This photo isn't from the Antarctic ice sheet – it's from the zoo. I went there with some friends last weekend. I was watching a baby penguin with its mother; she was feeding it. While she was doing that, another penguin came and stood next to them. I think it was the father. It was a really nice family picture.

I live on a farm in Texas near a big desert. Last week, I was helping my father on the farm when I saw these ants. There were hundreds of them, and they were carrying food back to their nest. The pieces of food were bigger than they were, so they were all helping the others. I watched them for a long time.

4

- Ask students to reflect on which tips from the HOW TO box helped them do Exercise 3b and to check them.

Extra activity

Divide the class into groups of three to use their notes to reconstruct the listening texts. If you wish, you could play the track again for students to feel more confident before doing this task.

REACT

5

- Divide the class into pairs to discuss which photo they liked best and why. Encourage them to explain to their partners how it made them feel.
- Invite volunteers to share their thoughts with the class.

WORK WITH WORDS

6a 38

- Refer students to the photos of wildlife. Play the track for them to listen and repeat the names of the animals.
- Highlight the pronunciation of *crocodile* (/ˈkrɒkədaɪl/), as students often find this word challenging.

AUDIO SCRIPT 38

See Student's Book, page 36.

6b 39

- Play the track for students to listen to the sounds and guess the animal.
- After checking answers as a class, elicit which animals don't make a sound.

ANSWERS

1 bear 2 bee 3 dolphin 4 frog 5 owl 6 parrot
7 snake No sound: ant, crocodile, turtle, penguin, spider

7

- Divide the class into pairs to write the names of the animals in the photos in the correct lists. Encourage students to add any more that they know.
- Write the list headings on the board and invite students to call out the names of corresponding animals.

ANSWERS

Land and water animals: *frog*, bear, dolphin, spider
Birds: owl, parrot, penguin
Insects: ant, bee (spiders are not insects)
Reptiles: crocodile, turtle, snake

Alternative procedure

You could make this into a competition to see which pair can think of the most animals for each category in five minutes.

MOVE BEYOND

Ask students to do the **Move Beyond** task on page 71.

Homework

Ask students to write about a photo they have of an animal, bird, insect, or reptile and describe the story behind it. (Alternatively, students can find a photo on the internet and invent a story to go with it.) Ask students to bring in their texts on separate sheets of paper. At the beginning of the next class, divide the class into groups and distribute the texts and photos for students to match them correctly.

GRAMMAR Past progressive and simple past

Talk about actions in progress and finished actions in the past *Page 35*

STAGE	TIME	FOCUS
GET STARTED		Check students' knowledge of the past progressive before teaching it.
READ		Read for specific information.
STUDY		Complete examples in grammar explanations of the past progressive tense and contrast the use of the past progressive and simple past using *when* and *while*.
PRACTICE		Recognize and produce the target language in written exercises.
WRITE AND SPEAK		Produce the target language in a writing and speaking task.

Get started

Elicit three different times from students and write them on the board (e.g., *7 a.m.*, *1:30 p.m.*, *7 p.m.*).

Ask students to write a sentence about what they were doing at each of these times. One of their three sentences should be false.

When students have written their sentences, divide the class into pairs to interview each other and try to identify the false statements.

Circulate and monitor to see if students are familiar with the form and use of the past progressive. This will show you how much extra help they might need with the grammar input of today's lesson.

Fast finishers

Fast finishers can tell their partners what they were really doing at these times.

READ Grammar in context

1

- Refer students to the photo and ask them to read the story to find the answer to the question.
- Elicit what the man in the photo is "wearing" and why. Ask students if they have heard about the "bee beard" competition or anything similar.

ANSWER

He's wearing a "bee beard" (hundreds of bees). It's a competition.

STUDY

2

- Refer students to the grammar explanation of the use of the past progressive.
- Ask students to work individually to look for examples from the story in Exercise 1 to help them complete the sentences.
- Encourage them to compare their answers in pairs before you check them as a class. Explain that we don't use the past progressive with stative verbs.

ANSWERS

was wasn't Were weren't

Extra activity

You may want to review the form of the past progressive. Start by eliciting from students how we form the present progressive. Point out that they only need to change *am/is/are* to *was/were*. Copy this table on the board for students to complete with the verb *speak*.

	I/he/she/it	You/we/they
Affirmative	*I was speaking.*	*You were speaking.*
Negative	*I wasn't speaking.*	*You weren't speaking.*
Question	*Was I speaking?*	*Were you speaking?*

Take this opportunity to recycle stative verbs, which students saw in Unit 2. Elicit examples of stative verbs (e.g., *know*, *like*, *hate*, *mean*, *prefer*, *need*, *realize*, *understand*, *want*) and remind students that they are not usually used in the progressive form.

3

- Ask students to work individually. Tell them to look at the examples from the story in Exercise 1 and complete the rules.
- Encourage them to compare their answers in pairs before you check them as a class.

ANSWERS

past progressive simple past past progressive simple past

PRACTICE

4

- Ask students to quickly skim through the conversation to get the gist of what it is about.
- Ask them to work individually to complete the conversation with the past progressive form of the verbs. Go over the example answer before they start. Remind students of the acronym QASV (question word, auxiliary, subject, verb) to help them formulate questions with the words in the correct order.
- Monitor students while they complete this exercise and offer support if necessary. They can refer to the **Grammar Database** if needed.
- Let students compare their answers in pairs before you check them as a class.

ANSWERS

2 wasn't sleeping 3 were watching 4 was flying
5 weren't talking 6 weren't moving 7 Was the owl holding
8 was carrying

5

- Divide the class into pairs to ask and answer questions about each other's activities at certain times yesterday.
- Draw students' attention to the model conversation and point out the difference between an open or *Wh-* question and a closed or Yes/No question (*Were you … ?*).
- Encourage a more confident pair of students to model an exchange for the rest of the class before they start.

6

- Ask students to complete the story. Before they start, go over the example sentence.

ANSWERS

2 were standing 3 saw 4 didn't know 5 swam
6 were watching 7 were getting 8 realized

Alternative procedure

Before doing Exercise 6, ask students to read the text and answer these comprehension questions: *Where was the narrator? Who was he with? What was the animal doing? What happened?* This will help them see that the text is a good model for the writing exercise in Exercise 7.

WRITE AND SPEAK

7

- Divide the class into pairs. Refer Student A to the monkey photo on page 75 and Student B to the elephant photo on page 76.

- Encourage them to make notes for a short story by answering the questions given. This will help them structure their texts.
- When students have written their notes, ask them to work in their pairs and take turns showing their photos to their partners and telling their partners the story about them.

Homework

Ask students to exchange photos and write a story about their partner's photo for homework. At the beginning of the next class, students can take turns reading their texts aloud and discussing similarities and differences.

LANGUAGE & BEYOND GET ORGANIZED

Use mind maps to organize information for a speech Page 36

STAGE	TIME	FOCUS
GET STARTED		Introduce the idea of mind maps.
READ		Discuss how to remember information. Read notes and organize information in the correct sections of a mind map.
DO		Read tips for making a mind map and make one in your own style.
REFLECT		Discuss the good things and bad things about mind maps.
EXTEND		Create a mind map to organize ideas for a presentation.

LIFE SKILLS

MIND MAPS

Mind maps are the creation of Tony Buzan, the memory expert. A mind map works the way your brain does, reflecting your thoughts. The basic principle is that human thought is characterized by expansion in multiple directions, so anything you write should start in the center of the page with related ideas branching out in all directions. Many people use different colored pens, pictures, or symbols to make their mind maps more memorable.

In the workplace, mind maps are often used in meetings for collaboratively brainstorming ideas and by managers to organize and prepare presentations.

Get started

Give students a good model as a guide for their discussion in Exercise 1 by talking about how you remember information (see example below).

Ask students to take notes on the different ways you remember things. Include information about three or four different techniques you use.

At the end of your presentation, elicit the ways that you mentioned in order to check students' comprehension.

Example presentation:

I use my phone a lot to write down things I have to remember. If I have to remember a long piece of information, I read it aloud into my phone to record myself and listen to it again. If I have to study for a test, I make a mind map. I write the main topic in a circle in the middle of a sheet of paper and then draw lines out from this circle and write subheadings. Then I just write down all the things that are important in each group. Sometimes I use different colored pens, and I draw pictures because it helps me remember.

You could draw an example of a mind map on the board.

READ

1

- Divide the class into pairs to discuss how they usually remember information.
- Encourage them to say whether their techniques work well.

2

- Refer students to Ryan's mind map and ask them to write the missing words along the branches.

ANSWERS
FACTS: description, statistics
PROBLEM: summary, causes
ACTION: why, what

3

- Ask students to read Ryan's notes and match them to the correct sections on the mind map.

ANSWERS
1 FACTS – statistics 2 ACTION – what 3 PROBLEM – summary
4 FACTS – description 5 PROBLEM – causes 6 ACTION – why

DO

4a

- Ask students to read the tips for making a mind map. You could choose different students to read the tips aloud to the class. Ask the class what Ryan hasn't done. (*He hasn't used symbols or images.*)

4b

- Encourage students to copy Ryan's mind map in their own styles, adding spaces and lines as necessary to include the information for Ryan's speech. Remind them to copy key words only.

REFLECT

5

- Refer students to the questions and discuss them as a class.
- Choose a student to read the **REFLECTION POINT** aloud and ask the class if they agree with it.
- Ask students how they could use mind maps to help them in their own lives.

EXTEND

6

- Divide the class into groups and ask them to choose one of the topics and create a mind map to organize their ideas.
- Circulate and monitor, helping students as necessary during this task.
- At the end of the exercise, ask students to exchange their mind maps with other groups for them to comment on and make suggestions.

Homework

At the end of the class, ask the groups to discuss and decide how to divide up the different areas of the mind map they made in Exercise 6 so that each student in the group can work on a section for homework. Monitor and support as necessary.

Tell students to work on their own area, elaborate on the ideas they thought of in Exercise 6, and prepare a short presentation. At the beginning of the next class, have students give a short presentation to their group for their section of the mind map.

SPEAKING I have a suggestion

Make and react to suggestions *Page 37*

STAGE	TIME	FOCUS
GET STARTED		Introduce the topic of the lesson: going green.
SPEAK		Talk about activities connected to the environment.
LISTEN		Listen to a conversation with expressions for making suggestions. Learn how to make suggestions and react positively or negatively to them (speaking subskill).
ACT		Prepare and present a conversation using expressions for making and reacting to suggestions.

Get started

Write these words on the board: *Transportation*, *Energy*, *Food*.

Encourage students to say which "green" ideas in these areas already exist in their country and how things could be improved to become more sustainable (*car sharing, electric cars, speed limits, bike rental, solar panels, wind power, buying local food, reducing packaging, organic food, etc.*).

SPEAK

1

- Divide the class into pairs and ask them to make a list of ideas for Save the Planet Day at their school. Draw students' attention to the example sentence on the list.
- Elicit suggestions from different students around the class.

LISTEN

2 40

- Have students close their books. Play the audio track for them to listen and find out what ideas the students have for Save the Planet Day.
- Check answers as a class and ask if the ideas are similar to or different from their ideas.

ANSWERS / AUDIO SCRIPT 40

Wear green clothes to school. Walk or bike to school.
Make something from recycled materials.
Collect money for Save the Dolphins.

Lucia: Hey. What should we do for Save the Planet Day next month?
Carl: We could wear green clothes to school – green socks or a green hat.
Rick: No way! I'm not going to wear green.
Lucia: Why don't we all walk to school?
Carl: Yes. Or ride our bikes here.
Rick: I don't know. I live really far away and I don't have a bike. Let's do a survey and ask people their opinions about the environment.
Lucia: That's pretty serious. What about making something from recycled materials?
Rick: That's a nice idea.
Carl: Yes, but it doesn't really help the environment. What could we do to really make a difference?
Lucia: I know! We could collect money for Save the Dolphins.
Carl: That's a great idea!

3 40

- Ask students to complete the conversation with the phrases in the box.
- Play the conversation again for students to listen and check.

ANSWERS / AUDIO SCRIPT 40

1 What should we 2 We could 3 Why don't we
4 What about 5 What could 6 We could
See Exercise 2 for audio script.

4 41

- Play the track for students to listen to the sentences from the conversation and repeat them.

AUDIO SCRIPT 41

1 What should we do? 2 We could wear green clothes.
3 Why don't we all walk to school? 4 Let's do a survey.
5 What about making something? 6 What could we do?

5 42

- Play the track for students to listen and decide if the reactions are positive or negative.
- Check the answers as a class.
- Play the track again for students to listen and repeat.

ANSWERS / AUDIO SCRIPT 42

1 No way! (N) 2 I don't know. (N) 3 That's pretty serious. (N)
4 That's a nice idea. (P) 5 That's a great idea! (P)

Extra activity
Ask students to practice the conversation in Exercise 2.

ACT

6 43

- Divide the class into pairs to prepare a conversation to decide what to do for a Save the Planet Day at your school. Ask them to include at least three suggestions and then to choose one of them. Refer students to the phrases in the PHRASEBOOK box and encourage them to use them in their conversations. Play the track for students to listen and repeat the phrases.
- Circulate and help students if necessary. Note good use of language and errors to give feedback to students before they present their conversations.

7

- Have students present their conversations to other pairs or to the class. Do they have any suggestions in common with other pairs? You may want to ask one or two pairs to perform their conversations in front of the class to end the exercise if they haven't done this already.

Homework

Ask students to use the internet to research more things that other schools are doing to be greener. Ask them to make a list of things that their school could do to be greener. Have students present their work to the rest of the class at the beginning of the next class.

WRITING A vacation story

Write a story with time expressions Page 38

STAGE	TIME	FOCUS
GET STARTED		Review the simple past and the past progressive and introduce key vocabulary.
SPEAK AND READ		Talk about diaries. Read a diary entry for specific information. Explore the use of time expressions (writing subskill).
PRACTICE		Produce target language in written exercises.
DISCUSS		Describe problems that might happen on a camping trip.
WRITE		Write a story about a camping trip.
SHARE		Take turns reading the stories. Decide which stories are scary, funny, or strange.

Get started

Play the *Grammar Auction* game. Divide the class into teams. Write some correct and incorrect simple past and past progressive sentences on the board; for example, *Last year I was to Paris on vacation. I slept in a tent when the rain started. He were staying on a campsite. I was sleeping when a noise woke me up. The dog chased me while I was riding my bike. The dog barked at the man. I rode my bike when I was falling off. He was riding a bike away from the scary dog while he was falling off his bike.* Use this opportunity to pre-teach vocabulary from the lesson.

Explain that the sentences are for sale and each team has 1,000 points to "buy" sentences. Read each sentence aloud and ask each team to offer an amount of points to buy the sentence if they think it is correct. The team that offers the most wins the sentence.

Keep track of how many points each team offers for each sentence. At the end of the game, tell students which sentences were correct. If a team bought a correct sentence, they win back double their points. If they bought an incorrect sentence, they lose twice the amount they paid. Ask teams to total up the points they have. The team with the most points wins.

SPEAK AND READ

MOVE BEYOND FOR TEACHERS

Personal diaries

There are a number of famous diaries that have provided an insight into the past. Many famous diary writers documented what was happening to them and in their countries at the time. There are several diaries that have remained bestsellers on literary lists throughout the world (e.g., *Anne Frank: The Diary of a Young Girl*). Through her personal diary, Anne Frank described her life in hiding with her family and four friends in Amsterdam during the German occupation in World War II.

1

- Ask students if they know of any famous diaries and invite them to share their knowledge of them with the class.
- Divide the class into groups and ask them to discuss the questions.
- Elicit answers from different students around the class.

2

- Encourage students to look at the photos and invite them to guess what they think the text is going to be about.
- Ask students to read the diary entry to find out why Lynn didn't sleep well.

ANSWER

Because first a strange noise woke her up, and then she found a field mouse in her sleeping bag.

Alternative procedure: less confident classes

In a less confident class, ask some comprehension questions about the text to check understanding. For example: *Where did they go on vacation?* (Utah / the desert); *What type of vacation was it?* (a camping vacation); *Where was she sleeping?* (in a tent); *What did she think the noise was at first?* (the rain); *What woke her up again?* (a mouse in her sleeping bag); *What did she do?* (she screamed and jumped out of the sleeping bag).

3a

- Focus students' attention on the tips in the HOW TO box.
- Ask them to underline all the time expressions in the tips.

3b

- Refer them back to the diary entry in Exercise 2 to find and underline examples of the time expressions.

ANSWERS

Yesterday we arrived ...
I'm feeling really tired today ...
... happened during the night
At first I thought ...
But then I realized ...
After a minute or two, the noise ...
Later I woke up again ...

PRACTICE

4

- Ask students to complete the description with expressions from the HOW TO box.
- Let students compare their answers in pairs before you check them as a class.

ANSWERS

2 At first 3 later 4 Then 5 After 6 Later

Fast finishers

Ask fast finishers to find one adverb (*really*, *loudly*, *around*, *away*), three verbs + prepositions/adverbs (*ride ... through*, *run toward*, *turn around*, *ride away*), four nouns (*afternoon*, *bike*, *forest*, *dog*, *seconds*, *minutes*, *man*), and two irregular past tense verbs (*saw*, *ran*) in the text in Exercise 4 and to write these in their notebooks.

DISCUSS

5

- Write the word *MIGHT* in large letters in the center of the board. Ask students to remind you what Lynn's problem was on her camping trip to Utah. As they describe her problem, complete a sentence on the board using *might* (e.g., *A field mouse might crawl into your sleeping bag*).
- Check the meaning of *might* (i.e., *to talk about a possibility*).
- Tell students you'd like them to talk about some other problems that might happen on a camping trip and set a time limit of three minutes.
- If you think they need some help thinking of ideas, write some prompts on the board (e.g., *weather*, *animals*, *food*, *accidents*).
- Elicit some ideas from students and write them on the board using the word *might*; for example:

Your tent		fall down.
A bear	MIGHT	eat your food.
There		be a storm.
You		get lost.

WRITE

6

- Explain to students that they are now going to write a story like the ones in Exercises 2 and 4 using one of the ideas on the board.
- Remind them that when they write a story, they should think about the people they are telling the story to and make sure they give them all the information they need to understand and enjoy the story.
- Refer them to the questions in Exercise 6 (Step 1) and explain that the answers to these questions give the background to their stories.
- Read through Step 2 with students and ask them what Lynn was doing and what problem interrupted her. (*She was sleeping when a strange noise woke her up.*)
- Ask students to point out examples of the past progressive / simple past in Lynn's story or in the story in Exercise 4.
- Finally, remind students that using time expressions helps the person reading or listening to their stories understand the order of events. Suggest that they refer to the expressions in the HOW TO box as they are writing their story.
- Set a time limit of 15 minutes for students to write.

SHARE

7

- Divide the class into small groups and ask students to read their stories to one another. Ask them to decide after each story if it was funny, scary, or strange.

Homework

Ask students to write a diary entry for a day between this class and the next. Students could read their diary entries to each other in pairs at the beginning of the next class.

VOCABULARY Landscapes and natural features

1

- Ask students to skim the text to get an idea of what it is about. Briefly elicit their ideas as a class.
- Ask students to read the text and choose the correct options.
- Check answers by choosing different students to read sections of the text aloud.

ANSWERS
1 ice sheet 2 coast 3 savannah 4 grass
5 streams 6 Lakes 7 countryside 8 fields
9 Desert 10 flowers 11 hill 12 forest

Wildlife

2

- Ask students to read the descriptions of wildlife under each heading and complete the words.
- Let students compare their answers in pairs before you check them as a class.

ANSWERS
1 dolphin 2 bear 3 frog 4 spider 5 bee
6 ants 7 parrot 8 penguin 9 owl 10 snake
11 crocodile 12 turtle

GRAMMAR Simple past

3

- Refer students to the prompts in parentheses and ask them to complete the conversation using the correct form of the simple past. Remind them to check whether the sentence is affirmative, negative, or a question to make sure they use the correct word order.
- When they have finished, choose a pair of confident students to read the conversation aloud for students to check their answers.

ANSWERS
1 did you go 2 didn't go 3 stayed 4 had
5 loved 6 went 7 got

Past progressive and simple past

4

- Give students 10 seconds to skim the story to see what it is about. Elicit any ideas from volunteers.
- Ask students to complete the story correctly with the past progressive or simple past form of the verbs.
- Let students compare their answers in pairs before you check them as a class.

ANSWERS
1 were visiting 2 saw 3 was eating
4 wasn't looking 5 stopped 6 were standing

Extra Resources

Go to the Teacher's Resource Center at mee2.macmillaneducation.com for:

- downloadable audio and audio scripts for the Student's Book and Workbook;
- videos and video scripts;
- extra vocabulary at two levels of difficulty;
- extra grammar at two levels of difficulty;
- CLIL lessons, with full teacher's notes;
- a life skills lesson, with full teacher's notes;
- Speaking Database materials;
- the Move Beyond Level 3 wordlist;
- tips for using the Grammar Database;
- and more!

Go to Workbook pages 108–119 for further practice material.

UNIT 4 WHAT'S COOKING?

IN THE PICTURE Inside the kitchen

Talk about food and cooking

Page 40–41

STAGE	TIME	FOCUS
GET STARTED		Practice the pronunciation of /uː/ in *food* (/fuːd/) and /ʊ/ in *cook* (/kʊk/) and introduce the theme of the unit.
WORK WITH WORDS		Recycle food vocabulary and learn new words to talk about kitchen equipment and cooking. Watch a video about a summer camp and decide whether you would like to go there.
SPEAK		Talk about food you like and what you know about cooking.

Get started

Write the following two sentences with blanks on the board and ask students to think of the words to fill in the blanks (the target words are *food* and *cook*).

That's my favorite restaurant. The ____ is always delicious.
You need to ____ potatoes for 20 minutes.

Drill the *oo* in *food* (/fuːd/) and tell students that the /uː/ sound is very common in English. Point out that the major characteristic of this sound is that your lips form a small circle.

Drill the *oo* in *cook* (/kʊk/) by asking students to create the sound by starting with /uː/ and then relaxing the lips to a /ʊ/. Drill both sounds, first chorally and then individually, using other suitable words such as the following: *tooth* (/tuːθ/), *took* (/tʊk/), *tooth* (/tuːθ/), *took* (/tʊk/).

Play *Pronunciation Maze*. Draw this pronunciation maze on the board and ask students to find a way across the maze, starting from *food* and moving through words in the /uː/ route across, up, or down until they get to *zoo*. Explain that the line must connect one word with another without other words between them, and that they will not necessarily use all of the words with the /uː/ sound.

hook	*foot*	*took*	*football*
food	*school*	*looked*	*soon*
good	*tooth*	*book*	*stood*
cool	*room*	*too*	*look*
wood	*notebook*	*choose*	*cook*
spoon	*hood*	*kangaroo*	*zoo*

ANSWERS
food, school, tooth, room, too, choose, kangaroo, zoo

Draw students' attention to the title of the unit and ask them what they think the unit is going to be about (*food, drink, and health*). Point out that *What's cooking?* can mean "What's happening?" or "What's going on?" in slang.

WORK WITH WORDS

1 RECALL

- Refer students to the example words in the table and elicit another example for each heading.
- Divide the class into pairs to brainstorm and add more words. Set a three-minute time limit for this.
- Write the list headings on the board and invite students to call out more words for you to write up.
- Highlight the pronunciation of *steak* (/steɪk/), as many students find this word difficult to pronounce. Drill the words, first chorally, and then individually.
- Ask students to do the **Work with Words** task on page 72.

Alternative procedure

You could make this into a competition to see which pair can think of the most correctly spelled words in three minutes. After three minutes, ask pairs to exchange lists.

Elicit food words from the class and write them on the board. Inform students that they can give one point for every correctly spelled word and two points for a correctly spelled word that no one else has thought of. Invite students to total up their points at the end of the exercise to see which pair has won.

MOVE BEYOND FOR TEACHERS

Tomato – vegetable or fruit?

Tomatoes are often called vegetables; however, a tomato is technically the fruit of the tomato plant.

2 44

- Refer students to the photos and explain that they are going to listen to someone giving instructions in the kitchen. Ask students to predict what they think the instructions could be for each photo.

- Encourage students to listen for any food words from Exercise 1 and use these to help them identify the correct photo. Play the track and ask them to write the letters for the photos (a–e) in the order they hear them.
- Let students compare their answers in pairs before you check them as a class.

ANSWERS / AUDIO SCRIPT 44

1 c 2 a 3 d 4 b 5 e

OK. So first you beat the eggs in a large bowl like this. After that, you chop an onion – carefully. Don't forget to do it on a cutting board. Then you heat some oil in a frying pan and fry the chicken. Here's some lemon juice. You pour the lemon juice into a saucepan and stir slowly. Now, with a knife, you cut some bread. I love the smell of fresh bread!

3 45

- Refer students to the words for kitchen equipment and ask them to find each item in one of the photos. Draw students' attention to the example before they start.
- Check answers as a class by choosing different students to point to the items.
- Play the track for students to listen and repeat.

ANSWERS / AUDIO SCRIPT 45

2 d 3 c 4 a; c; e 5 a; e

See Student's Book, page 40, for audio script.

Fast finishers

Ask fast finishers to find the silent letters in these words in Exercise 2 (*bowl*, *board*, *knife*).

4 46

- Play the track for students to listen and repeat the words.

AUDIO SCRIPT 46

See Student's Book, page 40.

5 47

- Refer students back to the words in Exercises 3 and 4 and explain that these are the answer options.
- After students have filled in the blanks, play the track for them to listen and check.

ANSWERS / AUDIO SCRIPT 47

2 chop 3 cutting board 4 frying pan 5 fry 6 pour 7 saucepan 8 knife

See Student's Book, page 40, for audio script.

6a

- Divide the class into pairs to match the verbs in Exercise 4 to some of the words they wrote in Exercise 1. Draw students' attention to the examples before they start.
- Encourage students to make a list of their collocations in their notebooks to study later.

6b

- In the same pairs, ask students to act out some of the actions. You could ask a pair of more confident students to demonstrate this activity first for the class.

Alternative procedure

Divide the class into two teams. A volunteer from each team comes to the front of the class and acts out cooking instructions for the team to guess. If the team guesses correctly, the team wins a point and a volunteer from the other team comes to the front. Set a time limit (e.g., two minutes). The team with the most points at the end of the time wins the game.

7 THE MOVING PICTURE

- Elicit the meaning of the acronym *NYC* (*New York City*). Explain to students that they are going to watch a video about a summer camp for teenagers.
- Play the video and encourage students to write down things they like and don't like about Passport NYC.
- Let students compare their answers in pairs and discuss whether they would like to go to Passport NYC and why or why not.
- In a class discussion, invite different students to report what their partner said.

VIDEO SCRIPT

Narrator: Are you a foodie? Do you love food? Join us at Passport NYC – the summer camp for teenage foodies. Spend the summer in New York City and learn to cook with some of the city's top chefs! At Passport NYC, teens from all over the world come to New York City to live, have fun, and learn about cooking with professionals.

Chef: You finish cooking in the curry sauce. OK? But right now what I've done is I've forced the sugars out of them ... brown them a little bit ... Everything hands on, that's the whole process. We don't want them to sit back and watch me cook. I know how to cook. We want them to be in the forefront and experience the unknown. To get really a sense of what it would be to work professionally in the kitchen, not just learning how to cook for home.

Zoe: Other campers are from everywhere. There's some from Mexico, and one of my roommates is from Taiwan, and D.C., and Jersey.

Aaron: It's a really, really, really good way to meet people that you really wouldn't normally hang out with that have the same interests as you and you start to make a whole new other group of friends.

Narrator: Come to New York City, learn to cook, make friends, and have fun.

SPEAK

8

- Refer students to the advertisement on page 41. Divide the class into pairs to answer the questions. Allow two minutes.
- Elicit different students' answers in a class discussion.

Alternative procedure

Try a mix of pair work and group work. Question 1 is more straightforward and suited to pair work. Questions 2 and 3 could be discussed in small groups. Alternating groupings gives students a chance to work with different students and varies the rhythm of work.

Extra activity

Recycle the simple present. Divide the class into groups to write about a typical day's activities at the Passport NYC summer camp. In a less confident class, brainstorm activities (e.g., *get up*, *have an English class*, *learn how to cook a new dish*, *clean the kitchen*, *have lunch*, *have a workshop with a famous chef*, *visit the Statue of Liberty*). Encourage students to start: *On a typical day at Passport NYC, we … .*

MOVE BEYOND

Ask students to do the **Move Beyond** task on page 72.

Homework

Ask students to write a diary entry for a day at Passport NYC. Encourage them to describe what they learned to cook, what they ate, and which famous chef they met.

READING Zach's favorite recipe

Use headings to find specific information Page 42

STAGE	TIME	FOCUS
GET STARTED		Play a game to recycle vocabulary from the previous lesson.
SPEAK AND READ		Discuss cooking and recipes. Use headings to find specific information in a recipe (reading subskill). Then read the recipe in more detail.
REACT		React to the text. Express personal opinions on the topic.

Get started

Play a game of *Twenty Questions* (see Games, page 33) using food and cooking vocabulary from the last lesson. Start by thinking of an item yourself, and after it is correctly guessed, divide the class into groups of three to continue playing.

SPEAK AND READ

1

- Elicit from students the meaning of the word *recipe* (*a set of instructions for cooking or preparing a particular food*) and drill its pronunciation (/ˈresəpi/).
- Divide the class into pairs to ask and answer the questions.
- Choose two or three students to report back to the class about their partners' answers.

Alternative procedure

Play a game of *Just a Minute*. Divide the class into pairs to take turns speaking for one minute (or as long as they can), answering the questions in Exercise 1. Their partner times them and gives them points out of 10 at the end. Points are taken off for long pauses and going off topic.

With a less confident class, elicit phrases that will help students gain some thinking time. Write them on the board for students to use; for example, *Let me think …* , *Well …* , *Let me see …* , *What I'm saying is …* . Using these phrases is better than silence or using their own language.

Monitor and note good use of language and errors to go over in a feedback session at the end of the game. Ask students to play this game again, using the same questions but with a different partner. At the end of the game, ask students if they spoke for longer the second time and felt more confident. Remind students that in many oral examinations, candidates are expected to speak on their own for a minute or more.

2a

- Focus students on the tips in the HOW TO box for using headings to find specific information.
- Elicit from students when they already use this technique (e.g., when researching a homework topic).

2b

- Refer students to the recipe and ask them to match the information asked for in 1–4 to the corresponding headings.
- Let students compare their answers in pairs before you check them as a class.

ANSWERS

1 Directions 2 Time 3 Ingredients 4 Level of difficulty

3

- Encourage students to reflect and say which tips in the HOW TO box they used and to check them.

4 48

Exam-type task

- Ask students to read the recipe again, this time in more detail, and decide if each sentence is correct or incorrect. Don't play the audio at this point. It is an extra feature, and a suggestion for using it in class is included at the end of the lesson.
- Check answers as a class. Ask students to justify their answers by identifying where they found the correct answers in the text or by correcting the information if a statement is incorrect.

ANSWERS

2 C (*TIP: Don't cut the omelette when it's very hot. Wait for it to cool [about 10 minutes].*)
3 I (*Before you pour the mixture into the frying pan, add some salt and pepper.*)
4 I (*500 g potatoes, one onion*)
5 I (*A Chinese omelette has vegetables and soy sauce.*)
6 C (*This is one of my favorite recipes because … it doesn't need a lot of preparation.*)

Extra activity

Divide the class into pairs to write two comprehension questions about the text to test another pair; for example, *How many people does the recipe serve? Why is the recipe easy? How long does it take to cook a Spanish omelette? What is in an Italian frittata?*

REACT

5

- Divide the class into pairs to discuss the questions and whether or not they think they can make a Spanish omelette.
- In a class discussion, ask if anyone has already made a Spanish omelette or knows any similar egg recipes.

Recorded reading text 48

Use the audio as an alternative warm-up to the lesson. Play the "About this recipe" section and ask if students can predict what the recipe is for.

MOVE BEYOND

Books closed. Divide the class into pairs and encourage students to explain the recipe to each other.

Homework

Ask students to write out their favorite recipe in English or to find an easy recipe on the internet and take notes about it. At the beginning of the next class, ask students to explain their recipe to a partner.

GRAMMAR Expressions of quantity

Talk about quantity — Page 43

STAGE	TIME	FOCUS
GET STARTED		Play a game to recycle food vocabulary and countable and uncountable nouns.
READ AND LISTEN		Read and listen to a conversation to decide which recipe two teenagers make for lunch.
STUDY		Use a conversation to complete rules about expressions of quantity and recycle countable and uncountable nouns.
PRACTICE		Produce target language in written exercises.
SPEAK		Produce target language in a speaking task. Interview a partner about his or her eating habits.

Get started

Play the *Picnic Drill* game. Tell students that you are having a picnic and that they can come if they bring the right thing. Start by saying: *I'm going on a picnic and I'm bringing some chocolate.*

Encourage students to continue by repeating what you said and adding another word; for example, *I'm going on a picnic, and I'm bringing some chocolate and some water.*

If students add an uncountable noun, tell them that they are welcome to come, but if they say a countable noun, say that you are sorry but they can't come. Continue this way until all students have worked out the puzzle.

READ AND LISTEN Grammar in context

1 49

- Elicit from students whether they remember the information about Spanish, Italian, Chinese, and Mexican omelettes from the previous lesson. Encourage them to look at the recipe on page 44 and check whether they were right.
- Tell students that they are going to read and listen to two teenagers talking about their lunch. Ask them to find out which omelette they decide to make.

ANSWER / AUDIO SCRIPT 49

An Italian omelette.
See Student's Book, page 45, for audio script.

STUDY

2

- Focus students on the table and ask them to complete it with the words in the box, using the conversation in Exercise 1 to help them. If necessary, go over the first answer as an example with the class.
- Let students compare their answers in pairs before you check them as a class, eliciting examples for each expression.

ANSWERS

a lot of = large quantity some = not large or small quantity
a few, a little, not much, not many = small quantity no = zero

3

- Refer students to the table and ask them to find which expression they can use before both countable and uncountable nouns and in all types of sentences – affirmative, negative, and questions.

ANSWER

a lot of

Extra activity

If students have forgotten the difference between countable and uncountable nouns, write these sentences on the board and ask them to choose the correct option.

1 *Countable nouns (e.g., potato, egg)* have / don't have *a singular and a plural form.*

2 Use / Don't use *"a/an" with uncountable nouns (e.g., food, pasta) or plural forms (e.g., potatoes, eggs).*

ANSWERS

1 have 2 Don't use

PRACTICE

4

- Focus students' attention on the photos and the example description for the first one. Ask students if the quantity of bread is a big, small, or medium amount (*medium*) and point out the corresponding use of *some*.
- Ask students to write similar short descriptions using the expressions of quantity in the box.
- Let students compare their answers in pairs before you check them as a class.

ANSWERS

2 a few 3 a lot of 4 a little 5 no

Alternative procedure: less confident classes

Break this into a two-part exercise. First, elicit the expression of quantity for each picture. Then recycle *there is / there are* and ask students to write complete sentences.

ANSWERS

1 There is some bread. 2 There are a few vegetables.
3 There are a lot of apples. 4 There is a little pasta.
5 There is no rice. / There isn't any rice.

5

- Ask students to skim the text to get a general idea of what it is about. Elicit their ideas.
- Ask students to read more carefully and choose the correct options in the text. Go through the example answer before they start.
- Let students compare their answers in pairs before you check them as a class, eliciting whether they correspond to countable (C) or uncountable (U) nouns.

ANSWERS
1 *much* (U) 2 any (C) 3 some (U) 4 little (U)
5 many (C) 6 a lot of (U)

6

- Ask students to work individually to choose a suitable word to complete each sentence. Go over the example answer before they start, eliciting or pointing out that the use of *but* means that a negative is necessary here.
- Let students compare their answers in pairs before you check them as a class.

ANSWERS
2 much 3 any 4 few 5 lot 6 some

SPEAK

7

- Divide the class into pairs and tell students to ask each other the questions in Exercise 6. Encourage them to decide whether their partners have good eating habits and to say why or why not.
- Discuss the questions as a class and ask students to think of the healthiest possible answers.

Homework

Recycle the simple present. Ask students to use Exercise 5 as a model to help them write a short text (80–100 words) about what they eat for breakfast during the week and on weekends.

LISTENING AND VOCABULARY What a waste!

Recognize facts and opinions *Page 44*

STAGE	TIME	FOCUS
GET STARTED		Introduce the idea of food waste and recycling.
SPEAK AND LISTEN		Listen to an interview about food waste and identify facts and opinions (listening subskill).
REACT		Compare and discuss opinions about food waste.
WORK WITH WORDS		Describe containers and amounts of food and practice the pronunciation of unstressed words.

Get started

Divide the class into pairs to make a list of all the things they have thrown in the trash since yesterday. Elicit a list of items and write them on the board.

Encourage students to think of the categories for sorting and recycling trash (e.g., paper, cardboard, glass, plastic) and ask students to say where each item on the list goes.

Refer students to the lesson title. Drill the pronunciation of the word *waste* (/weɪst/) and elicit its meaning (*to use, consume, spend, or expend thoughtlessly or carelessly*).

SPEAK AND LISTEN

1

- Divide the class into pairs or small groups and refer them to the photo to discuss what they think the people are doing. Ask them to choose option A, B, or C.
- Elicit answers from several groups and discuss the different options, but don't confirm the answer at this point.

2 50

- Explain to students that they are going to listen to an interview with Emma, one of the people in the photo.
- Play the track for students to listen and check their answers to Exercise 1 and also to write down what's on Emma's list.
- Let students compare their answers in pairs before you elicit the items on Emma's list and write them on the board.

ANSWERS / AUDIO SCRIPT 50

Exercise 1 B
Exercise 2 See underlined text below.

Reporter: It's a busy afternoon just after school, and there are a lot of students everywhere. But this group isn't just having a good time on their way home ... they're looking in trash cans outside the supermarket near their school ... Uh, why?
Emma: Well, every year the world wastes 30 percent of its food.
Reporter: Thirty percent? And nobody eats it?
Emma: That's right. Europe and North America waste about 100 kilograms of food a year per person. We're studying food waste in science class. This afternoon, we're looking at food in the supermarket trash cans. We're making a list of things the supermarket throws away.
Reporter: So what's on your list today?
Emma: Um ... <u>some bread</u> ... <u>a few apples</u> ... <u>two cartons of milk</u> ... um ... <u>a little cheese</u> – not much ... <u>a jar of jam</u> ... and <u>two packages of pasta</u>.
Reporter: So the supermarket just threw that away?
Emma: Yeah! Supermarkets throw away so much food – boxes of cookies, bottles of water, cans of soda, and old vegetables.
Reporter: Old produce ... yuck! I don't think people want to buy that!
Emma: Well, the supermarket can't sell it, but maybe they can donate it. In my opinion, it's wrong to waste good food.
Reporter: But is the food still good?
Emma: Sometimes it *is* good. Some supermarkets donate food before it goes bad. They give bread and cans of food to food banks. Sometimes they donate the produce to zoos or sell it to farmers for their animals. There are lots of ways not to waste food.

3a

- Ask students to read the tips in the HOW TO box.

3b 50

- Ask students to read the statements before they listen to the track again.
- Play the track and stop it after Emma's first speech in order to go over the example with the class.
- Then play the whole track for students to listen and decide which sentences are facts and which are opinions.
- Encourage students to compare their answers in pairs before you check them as a class.

ANSWERS
2 F 3 O 4 F 5 O

Extra activity
Ask some further comprehension questions to test students' full understanding of the listening text: *Where is the reporter?* (at a supermarket); *Does Emma act individually?* (No, she is part of a group against food waste.) *What does the group do?* (They make lists of food in supermarket trash cans.) *Who does Emma say supermarkets can donate food to?* (They can donate to food banks, zoos, or farmers.)

MOVE BEYOND FOR TEACHERS

Waste

In a year, more than 1 billion tons of waste is thrown away around the world. Waste amounts to around 100 kg per consumer in Europe and North America every year compared to consumers in sub-Saharan Africa and most of Asia, who throw away just 6–11 kg. Food waste is mainly due to retailers and consumers throwing edible food, particularly fruit and vegetables, into the trash can. Food loss and waste use up the world's resources – water, land, energy, and labor – and contribute significantly to greenhouse gas emissions.

4

- Ask students to reflect on which ideas from the HOW TO box helped them do Exercise 3b and to check them.

REACT

5

- Divide the class into pairs to discuss the questions and give reasons for their opinions. Encourage students to recycle phrases for giving opinions that they learned in Unit 1 (see Student's Book, page 15).
- Elicit opinions from different students around the class.

WORK WITH WORDS

6 51

- Ask students to match the phrases for containers and amounts to the pictures.
- Play the track for students to listen and check.
- Elicit or point out that most of the food items here are uncountable (e.g., *water*) but that by adding quantifiers, such as *a bottle of*, we make them countable (e.g., *three bottles of water*). Elicit other examples from students.

ANSWERS / AUDIO SCRIPT 51
2 e 3 d 4 c 5 b 6 f 7 g 8 h
See Student's Book, page 46, for audio script.

7 52 PRONOUNCE

- Play the track for students to listen to the phrases in Exercise 6 and decide which words are not stressed.
- Play the track again for students to listen and repeat.

ANSWER / AUDIO SCRIPT 52
a and *of* (In general, there is usually no stress on function words such as articles and prepositions.)
See Student's Book, page 46, Exercise 6, for audio script.

8

- Give students one minute to look at the pictures in Exercise 6.
- Ask them to close their books and make a list of all the items they remember.
- Draw students' attention to the model conversation and ask two volunteers to read it aloud to the class.
- Divide the class into pairs and tell them to ask and answer questions to check their lists. At the end of the exercise, ask students to look at Exercise 6 to check whether they remembered all the items.

MOVE BEYOND

Ask students to do the **Move Beyond** task on page 72.

Homework

Ask students to write a list of all the items in their imaginary perfect refrigerator. At the beginning of the next class, students can read their lists aloud to each other in pairs and decide whether their partners have a healthy or an unhealthy refrigerator!

GRAMMAR Indefinite pronouns

Use indefinite pronouns Page 45

STAGE	TIME	FOCUS
GET STARTED		Tell a funny story to introduce the idea of indefinite pronouns.
READ		Read and discuss interesting facts about waste.
STUDY		Complete grammar explanations of indefinite pronouns and discuss the use of *some*, *no*, *any*, and *every*.
PRACTICE		Produce target language in written exercises and discuss ideas about how to stop food waste at school.
WRITE AND SPEAK		Write a poem using target language and comment on other poems.

Get started

Write the names *Somebody*, *Anybody*, *Nobody*, and *Crazy* on the board and tell students a story to introduce the topic of the lesson:

There were four friends named Somebody, Anybody, Nobody, and Crazy. One day, Somebody and Anybody had a fight over Nobody. Crazy went to the police and said, "Officer, Somebody and Anybody are fighting over Nobody." The police officer said, "Are you crazy?" Crazy said, "Yes, I am."

Divide the class into pairs to try to reconstruct the story. Repeat the story if necessary.

Reconstruct the story as a class, eliciting parts from different students around the class.

Elicit the grammatical term for words such as *somebody*, *anybody*, and *nobody* (indefinite pronouns). Ask if students know any others (*e.g.*, *anything*, *everything*, *nothing*).

READ Grammar in context

1

- Refer students to the photo and ask them what they think it is (*a strangely shaped cucumber/pickle*). Ask students if they would buy it.
- Focus students' attention on the facts. Ask them to read them and decide which one they think is most interesting.

STUDY

2

- Refer students to the grammar explanation of indefinite pronouns. Ask them to work individually to choose the correct words to complete the rules.
- Let them compare their answers in pairs before you check them as a class.

ANSWERS

singular   some-   negative

3

- Go over the example in the table before asking students to complete the remaining sections.
- Check answers as a class.

ANSWERS

People: *somebody*, anybody, everybody, *nobody*
Things: *something*, anything, *everything*, nothing
Places: *somewhere*, *anywhere*, everywhere, nowhere

PRACTICE

4a

- Ask students to work individually to complete the indefinite pronouns by adding *some*, *any*, *every*, or *no*.
- Let students compare their answers in pairs before you check them by asking different students around the class.

ANSWERS

2 every(thing)   3 some(thing)   4 every(body)   5 any(thing)
6 some(where)

4b

- Divide the class into pairs to discuss whether any of the sentences in the conversation in Exercise 4a are true about them or their family.
- Invite volunteers to share their answers with the class.

5

- Refer students to the tips about food waste at school and go over the example with them.
- Ask students to complete the text with indefinite pronouns.
- Let students compare their answers in pairs before you check them as a class. Invite students to share and discuss their opinions of the tips.

ANSWERS

2 Everybody   3 anything   4 anybody   5 everything
6 anywhere

Fast finishers

Ask students to add another tip to the ideas on how to stop food waste at school (e.g., reusable lunchboxes, no prepackaged foods, drinks in reusable containers).

Extra activity

Play a game of *Three in a Row* with indefinite pronouns. (see Games, page 29). Draw a grid on the board and number the squares 1–9. Write the following sentences on the board and tell students that they need to correct a sentence in order to place their symbol in a square.

1 *She doesn't remember nothing about the accident.* (anything, everything)
2 *I don't want to eat everything now. I'm not hungry.* (anything)
3 *I don't understand something you say.* (anything, everything)
4 *I want to tell you anything.* (something, everything)
5 *The homework wasn't clear, and they understood everything.* (nothing)
6 *It is impossible to go somewhere in your lifetime.* (everywhere)
7 *The police searched the house, but they didn't find nobody.* (anybody, everybody)
8 *It was a great party. Nobody was dancing.* (Everybody)
9 *I don't know nobody in this city.* (anybody, everybody)

WRITE AND SPEAK

6a

- Focus students on the poem. Invite a volunteer to read it aloud. Elicit whether students like it or not and encourage them to give reasons.

6b

- Encourage students to write their own poems using the words in color and the ideas in the cloud.
- Ask students to exchange poems with a partner and to comment on each other's poems. Read the poem below aloud (or write it on the board) if you feel your class would benefit from it either before or after they write their own.

In my perfect world …
Nobody fights,
Everybody likes each other,
Nothing hurts.
Everything is cool.
Everywhere there is love and harmony.

Homework

Ask students to write an example sentence for each of the indefinite pronouns in Exercise 3. Ask each student to read one example in the next class.

LANGUAGE & BEYOND *RESPECT OTHERS*

Consider other people's needs and preferences *Page 46*

STAGE	TIME	FOCUS
GET STARTED		Recycle food vocabulary and introduce the topic of special diets.
READ		Match information about special diets to student profiles and list things they can't eat.
DO		Make a list of food for a party, considering special dietary needs.
REFLECT		Discuss special diets and how we can consider other people's needs and preferences.
EXTEND		Create a music playlist for a party, taking other people's tastes in music into account.

LIFE SKILLS

CONSIDERING OTHER PEOPLE'S NEEDS AND PREFERENCES

Considering other people's needs means taking into account how decisions and actions may affect them. Encourage students to think of times when they felt their own needs were not considered and invite them to say what happened and how they felt. Remind students that we should not consider other people's needs just to make ourselves feel good or earn recognition. Point out that considering other people's needs is a sign of maturity and an important skill for working in a team and creating strong friendships.

MOVE BEYOND FOR TEACHERS

Special diets

Vegetarians and vegans choose their diet for a variety of social, religious, lifestyle, moral, environmental, and health reasons. Some people may have an allergy and have to be careful because they can get very sick if they eat the wrong kinds of food. Some people cannot digest gluten, which is found in wheat, so they need to have a gluten-free diet.

Get started

Divide the class into pairs to write a list of food items beginning with each letter of the alphabet with the exception of *u*, *x*, and *z*. Set a three-minute time limit for this.

When the time is up, elicit food items for each letter and write them in a list on the board. Encourage students to write down any new items in their own lists. Ask if there is anything on the list that students are allergic to or can't eat.

READ

1

- Explain to students that a group of American students is coming to the school and three of them have special diets.
- Focus students on the profiles and the phrases in the box. Ask students to read and complete the profiles with the correct phrase.

ANSWERS

Asha is a vegetarian.
Carmelo is allergic to eggs.
Lucy can't eat gluten.

2

- Divide the class into pairs to make a list of the foods they can see in the photos.
- Ask them to consider the visitors' special diets and decide which foods they can't eat, marking them with their initials.

ANSWERS

1 chicken wings (A) 2 pasta salad (L) 3 cake (C, L)
4 sushi (A) 5 cheese
6 pizza (L, and A if it has a meat or fish topping) 7 sandwiches (L, A if they have meat or fish filling, and C if they are egg sandwiches)

DO

3

- Explain to students that the class is organizing a party to welcome the group of American students.
- Divide the class into small groups to make a list of food for the party, including options for Asha, Carmelo, and Lucy. Encourage students to also consider the needs and preferences of other students in their class.
- Refer students to the PHRASE BYTES box and encourage them to recycle phrases for making suggestions that they learned in Unit 3.
- Monitor and note good use of language and errors to go over in a feedback session at the end of the activity.
- In a class discussion, elicit ideas that take into account the needs and preferences of the American students and of students in the class.

REFLECT

4

- Discuss each of the questions with the class. Choose a student to read the REFLECTION POINT aloud and invite students to say whether they agree with this.

EXTEND

5

- Divide the class into groups and ask them to make a music playlist for the welcome party. Encourage them to consider the preferences of other people in the class by asking some classmates if necessary. Set a time limit of five minutes.
- Invite students to pass around their playlists for other groups to comment on.

Homework

Ask students to write a short conversation between two teenagers who are discussing the needs and preferences of friends with special diets for a party. Remind them to include all the phrases from the PHRASE BYTES box and the vocabulary from the lesson.

SPEAKING At a restaurant

Express preferences when you order food Page 47

STAGE	TIME	FOCUS
GET STARTED		Recycle word stress in questions and practice falling intonation in *Wh-* questions.
SPEAK		Talk about types of restaurants and favorite restaurant meals.
LISTEN		Listen and complete a conversation with food items. Learn how to make polite requests when ordering food (speaking subskill).
ACT		Prepare and present a conversation using polite expressions.

Get started

Books closed. Read aloud the two questions from Exercise 1 at a natural speed and ask students to say how many words there are in each sentence (contractions count as one word).

Elicit which words are not stressed in the questions.

Drill the questions and recycle unstressed words and falling intonation in *Wh-* questions.

SPEAK

1

- Divide the class into pairs and ask them to discuss their answers to the questions.
- Invite different students to share their answers with the class.

LISTEN

2 53

- Have students close their books. Play the conversation for them to listen and find out what Rick and Sandy order. Ask them to take notes.
- Let students compare their notes in pairs.
- Ask students to read the conversation in their books and try to complete it from their notes.
- Play the track again for students to listen and check their answers.

ANSWERS / AUDIO SCRIPT 53

2 salad 3 cheeseburger 4 fries 5 water 6 milkshake

Server: Hi. Are you ready to order?
Rick: Yes. I'd like the chicken sandwich, please. Can I have it without onions?
Server: Of course. Would you like some fries with it?
Rick: No, thanks. I'd rather have salad.
Server: OK.
Sandy: I'd like the cheeseburger, please. And I'd prefer fries with it.
Server: OK. Would you like anything to drink?
Rick: Do you have any fresh orange juice?
Server: No, but we have milkshakes and sodas.
Rick: Um ... I'll have some water.
Sandy: I'd like a milkshake, please.

3a

- Refer students to the tips about being polite in the HOW TO box.

3b 53

- Focus students on the sentences and ask if they sound polite or not (*they don't*).
- Ask students to look back at the conversation in Exercise 2 to find more polite versions of sentences 1–6. Go over the example sentence before they start.
- Check answers as a class by choosing different students to read sentences.
- Play the conversation again and point out that intonation is also important.

ANSWERS

2 Can I have it without onions?
3 Would you like anything to drink?
4 No, thanks. I'd rather have salad.
5 Are you ready to order?
6 I'll have some water.

ACT

4 54

- Divide the class into groups of three or four to role-play a conversation in a restaurant. Ask them to choose one person in the group to be the server.
- Invite students to choose what they would like to order from the menu. Refer them to the phrases in the PHRASEBOOK box and encourage them to use them in their conversations, together with the expressions in Exercise 2. Play the track for students to listen and repeat.
- Monitor while the servers take their group's order and note good use of language and errors to go over in a feedback session at the end of the exercise.

Extra activity

Ask students to perform their conversations for another group. Tell the other group to listen and write down what each student orders.

Homework

Write an example conversation on the board between a server and customer with both people using impolite speech (e.g., "*What do you want?*" "*I want fries.*") Ask students to copy the conversation and then rewrite it using polite language.

WRITING My favorite recipe

Order ideas

Page 48

STAGE	TIME	FOCUS
GET STARTED		Recycle cooking verbs and introduce the idea of sequencing instructions.
SPEAK AND READ		Identify sequencing words in the text and read and order a recipe (writing subskill).
PRACTICE		Produce target language in a written exercise.
DISCUSS		Discuss a recipe you know how to prepare.
WRITE		Write instructions for your recipe.
SHARE		Share your recipe with your classmates.

Get started

Divide the class into pairs and discuss how to make a strawberry and banana milkshake. Elicit instructions from students and use this opportunity to recycle cooking verbs (*chop*, *pour*, *stir*, *cut*) and to introduce the word *mixture*.

Write the instructions below in random order on the board and ask students to number them 1–6. Ask students if they know any sequencing words to order the instructions.

ANSWERS

Cut the leaves off and clean the strawberries. (1)
Chop the banana. (2)
Put the banana and strawberries in a blender. (3)
Add ice and milk. (4)
Blend the mixture. (5)
Pour the milkshake into a glass. (6)

SPEAK AND READ

1

- Focus students' attention on the expressions in the PHRASE BYTES box and ask them if they would like to eat the pancake and say why or why not as a class.

2a

- Ask students to read the tips in the HOW TO box.

2b

- Refer students back to the recipe in Exercise 1 to find and underline examples of the sequencing words.

ANSWERS

After that, Finally, Next, First, Then

3

- Ask students to read the recipe in Exercise 1 and put the steps in the correct order.

ANSWERS

1 First, put the flour in a bowl with a little salt.
2 Next, make a hole in the middle of the flour. Add the eggs and stir together with the flour.
3 After that, pour in the milk and beat it with the flour and eggs.
4 Then leave the pancake mixture for 15–20 minutes.
5 Finally, heat a little oil in a frying pan. Pour in some mixture and fry the pancakes on both sides until they're golden brown.

PRACTICE

4

- Ask students if they have ever eaten black bean and corn salad and elicit any ingredients they may know.
- Ask them to complete the recipe for black bean and corn salad using the sequencing words from Exercise 2. Remind them that in some cases more than one answer is possible.

ANSWERS

2 Next, / After that, / Then
3 Next, / After that, / Then
4 Next, / After that, / Then
5 Finally,

DISCUSS

5

- Ask students to say some things that they know how to cook. If students say they can't cook, encourage them to talk about how they make their favorite sandwich or burger.
- Divide the class into pairs to talk about the recipes of things they can make.

WRITE

6

- Tell students they are going to write one of the recipes they have talked about.
- Point out that the recipe for pancakes is divided into three different sections: Ingredients, Directions, and My tip.
- Refer students to the HOW TO box and encourage them to use the sequencing words in their recipes.
- Finally, suggest that a tip will give their recipe a personal touch and make it much more interesting for the reader.

SHARE

7

- Divide the class into pairs or small groups to read and comment on each other's recipes.
- Make a class recipe book. Encourage students to choose their favorite recipes and try cooking them at home.

Homework

Ask students to write a recipe for a friend with a special diet or preference. Tell them to include sequencing words. At the beginning of the next class, have students read their recipes for a partner to guess the special diet or preference.

VOCABULARY Kitchen equipment and cooking verbs

1

- Refer students to the picture and ask them to describe what is happening in the kitchen.
- Ask students to look at the instructions each person received and to choose the correct options to complete them.
- Choose different students to read Phil, Sue, and Lynn's instructions aloud while the rest of the class checks their answers.

ANSWERS
1 Chop 2 knife 3 cutting 4 fry 5 frying
6 Heat 7 saucepan 8 pour 9 stir 10 Beat
11 bowl 12 cut

Containers and amounts

2

- Ask students to complete the words on the shopping list for a party. If necessary, point out that they should check whether the items need to be singular or plural before they write them.
- Let students compare their answers in pairs before you check them as a class by choosing different students to read the answers aloud.

ANSWERS
1 carton 2 box 3 jar 4 cartons 5 loaves
6 pieces 7 cartons 8 cans

GRAMMAR Expressions of quantity

3

- Refer students to the expressions of quantity in the box and ask the class to use them to complete the phone conversation.
- Choose a pair of confident students to read the conversation aloud for the rest of the class to check their answers.

ANSWERS
1 much 2 lot 3 few 4 some 5 little 6 any
7 no 8 many

Indefinite pronouns

4

- Refer students to the picture and ask them to describe what they think is happening.
- Encourage students to complete the text with the correct indefinite pronouns.
- Let students compare their answers in pairs before checking them as a class.

ANSWERS
1 everybody 2 Nobody 3 somebody 4 everything
5 nothing 6 everywhere 7 anybody

Extra Resources

Go to the Teacher's Resource Center at mee2.macmillaneducation.com for:

- the Speaking section of the Progress Check 3&4;
- a downloadable project linked to Units 3–4;
- downloadable audio and audio scripts for the Student's Book and Workbook;
- videos and video scripts;
- extra vocabulary at two levels of difficulty;
- extra grammar at two levels of difficulty;
- culture lessons, with full teacher's notes;
- a life skills lesson, with full teacher's notes;
- Speaking Database materials;
- the Move Beyond Level 3 wordlist;
- tips for using the Grammar Database;
- and more!

Go to the Workbook pages 120–131 for further practice material.

PROGRESS CHECK 3&4

Preparing for the Progress Check

Vocabulary review

- Divide the class into four teams (call them A, B, C, and D) and give each team a category from the following: *Landscapes and natural features*, *Wildlife*, *Kitchen equipment and cooking verbs*, *Containers and amounts*. Tell students to find their category in the Unit Reviews (pages 39 and 49).
- In their teams, students devise clues for six of the words in their category; for example, *It's a very hot place* (desert) or *This animal is green* (frog). One member of each team writes down the clues.
- Once each team has written six clues, Team A reads their clues aloud. Each correct guess earns one point for that team. Keep score on the board.
- When Team A has read all their clues aloud, the other teams take turns reading their clues aloud. The team with the most points at the end is the winner.

Grammar review

- Ask students to look back through Units 3 and 4. Tell them to put their hands up when they find a grammar point they have studied in these units. Ask the first student who put a hand up to write one grammar heading on the board.
- Repeat with three more students until you have the following on the board: Unit 3 – Simple past; Past progressive and simple past; Unit 4 – Expressions of quantity; Indefinite pronouns.
- Ask the following questions about the grammar points and elicit a variety of examples from students:

  When do we use the simple past? (to describe completed events in the past)

  When do we use the past progressive? (to talk about actions in progress in the past)

  What are some examples of expressions of quantity? (*some*, *a few*, *any*, *many*, *a lot of*, etc.)

  What are the indefinite pronouns? (*everyone*, *everybody*, *something*, *somewhere*, *nothing*, *nobody*, etc.)

Optional warm-up activities

READ Exercise 1

- Direct students to the main text in Exercise 1 and ask the following question: *What activities can the students choose from?* (forest visit, walk by the ocean, etc.)
- Ask students to tell you which activities they enjoy and why. Then ask them which activities they don't like and why.
- Explain that they have to choose activities for different people based on their likes and dislikes.

LISTEN Exercise 2

- Refer students back to some fill-in-the-blank listening exercises they have recently done (Exercise 2, page 37, and Exercise 2, page 47) and remind them that they can usually predict what kind of word or phrase they need to write (*adjective*, *noun phrase*, *verb phrase*, etc.).
- Divide the class into pairs or small groups and ask them to look carefully at Exercise 2 on page 51 and work out what kind of information is missing from each blank.
- Write 1–5 on the board and, for each blank, ask students to tell you what information you should write down.

WRITE Exercise 3

- Refer students back to the work they did on writing stories on page 38 and ask: *How do you write a good story?* Elicit tips from the HOW TO box on page 38 and make sure students remember that the main tense for their stories should be the simple past, which they can also combine with the past progressive.
- Look at Exercise 3 with the class and point out that the example sentence has the two past tenses combined.
- Divide students into pairs and ask them to come up with a plot for a story based on the first sentence given. Allow up to five minutes for this before asking a few pairs to tell you their stories.

Doing the Progress Check

READ

1

- Remind students of the exercises they did on page 48, in which three people had special dietary needs. Then look at Exercise 1 in the Progress Check and ask: *What do these people need?* (a suitable vacation activity).
- Go through the **Test-Taking Tips** one by one and make sure students know how to do this kind of multiple-matching task.
- Revisit the HOW TO boxes on pages 32 and 42, to remind students that they've done tasks similar to this before.
- Allow 10–15 minutes for this section.

ANSWERS
1 G 2 E 3 A 4 D 5 F

LISTEN

2 55

- If you have decided not to do the full warm-up, encourage students to spend a minute or two predicting what they might hear in the blanks.
- Go through the **Test-Taking Tips** and the HOW TO boxes on pages 34 and 44, making sure that students understand that they have to write a word, a number, or a short phrase in each blank.
- Point out that they will hear the track twice.

ANSWERS / AUDIO SCRIPT 55

1 Vegetarian 2 environment 3 potatoes 4 allergic to 5 19.99

Restaurant owner: Welcome, everybody. Can I just tell you something about the restaurant? My name's Jarek, and I'm one of the owners. As you probably know, this is a vegetarian restaurant. We don't use any meat, meat products, or fish in our dishes – no meat or fish at all.
When we opened the restaurant, we wanted to offer fresh, healthy food. In our opinion, it's important to know where everything on our menu comes from. We think it's also bad for the environment to transport food a long way. So we decided to buy only local food. We use mushrooms from the local forest, and all our other vegetables come from our own garden. We buy our dairy products from local farms and bake all our own loaves of bread.
The lunch menu today includes soup, a main course, and dessert. For the main course, we have pancakes with vegetables in a cream sauce and potatoes. If you'd rather have rice instead of potatoes, we can do that. The other choice is an omelette with onions, tomatoes, and spices. That comes with a bowl of salad and bread.
For dessert, you can have a piece of chocolate cake with chocolate sauce or ice cream with fruit.
If you're allergic to anything or can't eat flour, please tell your waiter or waitress; we can make something different for you.
To drink, I'd like to recommend the apple juice. We make our own juice from the apples in our garden behind the restaurant, and we think it tastes fantastic. We also have milkshakes.
Oh, I forgot to say that the fixed lunch menu costs nineteen dollars and ninety-nine cents.
Somebody will come and take your order soon, but I'll be happy to answer any questions now.

WRITE

3

- Go through the **Test-Taking Tips** for the writing task. Refer students back to the writing exercises and the **HOW TO** box on page 38. Ask them to tell you what they learned from these tasks and make sure they know how to use time expressions correctly.
- Point out that their stories must begin with the exact sentence given and must continue logically from there.
- Remind the class that the main tense they will use here is the simple past although they can also use this alongside the past progressive, as in the opening sentence of the story.
- Finally, remind students that they must leave enough time to write a satisfactory ending, pointing out that they can lose a lot of credit if their stories are incomplete. Also point out that their stories should be within the word limit given.
- Allow up to 20 minutes for the task; remind students when they have five minutes left.

MODEL ANSWER

I was eating dinner with my parents when something strange happened. First, somebody screamed outside. It was a very loud scream. After that, we heard a car. It was driving away very fast.
We ran outside, but there was nobody there. Then I looked in the street and I found a small ring. It was very pretty and it had the name "Valeria" on it.
Later, the police came, but they didn't find anything and we didn't hear from them again. I thought about that evening for weeks. Who was Valeria? And why did she scream?

After the Progress Check

Optional game

- Tell students that they are going to write a story together. On a clean sheet of paper, each student writes the first line of a story (it can be on any subject, but suggest that they write about the topics that they have covered in the book). Students then pass their papers to the students on their right, who read the beginning and add one sentence. They continue in this way, adding one sentence each time until they have six or seven sentences. Then ask students to read aloud the stories they started; then ask the rest of the class to suggest suitable endings.

Feedback and extension

READ

- Where students made mistakes, focus attention on the links between the people (1–5) and the activities (A–H). Do the first one as an example on the board as follows:

Victor:

- *loves being by the coast (B, E, and G are all near the coast)*
- *hates going in the water / didn't learn to swim (E is not suitable because it asks for good swimmers)*
- *doesn't like any sports or being active (he won't like B because it's a five-kilometer walk)*

That leaves G, which is on the beach with friends but without swimming or being active.

- In pairs, students discuss the correct answers for the other people. Tell them to mark the important phrases in their books.
- When they are ready, ask different pairs to explain and justify the correct answers. Students can also tell you why they eliminated certain answers; for example, *A (the forest visit) isn't good for Victor because it isn't by the coast.*
- As an extension of this type of task, divide the class into two groups. Ask the members of the first group to write their own requirements for an activity (similar to items 1–5 in the exercise). Their requirements should have both likes and dislikes. The members of the second group should each devise an activity similar to A–H in the exercise.
- After about 10 minutes, the members of the first group take turns reading aloud what they have written. Those in the second group then say if they have something suitable. Students discuss which activity is most suitable and why.

LISTEN

- If students made mistakes, play the track again, pausing before each answer is revealed.
- As an alternative feedback exercise, make enough copies of the audio script so that each pair of students can go through and circle the answers in the text. Ask individual students to tell you where they went wrong and what they need to listen more carefully to.
- To give further practice on the topic of food, divide the class into pairs or small groups. Ask students to look at the listening task they have just done. Tell them that you want them to create something similar.
- Ask each pair or group to draw a table on a piece of paper with space for writing and with the following headings: *Type of restaurant*, *Owner's opinions*, *Lunch menu*, *Drinks*, *Price of lunch menu*.
- Tell the class to look through Unit 4 for some interesting ideas for their restaurant, which they should write down in the table. They can also use ideas of their own.
- After a suitable time (5–10 minutes), students should switch partners and take turns telling their new partners about their restaurants. The partners should make notes and then report back to the class.

WRITE

- Point out where students lost credit in their stories, explaining the importance of:
  - correct use of tenses,
  - effective use of linking devices (*so*, *but*, *then*, *later*, *after that*, etc.),
  - correct sentence formation, and
  - a suitable progression of events and an ending.
- To give further practice in story writing, create a story with the class. Write a suitable story beginning on the board; for example, *I was getting ready for bed when suddenly I heard a noise outside.*
- Ask a volunteer to come to the board and write the second sentence. Continue in this way until the story is completed.
- If there is time, several stories can be written in this way. Students will probably find it easier to create sentences on topics that they have studied (*Applications [Apps]*, *Computer parts*, *Homes and household chores*, *Free-time activities*, *Landscapes and natural features*, *Wildlife*, and *Cooking*). Below are some suggestions for beginning new stories. One of these could also be assigned for homework.
  - *I was surfing the internet when I got an unusual message on my computer.*
  - *I was doing some chores around the house when I noticed something strange.*
  - *I was getting ready to go to school when my basketball coach called.*
  - *One day we were walking through a forest when I thought I heard something.*
  - *While I was cooking dinner one evening, I had a little accident.*

5 WHO AM I?

IN THE PICTURE Different people

Talk about somebody's personality *Pages 52–53*

STAGE	TIME	FOCUS
GET STARTED		Brainstorm ideas within the topic of identity.
WORK WITH WORDS		Recycle personality adjectives and learn a new set. Watch a video and listen for specific information.
SPEAK		Role-play a character and invent a personality profile.

Get started

If possible, prepare for this activity by asking students to bring some of the items to class. This will make the activity more dynamic.

Write the title of the unit on the board: *Who am I?* Ask students to think of three items that say something about who they are.

Divide the class into pairs and explain that you want them to tell each other what the items are and what the items say about them.

Demonstrate the task by telling them about three items that say something about you (e.g., a photo of your family, your favorite soccer team scarf, something that is related to a hobby you do, an item that you treasure for some particular reason).

At the end of the activity, have a class discussion about the kinds of things people chose to represent their identities.

WORK WITH WORDS

1 RECALL

- Divide the class into pairs and refer them to the speech bubbles.
- Ask them to match the speech bubbles to the correct personality adjectives in the box. Go over the example answer before they start. Set a time limit of three minutes for this.
- Check answers as a class by choosing different pairs to give the answers.
- Ask students to do the **Work with Words** task on page 73.

ANSWERS

2 calm 3 friendly 4 funny 5 confident 6 shy
7 rude 8 serious

2 56

- Focus students on the pictures of the people and the adjectives that describe them.
- Explain that they are going to hear some questions and that they should answer them by saying the correct names.
- Play the audio for students to listen and respond orally.
- You could play the track again for students to write down the adjectives they hear. This will give them additional support for Exercise 3.

ANSWERS / AUDIO SCRIPT 56

1 Who's sensitive? (Linda)
2 Who's patient? (Jessica)
3 Who's generous? (Eduardo)
4 Who's ambitious? (Julia)
5 Who's brave? (Eric)
6 Who's smart? (Tony)
7 Who's kind? (Al)
8 Who's creative? (Sandra)
9 Who's cheerful? (Elena)
10 Who's competitive? (Jeff)

3 57

- Explain to students that they are going to hear 10 descriptions of people and after each description they should write (in their notebooks) the adjective from Exercise 2 that matches it.
- Divide the class into pairs, but ask them to write the answers individually the first time they listen. Play the track. Then ask them to compare their answers in pairs.
- Play the track again, eliciting the answer after each description.

ANSWERS / AUDIO SCRIPT 57

1 He often helps me when I have a problem. (*kind*)
2 You can ask him anything. He always knows the answers. (smart)
3 She paints and makes her own clothes and everything. (creative)
4 He's not afraid of scary situations. (brave)
5 You know, she cries when she watches sad movies. (sensitive)
6 She wants to earn a lot of money and work for a big company. (ambitious)
7 She never worries about anything at all. She always has a smile! (cheerful)
8 He always has to be the best when we play a game. (competitive)
9 He always gives people money when they need it. (generous)
10 She doesn't get angry when you don't understand. She just explains it again. (patient)

4

- Go over the example answer first and point out that students should read the sentences and complete each description with the appropriate adjective from Exercise 2.
- Let students compare their answers in pairs before you check them as a class.

ANSWERS
2 brave 3 generous 4 competitive 5 ambitious
6 sensitive

Fast finishers
Fast finishers can write one or two sentences of their own with blanks for the remaining adjectives. They can test the other students in the class by reading their sentences aloud, substituting a beep sound for the adjective.

5

- Draw students' attention to the model text and ask a volunteer to read it aloud.
- Ask students to write a similar description of their own personality using the adjectives in Exercises 1 and 2. Encourage students to give reasons in their descriptions, as in the model. Set a time limit of five minutes.
- Monitor students as they are working and offer individual attention and advice.

Extra activity
Ask students to write their descriptions in Exercise 5 on strips of paper. When they have finished, collect the strips of paper and redistribute them. Divide the class into small groups for them to take turns reading the descriptions they were given and deciding as a group which classmate they think each description refers to. Complete the activity by selecting one student from each group to read one of their descriptions aloud and say who they think wrote it. Students check with the supposed author to see if they were right.

6 THE MOVING PICTURE 58

- Tell students they are going to listen to five people talking about their personalities. They must match each person in the video to the picture showing the same personality adjective in Exercise 2. Play the audio track on its own the first time, and then play the video.
- Let students compare their answers in pairs before you check them as a class.

ANSWERS / AUDIO / VIDEO SCRIPT 58
1 Judy & Tony (smart) 2 Ben & Eric (brave)
3 Mariana & Sandra (creative) 4 Samuel & Elena (cheerful)
5 Paula & Eduardo (generous)

Judy: Hi, I'm Judy. I have this great new phone with a lot of great apps. My favorite is this math game. It's amazing. I can't stop playing it!
Ben: Hi, I'm Ben and I'm not really scared of anything – not spiders, not snakes, nothing! I'd love to go skydiving or try some extreme sports! I'd like to be a pilot or an astronaut when I get older.
Mariana: Hi, everyone, I'm Mariana. As you can see, I love to make jewelry. I love all kinds of art. I'm really into designing things. I drive my mom crazy because I'm always collecting boxes and things so I can use them for my art.
Samuel: Hi, I'm Samuel, but call me Sammy. I'm a really nice person and I think I'm a really good friend. I try to see the good side of everything and stay positive. If you're worried about something, come and talk to me. I can make you laugh. You won't stay down when I'm around.
Paula: Hi there, I'm Paula. I love to give things to people. I'm always sharing things with my brothers and my friends. Mom says that sharing is important. Here – you want some candy?
Young man: Sure. Thank you.

Extra activity
Dictate or write some comprehension questions on the board and ask students to write down the answers as they listen; for example, Speaker 1: What is she doing? (*playing a game on her cell phone*); Speaker 2: What does he want to do when he's older? (*be a pilot or an astronaut*); Speaker 3: What drives her mom crazy? (*She always collects boxes and things for her art*); Speaker 4: What do you do if you're worried about something? (*come talk to him*); Speaker 5: Who does she share things with? (*her brothers and her friends*).

SPEAK

7

Exam-type task

- Divide the class into pairs and invite them each to choose one person from the pictures. Ask them to imagine that they are that person and to invent a profile.
- Check the meaning of *profile* (i.e., *a description of a person that contains details about that person*).
- Give students two minutes of quiet preparation time to think about how they will answer each of the four questions.
- Finally, ask them to take turns presenting their profiles to their partners.

MOVE BEYOND
Ask students to do the **Move Beyond** task on page 73.

Extra activity 58
Play the video again and ask students to take notes in their notebooks about the things the people like.
At the end of the video track, set a time limit of two minutes for students to compare their notes in pairs before you check them as a class.

ANSWERS
1 Judy – her cell phone, apps, the math game
2 Ben – skydiving, extreme sports
3 Mariana – jewelry, art, designing things
4 Samuel – talking, making people laugh
5 Paula – giving things to people, sharing

Homework
Refer students to the task in Exercise 1 on page 52.
Ask students to write a speech bubble to match each of the new adjectives they have learned in this lesson; for example, for *sensitive*: *"When I see a sad movie, I want to cry!"*

READING Doodles and me

Identify the goal of a text

Page 54

STAGE	TIME	FOCUS
GET STARTED		Recycle personality adjectives.
SPEAK AND READ		Analyze a partner's doodles. Identify the goal of a text (reading subskill). Read for specific information.
REACT		React to the text. Express personal opinions on the topic.

Get started

Divide the class into pairs to brainstorm as many personality adjectives as they can in two minutes.

Ask which pair has the longest list and have them read their words aloud. Find out if any students have words that are not on pages 52–53.

Ask for some volunteers to act out particular personalities in front of the class so that other students can guess the adjectives.

SPEAK AND READ

1

- Ask students if they ever draw little pictures or designs during class or while other people are speaking.
- Explain that in English these are called *doodles* (/ˈduːd(ə)lz/). Point out that the word *doodle* is also a verb: *When he's bored, he sometimes doodles on a piece of paper.*
- Ask students to open their books to page 56 and follow the instructions in Exercise 1.
- Give them one minute to draw their own doodles in their notebooks. They shouldn't think about it too much, but just let their hand and pen move naturally.
- Divide the class into pairs. Before they discuss their doodles, focus their attention on the phrases in the PHRASE BYTES box and encourage them to use the phrases in their conversations. Set a time limit of two minutes for pairs to discuss each of their doodles.
- Ask for volunteers to report back to the class about their conversations.

2a

- Explain to students that they are going to read a text about doodles. Remind them that when we read, it is important to quickly identify the main goal of a text, as this will help us understand the content.
- Refer students to the HOW TO box. When they have read it, ask them to cover the box and to tell you what they remember about the tips in their own words.

2b 59

- Ask students to read the text about doodling and identify the goal of the text from the options A, B, or C. Set a strict two-minute time limit to discourage students from reading the text in detail at this stage. Don't play the audio at this point. It is an extra feature, and a suggestion for using it in class is included at the end of the lesson.
- At the end of two minutes, ask students to stop reading even if they have not finished the complete text. Ask them to talk to their partners about the goal of the text and decide on option A, B, or C.
- Check the answer as a class.

ANSWER

B

3

- Ask students to reflect on which tips in the HOW TO box helped them decide on the goal of the text and to check them.

4

- Ask students to read the text again, this time in more detail, and write the correct meanings of the types of doodles on the list.
- Set a time limit of five minutes for this and let students compare their answers in pairs as they finish.
- Choose individual students to read their answers aloud.

ANSWERS

2 You're serious.
3 You're emotional.
4 You're ambitious and you work hard.
5 You're scared of trusting people.
6 You're kind and friendly.
7 You like being free and aren't interested in doing difficult tasks.
8 You think about yourself a lot.

Fast finishers

Ask students to scan the text again and add more types of doodles and their meanings to the list in Exercise 4.

REACT

5

- Divide the class into pairs to discuss the questions.
- End the exercise by taking a quick poll to see if the class thinks that doodles tell us something about the person who drew them.
- Ask individual students to give some of their reasons.

Extra activity

Ask students to go through the text and make a list of all the personality adjectives. When they have completed their lists, ask them to test each other on the meaning of the adjectives; for example, *This adjective describes someone who is always happy and smiling* (cheerful).

Recorded reading text 59

The audio track could be used as an alternative in Exercise 4 if extra listening practice is needed. Ask students to cover the text and then play the track and ask them to complete the exercise. Students can then check their answers against the text.

Homework

Ask each student to write a short description of their partner's original doodle, their original interpretation, and any changes they made to their ideas after reading the text. They should finish with their opinion about whether doodles say anything about the person who draws them. You might like to give students a template to work from. For example:

> ________ 's doodle was ________.
> Before I read the text, I said that ________.
> The text said that ________.
> This was the same as / similar to / different from my ideas.
> I think that doodles ________.

GRAMMAR Adjectives with prepositions + *-ing* form

Express your feelings about doing things *Page 55*

STAGE	TIME	FOCUS
GET STARTED		Review names of parts of speech.
READ AND LISTEN		Read and listen for specific information.
STUDY		Use a text to find examples of adjective + preposition patterns.
PRACTICE		Produce target language in written exercises.
SPEAK		Produce target language in a speaking task. Express feelings about doing things.

Get started

Write this sentence on the board and ask students to copy it into their notebooks: *Give your opinions about doing things.*

Ask them to look at the sentence and to follow the instructions that you read aloud:

In this sentence there are two nouns, a verb, an -ing *form, a preposition, and a possessive adjective. Underline the two nouns. Put a circle above the verb. Put a star above the* -ing *form. Write the number 1 above the preposition. Write the number 2 under the possessive adjective.*

Let students compare their answers in pairs before you mark the sentence on the board for them to check.

Elicit some other examples of each type of word.

ANSWER

0 1 *
Give your opinions about doing things.
2

READ AND LISTEN Grammar in context

1 60

- Elicit from students the names of famous comic books, or TV shows or movies that were originally comic books (e.g., *Batman*). Ask them if they like reading comic books.
- Play the track for students to read and listen to the conversation. Ask them to find out what Diego is good at, and what he was scared of and why.
- Give students 30 seconds to check their answers in pairs before you check them as a class.

ANSWER / AUDIO SCRIPT 60

Diego is good at drawing and art. He was scared of showing his parents his first comic book because he was worried about hearing their opinion.
See Student's Book, page 57, for audio script.

STUDY

2

- Write the sentence *I'm happy about going on vacation* on the board and elicit which word is an adjective (*happy*) and what type of word follows it (*a preposition*).
- Refer students to the table and go over the example, asking them to locate the phrase *bad at* in the conversation.
- Ask students to complete the table with the correct preposition for each adjective.
- Check answers as a class, inviting students to read the full sentence aloud in each case.

ANSWERS

Adjective	Preposition
bored	with
excited	about
good / not bad	at
interested	in
scared	of
tired	of
worried	about

3

- Refer students to the grammar explanation in the box. Ask them to look back at Exercise 1 and complete the examples with suitable words.
- Check and discuss answers as a class.
- Remind students that sometimes there are spelling changes when we add *-ing* to a verb and refer them to the **Grammar Database** on page 68 to review when these changes happen.

ANSWERS
art drawing

PRACTICE

4

- Focus students on the photo of Rachel and the picture she made below. Ask students what they think she's good at (*using a computer to create art*).
- Ask students to complete Rachel's sentences using the correct prepositions and the *-ing* form of the verbs.
- Let students compare their answers in pairs before you check them as a class.

ANSWERS
2 in taking 3 about using 4 at creating 5 with changing
6 of trying

Extra activity
Divide the class into pairs to discuss these questions:
Are you interested in taking photos, like Rachel? Who or what do you take photos of? Do you use photo software? Are you scared of trying new things?

5

- Focus students on the pictures and emoticons and ask them to write sentences using the phrases in Exercise 2 and the *-ing* form of the verbs in the box. Set a time limit of four minutes for this.
- Ask fast finishers to write their answers on the board.
- Check the answers as a class, correcting the ones on the board if necessary.

ANSWERS
2 I'm bad at / not so good at singing. 3 I'm interested in cooking.
4 I'm tired of running. 5 I'm scared of dancing.
6 I'm excited about skiing.

SPEAK

6

- Give students a minute to think about their answers to the questions.
- Then divide the class into pairs to take turns asking and answering the questions.

Alternative procedure
Create a space in the classroom for students to mingle. Ask them to talk to six different people, one for each question. Encourage them to find out a little bit more about the answers they get by asking follow-up questions. For example:

A: *What are you excited about doing in the future?*

B: *I'm excited about going on vacation with my family in August.*

A: *Oh, really? Why?*

B: *We're going to the beach for two weeks, and I love swimming in the ocean and sunbathing.*

MOVE BEYOND

Ask students to write their own answers to the questions in Exercise 6 in their notebooks, making sure they write complete sentences.

Extra activity
Dictate the sentence stems below for students to write in their notebooks. Ask them to complete the sentences with endings that are true for them. Give students time to read their sentences aloud in pairs or small groups.

I'm interested in learning English because …

Some people are worried about the future because …

My parents worry about me because …

Sometimes I'm bored with doing schoolwork because …

Homework

Ask students to think about their best friends and choose four of the questions from Exercise 6 to rewrite in the third person singular. Then ask them to write answers about their friends, adding an extra sentence to each answer to explain more; for example, *What is he good at doing? He's good at singing. He sings in a choir, and he also plays the piano.* Choose three or four students to read their descriptions aloud in the next class.

LISTENING AND VOCABULARY Where do I belong?

Recognize when speakers need time to think

Page 56

STAGE	TIME	FOCUS
GET STARTED		Recycle names of countries. Discuss the meaning of *belong*.
SPEAK AND LISTEN		Talk about where you and your parents were born and what language(s) you speak. Listen for specific information. Recognize when speakers need time to think (listening subskill).
REACT		Order a list of things that make someone feel they belong to a place. Compare and discuss choices.
WORK WITH WORDS		List countries, nationalities, and languages. Identify word stress.

Get started

Divide the class into small groups to brainstorm the names of as many countries as they can in two minutes.

Elicit the names of three countries from each group, one by one, telling them not to repeat any that have already been mentioned.

Find out whether students think they'd be happy if they suddenly had to move to another, very different country. Ask them to say why or why not. Try to introduce the idea of belonging or not belonging and write the word *belong* on the board. Elicit or explain its meaning (*to feel happy and comfortable in a particular place or with a particular group of people*). Draw their attention to the title of the lesson, *Where do I belong?*

SPEAK AND LISTEN

1

- Divide the class into pairs to ask and answer the questions. Refer them to the expressions in the PHRASE BYTES box and encourage them to use them in their discussions.

Extra activity

Depending on your students' L1, they may have difficulty with the expression *be born*. If so, set up a substitution drill, writing the following prompts on the board and eliciting the sentence from the group or from chosen students:

+ I / in 2000.

+ My parents / in a small town.

? your sister / in 2004?

? you / in a hospital?

– My grandparents / in Spain.

– Shakespeare / in London.

ANSWERS

I was born in 2000.

My parents were born in a small town.

Was your sister born in 2004?

Were you born in a hospital?

My grandparents weren't born in Spain.

Shakespeare wasn't born in London.

2 ▶61

- Focus students' attention on the pictures of Joshua, Amelie, and Hiro, students at an international school in Mexico. Ask what countries they think they come from.
- Ask students to listen to the three students speaking and to match them to the countries of their parents and the languages they speak. Go over the example, playing Joshua's part of the audio before you play the full track.
- After they have listened, let students compare their answers in pairs.
- Ask them if they would like to listen again before you check the answers as a class.

ANSWERS / AUDIO SCRIPT ▶61

(See underlined text below for answers.)

Interviewer: Tell me where your parents are from and what languages you speak.

Joshua: My dad's from the USA, and my mom's from Brazil. English is my favorite language because we speak it at home. Spanish is hard for me, and I don't speak Portuguese … like, just a few words.

Amelie: My mom's from France and my dad's from Egypt. French is my favorite language because … well … I just like it. But I speak Arabic and Spanish too.

Hiro: My parents come from Japan. I speak Japanese at home because my parents don't want me to forget our language. But Spanish is the easiest language for me because I … um … speak that at school. I think English is hard.

Interviewer: What are you going to do when you graduate from high school?

Joshua: I'm going to go to college.

Amelie: Um … I definitely want to visit different places in the world.

Hiro: I don't know.

Interviewer: Where do you think you'll live in the future?

Joshua: I'm going to live in the USA. I grew up there.

Amelie: Uh, I was born in Mexico and my friends are here. But I don't know if I'll live here. I might live in France.

Hiro: It will be hard for me to live in Japan now. I feel I belong in Mexico because … you know … I was born here and my friends live here.

3a

- Find out if students noticed Joshua, Amelie, and Hiro hesitating sometimes before answering the questions in the interview. Elicit or explain the meaning of *hesitation* (*a pause before doing something*).
- Ask students why we sometimes hesitate when we are speaking (*to give us time to think or if we're not sure what we want to say*).
- Refer students to the tips in the HOW TO box.
- Ask students why they think it's important to listen carefully after a hesitation (*the hesitation gives the speaker time to think, and when they start to speak again, it is usually to contribute some information that is important to the conversation*).

3b ▶61

Exam-type task

- Give students one minute to read the sentences and options. Go over the example with the class before they complete the exercise.
- Play the track for students to listen and choose the correct options.
- Check answers as a class.

ANSWERS

2 B 3 C

4

- Encourage students to reflect and say which tips in the HOW TO box helped them answer Exercise 3b and to check them.

REACT

5

- Ask students to think about what makes a person belong to a place. Focus their attention on the ideas on the list.
- Ask them to put the ideas in order from 1 to 5, where 1 = most important.
- Let them compare their choices in pairs and explain to each other why they ordered the options as they did.

Alternative procedure: more confident classes

Write these sentence stems on the board:

All of us … because …

Some of us … because …

Most of us … because …

None of us … because …

Divide the class into groups of six to eight. Ask them to discuss their rankings and reasons for their choices and to write some sentences using the sentence stems to summarize their group's opinions on belonging. Each group should then elect a spokesperson to report back to the class. For example, *All of us think that speaking the same language is important. If you can't communicate with your classmates or neighbors, it's difficult to feel like you belong to a place. None of us think the weather is very important because you can adapt to different weather without many problems.*

WORK WITH WORDS

6 ▶62

- Ask students to copy the table in their notebooks. Also ask them to copy the countries in the box in the first column.
- Divide the class into pairs to fill in the other columns. Set a time limit of four minutes for this.
- Play the track for students to listen and check their answers.
- Ask students to tell you the three countries on the list in which the nationality and language differ.

ANSWERS / AUDIO SCRIPT ▶62

Country	Nationality	Language
Brazil	Brazilian	Portuguese
China	Chinese *	Chinese
Egypt	Egyptian *	Arabic
France	French	French
Germany	German	German
USA	American	English
Japan	Japanese *	Japanese

Three countries where the language is not the same as the nationality are: Brazil, Egypt, and the USA.

7 ▶63 PRONOUNCE

- Play the track for students to listen and underline the stressed syllable in each word.
- Point out that the stress sometimes changes when the word takes a suffix to make it into a nationality or language. Give an example (*China* – *Chinese*) and ask students to find other examples where the stress changes.
- Play the track again for students to listen and repeat.

ANSWERS

Stressed syllables are underlined in the Exercise 6 answer key. The stress changes in the nationalities are marked with *.

Extra activity

Play a game of *Bingo* with languages and countries. To win the game, the student who shouts *Bingo!* first must read the languages and the corresponding countries aloud with the correct stress.

8

- Divide the class into pairs. Refer Student A to the quiz questions on page 75 and Student B to the ones on page 76.
- Encourage them to take turns asking each other the questions, checking the answers to see who can answer the most correctly.

MOVE BEYOND

Ask students to do the **Move Beyond** task on page 73.

Extra activity

Ask students to look at the table they completed in Exercise 6 and choose the following: two countries they would like to visit, a language they think would be difficult to learn, a language they think would be easy to learn, and two famous people from two different countries.

Ask students to compare their answers in pairs and give reasons why they chose that famous person and what they know about him or her.

Homework

Ask students to write their answers to some of the questions from the extra activity above. Give them these prompts:

I'd like to visit (country) *because …*

I'd like to learn (language) *because …*

(famous person) *is* (nationality). *He/She …*

In the next class, divide the class into small groups to exchange their answers.

GRAMMAR Hopes, plans, and predictions

Talk about your hopes and plans, and predict events in the future

Page 57

STAGE	TIME	FOCUS
GET STARTED		Define *hopes*, *plans*, and *predictions*.
READ AND LISTEN		Read and listen for specific information.
STUDY		Categorize sentences from the text as hopes, plans, or predictions. Choose the correct options to complete rules and examples. Deduce the meaning of *definitely*, *probably*, *may*, and *might*.
PRACTICE		Recognize and produce target language in written exercises.
SPEAK		Produce target language in a speaking task about personality.

Get started

Write on the left-hand side of the board:

Thc future

definitely ... It's already decided!

likely ... I think it's probable.

maybe ... I really would love to, but I don't know if it's possible.

Write on the right-hand side:

Predictions

Hopes

Plans

Divide the class into pairs to match the descriptions to the words on the right.

ANSWERS
Plans: definitely ... It's already decided!
Predictions: likely ... I think it's probable.
Hopes: maybe ... I really would love to, but I don't know if it's possible.

READ AND LISTEN Grammar in context

1 64

- Ask students to read the instructions. Check that they understand what information they need to look for.
- Play the track for students to read and listen to the interview. Ask them to write down where Fernanda thinks she will live in the future and why.
- Check and discuss answers as a class.

ANSWERS / AUDIO SCRIPT 64
The USA; because her parents are going to stay in the USA.
See Student's Book, page 57, for audio script.

STUDY

2a

- Divide the class into pairs to decide if each sentence (1–8) in the interview expresses a hope, a plan, or a prediction.
- Check answers as a class.

ANSWERS
1 plan 2 plan 3 prediction 4 prediction 5 prediction
6 hope 7 plan 8 prediction

2b

- Focus students' attention on the grammar explanation and ask them to choose the correct options. Remind them to use the examples from the interview to help them.
- Check answers as a class.

ANSWERS
be going to will will
am is are

3

- Refer students back to Exercise 1 and ask them to underline the words *definitely*, *probably*, *may*, and *might*.
- Then ask them to use those examples to help them choose the correct answers in the Study box.
- Elicit answers from different students around the class.

ANSWERS
definitely = 100 percent sure
probably = 75 percent sure
may/might = 50 percent sure

- Point out that *probably* and *definitely* go after *will* but before *won't*; for example, *I'll probably finish my homework in one hour. I definitely won't see you next week.*

PRACTICE

4a

- Go over the example with the class and check that they understand that the answer is *going to* because it refers to a plan.
- Ask students to work individually to read the sentences and choose the correct options.
- Let them compare their answers in pairs before you check them as a class.

ANSWERS
2 'm going to finish 3 'll get 4 may live 5 'll definitely work
6 'll probably be

4b

- Ask students to look at the sentences again and decide what adjective best describes Alex's personality.

ANSWER
ambitious

5

- Go over the example answer with the class before asking students to put the remaining sentences in order.
- Invite fast finishers to write the questions on the board.
- Check the questions on the board as a class and make any necessary corrections.
- Finally, ask students to write answers that are true for them.

ANSWERS
2 What are you going to do on the weekend?
3 What do you hope you'll do when you graduate from school?
4 Where might you live in the future?
5 What other things will you probably do?
6 What won't you probably do?

SPEAK

6

- Refer students to the personality adjectives in the box and ask them to choose one but not to tell anyone.
- Give them three or four minutes to prepare how they will answer the questions in Exercise 5 as their chosen "personality." Encourage them to be as creative as they like with their answers. You could provide some examples. For example:

What are you going to do this evening?
lazy = *I'm going to lie on the sofa and watch TV.*
brave = *I'm going to parachute from an airplane.*

- Divide the class into pairs to take turns asking and answering the questions in order to guess which personality adjective their partner has chosen.

Extra activity

Ask students to work in pairs to read to each other the answers they wrote in Exercise 5 about their own futures. For each of the answers, their partners must ask an extra question. For example:
A: This evening I'm going to watch television.
B: What are you going to watch?

Homework

Ask students to write five sentences about their future 20 minutes from now, and five sentences about their future 20 years from now. Encourage them to think of hopes, plans, and predictions.

LANGUAGE & BEYOND KNOW YOURSELF

Recognize what you're good at *Page 58*

STAGE	TIME	FOCUS
GET STARTED		Learn the meaning of *skills*. Give one or two personal examples.
READ		Read a list of skills and choose the most important one. Categorize skills.
DO		Make a list of personal skills. Read and categorize a partner's list.
REFLECT		Talk about the importance of recognizing skills.
EXTEND		Plan and present a talent show program.

LIFE SKILLS

RECOGNIZE WHAT YOU'RE GOOD AT
It is important that students can identify the skills they possess and that they reflect on how these skills could be used in different ways, not only for learning, but also for life in general. It is equally important for students to understand that each individual has a different range of skills. Worrying about what they can't do is less productive than focusing on what they can do! You may find your students are not used to this type of personal reflection and need a lot of support and encouragement.

Get started

Ask students to tell the person next to them two skills that they have (things that they are good at doing). Remind them to use the *-ing* form of the verb. Write a couple of examples on the board; for example, *I'm good at dancing. I'm good at playing video games.*

READ

1

- Ask students to read Patrick's list. Ask if there are any items on the list they didn't understand.
- Elicit or clarify the meaning of *lyrics* (the words of a song); *patient* (you don't get angry or annoyed easily when other people don't behave the way you'd like them to); *fixing* (making something work if it is broken); *being on time* (punctual; always there at the time you have to be there); *clean* (arranged and organized).
- Ask students to look at the list again and decide which is Patrick's most important skill.
- Let students compare and explain their choices in pairs before you invite different students to share their answers with the class.

2

- Go through the skills categories with the class.
- Ask students to read Patrick's list again and categorize each of the skills by writing a letter or letters next to it. Set a time limit of three minutes for this.
- Let students compare their answers in pairs before you ask for examples of each category as a class. If students disagree with the categories other students have chosen, encourage them to give reasons for their choices.

DO

3

- Ask students to make a list of as many things as possible that they are good at. Remind them to use the *-ing* form of the verb. Set a time limit of five minutes for this.
- Monitor as students work and offer advice and encouragement.

4

- Divide the class into pairs. Ask them to exchange lists with their partners and to categorize each of their partners' skills according to the categories in Exercise 2.
- Encourage students to tell their partners which categories they are strongest in.

5

- Before students hand back the lists, invite them to add at least three more items according to what they know about their partners' skills.
- Ask them to read what their partner has written and to tell their partners if they agree with the suggestions added.

REFLECT

6

- Focus students' attention on the REFLECTION POINT and invite a volunteer to read it aloud.
- Divide the class into pairs to answer the questions before you discuss them as a class.
- Before you introduce each question, read the corresponding point in the REFLECTION POINT box aloud. Then invite students to share their opinions. If the following points do not come up in the discussion, you could mention them at an appropriate moment.
  - Often people don't recognize what they are good at because it comes easily and naturally to them. So it's important to take time to really think about all the things you're good at. If you're ever feeling stressed about something you can't do, that's a good time to remind yourself of all the things you *can* do!
  - Doing the things you are good at gives you a boost of positive energy and can inspire other people as well. Try to think of ways to use your skills in different areas of your life.
  - Sometimes it's really helpful to hear another person's perspective on the things you do well. Other people see things that you just take for granted. Everyone likes to hear when they've done something well, so tell them – it doesn't cost anything!

EXTEND

7

- Divide the class into groups of four to six to design a program for a "Real Talent Show." Ask students to think of something they can each do. Stress that students can include skills such as the ones they have discussed during the lesson, come up with other ideas for acts based on their everyday skills, or even use something silly that they are good at doing! Set a time limit of seven minutes for this.
- Invite each group to present their programs to the class.
- After each presentation, invite students to say (or vote on) which act they would most like to see.

Extra activity

Ask students to write up their talent show programs, incorporating design elements or illustrations. These could be displayed in the classroom later.

Homework

Ask students to reflect on their own skills and how these help them learn English. Point out that these can involve specific classroom skills; for example, *I'm good at spelling, so this helps me when I check my written work.* They can also be more general; for example, *I'm confident, so this helps me take opportunities to speak to English-speaking people.* Suggest that they choose six skills to write a sentence about.

SPEAKING Can I help?

Offer help and express spontaneous decisions *Page 59*

STAGE	TIME	FOCUS
GET STARTED		Play a memory game using *I'll* + verb.
SPEAK		Use pictures to predict details of a situation.
LISTEN		Listen for specific information in two conversations. Complete the conversations with phrases for offering help and expressing spontaneous decisions (speaking subskill).
ACT		Role-play talking about problems and offering help.

Get started

Divide the class into groups of four to six to play a memory game.

Tell students they are going to plan a party and each student must say what they will do to help. Before they state their contributions, they must remember what everyone who went before them said. Anyone who can't remember or who makes a mistake is out of the game.

For example:

Student 1 (Alicia): I'll bring the drinks.
Student 2 (Marco): Alicia will bring the drinks, and I'll decorate the house.
Student 3 (Karen): Alicia will bring the drinks, Marco will decorate the house, and I'll make a cake.

SPEAK

1

- Refer students to the PHRASE BYTES box and encourage them to use these phrases in their discussion.
- Divide the class into pairs to look at the photos and answer the question, making predictions about the situations based on, for example, the facial expressions.

LISTEN

2 ▶65

- Have students close their books. Play the audio track for them to listen and find out what problem Sam and Lynn each have.
- Play both conversations and then ask students to compare their answers in pairs.
- Elicit answers as a class and find out if their predictions from Exercise 1 were right.

ANSWERS / AUDIO SCRIPT ▶65

1 The lyrics of Sam's song are in Spanish. He doesn't speak Spanish.
2 Lynn is trying to learn lines for the school play. She can't remember them.

1
Karina: What's wrong?
Sam: I downloaded this great song, but the lyrics are in Spanish. You know I don't speak Spanish.
Karina: But I understand Spanish. Would you like me to listen to the song and translate it?
Sam: That would be great, thanks. You're so smart!
Karina: No problem.

2
Al: What's wrong?
Lynn: I'm trying to learn these lines for the school play. I can't remember them.
Al: Don't worry, I'll help you. I can practice the lines with you. I'll come over to your house later.
Lynn: Thanks! That's really generous of you.

3 ▶65

- Ask students to close their books and take turns telling their partners from memory what Karina and Al are going to do to help.
- Ask students to open their books and complete the conversations with the expressions in the box.
- Play the track again for students to listen and check their answers.

ANSWERS

Karina is going to listen to the song and translate the lyrics.
Al is going to practice the lines with Lynn.
1 Would you like me to listen 2 I'll help 3 I can practice
4 I'll come

ACT

4 ▶66

- Set up the role-plays by telling students they are going to act out some similar conversations in which one person explains the problem and the other offers help.
- Refer students to the phrases in the PHRASEBOOK box. Play the track for students to listen and repeat. Encourage them to use the phrases in their conversations. You could suggest they begin their conversations in the same way as in the conversations above, with the phrase *What's wrong?*
- Give students two minutes to read the situations and think about what they will say. Tell them to alternate between the role of asking for help and the role of offering help.
- Encourage students to stand up if appropriate for the situation in order to act it out more naturally. Monitor and note good use of language and errors to go over in a feedback session at the end of the exercise.
- After the feedback session, invite volunteer pairs to perform one of their conversations for the class.

Extra activity

Ask students to assess their performance after the role-play in Exercise 4 and think about how they can improve next time.

Homework

Ask students to write out two of the conversations they acted out in Exercise 4. They can use ideas from their improvisations or invent new ones.

WRITING Time capsule

Use *because* and *so* Page 60

STAGE	TIME	FOCUS
GET STARTED		Make predictions about the future.
SPEAK AND READ		Talk about attitudes about the future. Read predictions that a girl has written for a time capsule. Explore the use of *because* and *so* (writing subskill).
PRACTICE		Produce target language in a written exercise.
DISCUSS		Make predictions about your future.
WRITE		Write predictions about yourself for a time capsule.
SHARE		Make a list of hopes and predictions as a class.

Get started

Divide the class into pairs to each make three predictions about things their partners will do in the future.

Encourage them to say whether they agree or disagree with their partners' predictions. For example:

A: *I think you'll be a famous film director.*
B: *Well, maybe that will happen, but I think I'll probably be an actor rather than a director. I think you might travel to a lot of different countries because I know you're interested in other countries.*
A: *Yes. I hope I'll travel all around the world!*

SPEAK AND READ

1

- Ask students to think about how they feel about the future and to choose the option that best matches their feelings.
- Conduct a poll to see how many students chose A, B, or C.
- Ask students who completed option D to share their ideas with the class.

2a

- Focus students' attention on the HOW TO box about the use of *because* and *so*. Check that they understand the difference between the two words.

Alternative procedure

Try to pick up on some of your students' ideas from the speaking activity in Exercise 1 to write examples of sentences with *because* and *so* in them on the board; for example, *I'm worried about the future because it might be difficult to find a job. I want to get a good job, so I'm going to go to college.*

Circle the linking words *because* and *so* and underline what comes after them. Focus on the two sentences and, for each one, ask if the underlined section is a reason for or a result of the beginning of the sentence (*because* is followed by a reason, *so* is followed by a result).

2b

- Ask students if they think it might be interesting to write predictions for a time capsule to be read in the future and, if so, why (*because a person could read about the plans they had and compare them with his or her real situation several years later*).
- Explain to students that they are going to read predictions that Adele has written about her future and write answers to the questions in their notebooks. Set a time limit of five minutes for this.
- Check answers as a class.

ANSWERS

1 She hopes she'll improve in math. She hopes she'll still be best friends with Emilia, Gina, and Lucia.
2 She'll probably get another dog. She might study biology. She'll probably continue taking art.

PRACTICE

3

- Go over the example answer with the class before asking students to complete the remaining sentences with *because* or *so*.
- Choose individual students to read their answers aloud.

ANSWERS

2 because 3 so 4 so 5 because

DISCUSS

4

- On the board, write *MY LIFE* in a circle, with linking circles containing categories such as: *friends, school, hobbies, sports, pets, vacations, family, home.*
- Ask students which of these categories Adele makes predictions about (i.e., pets, school, friends, hobbies).
- Divide the class into pairs or small groups to make predictions about what will happen to them in three years' time.
- Write some sentence stems on the board as prompts (e.g., *I hope I'll... , I'll probably... , I probably won't ... , I might ...*).

WRITE

5

- Tell the class they are going to make a time capsule and include their predictions about their lives in three years' time.
- Explain that you'd like them to write five predictions or hopes like the ones they have just discussed.
- Refer them to the prompts on the board and remind them to use these structures to make predictions about the future.
- They should also give reasons for why they think their predictions will come true or describe the results of their predictions. Refer them to the HOW TO box and review the use of *because* for a reason why and *so* for a result.
- Refer them to page 55 to find more adjective + preposition combinations to use as they are writing their predictions.

SHARE

6

- Ask students to stand up and move around the room and talk to different classmates and share their predictions to find out if they have written similar things.
- Make sure they speak to a number of different people. You could ensure this by clapping your hands every couple of minutes and calling out: *Change!*
- Have a feedback session to find out what predictions were similar throughout the class.

Extra activity

Ask students: *Why are you learning English?*

Divide the class into pairs to write reasons for learning English (using *because*) and results of learning English (using *so*). Encourage them to write as many as possible. Allow five minutes before sharing them with the rest of the class. Examples: *I'm learning English ...*

- ... *because it will be useful in the future.*
- ... *so I'll be able to understand song lyrics.*

Homework

As a way of wrapping up the unit, ask students to collate work that they have done during the unit and make a PowerPoint presentation, booklet, or poster that says something about their identities. Encourage them to use photos or any other visual material that they wish. Some of the things they could include are:

- a short description of their personalities;
- an example of a doodle and an analysis of what this says about them;
- some information about how they feel about doing certain things;
- information about where they belong and why;
- their hopes and plans for the future;
- things they are good at (skills).

Display their work around the class.

VOCABULARY Personality adjectives

1

- Refer students to the pictures and information about the three students from different countries.
- Ask them to read the sentences and complete the personality adjectives, pointing out that they should look for the clues in the sentences; for example, *Fleur says she likes to win, which means she is competitive*.
- Check answers as a class by choosing different students to read a sentence aloud. As they do so, monitor pronunciation of individual sounds and word stress and correct as necessary.

ANSWERS
1 competitive 2 ambitious 3 brave 4 cheerful
5 smart 6 patient 7 generous 8 creative
9 kind 10 sensitive

Countries, nationalities, and languages

2

- Ask students to complete the sentences by writing the correct nationalities or languages, reminding them that in some cases the nationality and the language are not the same.
- Let students check their answers in pairs before you invite different students to write the answers on the board for the class to check.

ANSWERS
1 French 2 Arabic 3 Italian 4 Spanish
5 Chinese 6 Vietnamese 7 Japanese 8 Russian
9 German 10 Spanish 11 Portuguese 12 English

GRAMMAR Adjectives with prepositions + *-ing* form

3

- Refer students to the sentences about Paul and ask them to first choose the preposition that goes after each of the adjectives (two options are given) and then to complete the sentences using the *-ing* form of the verb.
- Let students compare their answers in pairs before you check them as a class, each time eliciting the spelling of the *-ing* form of the verb.

ANSWERS
1 of talking 2 at telling 3 about taking
4 with watching 5 about going 6 in playing

Hopes, plans, and predictions

4

- Ask students to read the interview with Karin and complete it with *going to*, *'ll*, *won't*, or *might*.
- Check answers as a class and encourage students to explain their choices; for example, *In number 1, I put* going to *because the sentence starts with* I'm *and you can't use this with* will *or* might.

ANSWERS
1 going to 2 going to 3 'll/might 4 might
5 going to 6 'll 7 won't 8 'll

Extra Resources

Go to the Teacher's Resource Center at mee2.macmillaneducation.com for:

- midterm tests;
- downloadable audio and audio scripts for the Student's Book and Workbook;
- videos and video scripts;
- extra vocabulary at two levels of difficulty;
- extra grammar at two levels of difficulty;
- CLIL lessons, with full teacher's notes;
- a life skills lesson, with full teacher's notes;
- Speaking Database materials;
- the Move Beyond Level 3 wordlist;
- tips for using the Grammar Database;
- and more!

Go to Workbook pages 132–143 for further practice material.

PROGRESS CHECK 5

Preparing for the Progress Check

Vocabulary review

- Draw a table on the board with the following headings: *Personality adjectives*; *Countries, nationalities, and languages*.
- Elicit one or two examples for each category and write them on the board.
- Divide the class into pairs or small groups. Tell them to look back through Unit 5 and find more examples from each vocabulary category.
- After five minutes, encourage students to come to the board and write their answers. Stop them when you have five or six words in each category.
- Finally, ask students to look at the Progress Check. Ask them to look at the multiple choice items in Exercise 2 and tell you which vocabulary they might hear in the listening section (*personality adjectives*).

Grammar review

- Divide students into pairs and ask them to refer to the grammar pages (pages 55 and 57).
- Remind students of the grammar they have studied in Unit 5 (adjectives with prepositions + *-ing* form; hopes, plans, and predictions).
- Write the following two sentences on the board, pointing out that each sentence contains both of the grammar points (underlined) from Unit 5: *<u>I'm not very good at playing</u> the piano, but <u>I'm going to improve</u>.*
  <u>I'm excited about going</u> to the party, and <u>I might wear</u> my new shirt.
- Ask each pair to write as many sentences as they can containing both of these grammar points, using the sentences on the board as a model. Allow five minutes before asking how many sentences each pair has made. Write some of the sentences on the board.

Optional warm-up activities

READ Exercise 1

- Students may not be very familiar with this type of reading task, so they may need help. If you are not planning to do this under test conditions, do the first paragraph as a class activity.
- Ask students to read the first paragraph and look at the first three blanks. Go through the multiple-choice options one by one and ask the following:
  In number 1, we go to museums to learn about art or to do art? (learn)
  In number 2, at a science museum, there is no guarantee that you will or won't be interested in what you see, so the more likely answer is what? (might)
  In number 3, ask yourself, why are science museums great ... which word would you start the answer to that question with? (because)
- Point out the importance of reading to the end of the paragraph or text before filling in the blanks.
- Doing the first paragraph as a class should help students gain the confidence to attempt the rest on their own. If it is clear that they are still having difficulty, encourage them to discuss the second paragraph (questions 4–5) with a partner.

LISTEN Exercise 2

- Read the task instructions with the class and make sure they realize that they have to check A, B, or C for each sentence.
- Point out that they are going to hear someone giving advice to students on making career decisions.
- Ask students to look at the first item while you write the following on the board: *You'll need to ... , You're going to ... , I think you should ... , You will probably / might ... .*
- Ask the class to suggest how a career counselor might express each of the options in the first item (e.g., *You'll need to choose what job you want to do*; *You're going to decide what new subjects to study next year*; *You will probably study math and science next year*).
- Divide the class into pairs or small groups and ask them to discuss how the career counselor might phrase each of the options in the other items. After two or three minutes, ask students to tell you their ideas.
- Finally, point out to students that they are now prepared for what they will hear and they know exactly what to listen for.

WRITE Exercise 3

- Students did sentence transformations in the Progress Check for Units 1 and 2. Ask them what they remember and what the purpose of this exercise is (to fill in the blank so that both sentences mean the same thing although they are expressed in a different way).
- Remind the class of the grammar points they covered in Unit 5 (see the **Grammar review**). Explain that they should expect to see some of those points in this exercise.
- Do the first item with the class by asking them which word comes after *good/bad* when we're talking about activities (*at*). Explain that *good at languages* is possible. However, students have learned that *good at* can be followed by the *-ing* form of a verb. Remind them of this and ask them which *-ing* form they need to use (*learning*).

WRITE Exercise 4

- Refer students back to Exercise 3 on page 60 and the writing they did on that page. Point out that the task in the Progress Check asks them to write about their plans.
- Ask pairs of students to make a list of things they could plan to do on Saturday.
- After a minute or two, ask them how the weather might affect their plans. If necessary, prompt with questions such as: *What will you do if it rains / if it's sunny?*
- Ask pairs to suggest why they can't meet on Sunday.
- Finally, ask students to suggest a good way to begin and end their messages.
- Bring all the above points together by constructing a model on the board with the class. Remind students to include all the information required in the task. First, invite one student to suggest a suitable greeting, which the student writes on the board. Ask other students to add sentences one at a time, before the last student suggests a way to end the message.

Doing the Progress Check

READ

1

- Go through the **Test-Taking Tips** with the class and remind them of the work they did to identify the goal of a text using the HOW TO box on page 54.

- Advise students to read the whole text before filling in any blanks. Encourage them to use the general meaning to help them find the specific answers.
- Remind students that they can usually eliminate one or more of the answers that clearly do not fit.
- Allow about 10 minutes for this section.

ANSWERS
1 B 2 D 3 A 4 D 5 B

LISTEN

2 67

- Encourage students to read all the items and answer options so that they can try to predict what they will hear.
- Go through the **Test-Taking Tips** for the listening task, briefly referring students back to the work they did on page 56.
- Remind them that the answers usually appear in the same order as the items, so when they have heard the answer to one items, they should prepare for the next.
- Point out that they will hear the speech twice.

ANSWERS / AUDIO SCRIPT 67

1 B 2 A 3 C 4 B 5 A

Maggie Thompson: Good morning, everyone. Sit down, please. No, don't get your books out. You won't need them. My name's Maggie Thompson, and I'm the school's career counselor. Now, I know what you're thinking: "I'm too young to think about what job I'm going to do after school." And you're right.

However, later this year you'll need to make some important decisions. You're all going to continue studying subjects like math and science, but you're also going to choose some other subjects. Now, these choices might influence what you do in the future, so I think you should start thinking about which ones to take.

So, what's the best way to do this? I think there are three things you can do. The first is to think about what you're good at doing – but also what you're *not* good at. For example, if you're good at learning languages, choosing Arabic or Chinese will be a good choice. You'll probably get good grades, and speaking a foreign language might help you get the job you want one day. But if you're scared of speaking in public, drama might be a good option. Because if you're shy, drama will help you to become more confident, and communicate better.

The second thing you should do is talk to teachers of new subjects. That way you'll get a better understanding of what the different subjects are about. And with that in mind, your teacher is going to invite other teachers to your class over the next few weeks. They'll talk to you about their subjects, and you'll also have the chance to ask questions.

And finally, you should talk to your parents. I'm sure they'll give you good advice, but when you talk to them, you shouldn't be afraid of telling them what *you* would really like to do. You might think a subject you're interested in taking isn't serious enough, but it's important to be open and honest. You might be surprised by their reaction!

Finally, I have, um, a form to hand out. Um ... Now ... Oh, now please listen carefully to what I'm going to say. Take these forms to your parents. Then ask your parents to sign the first page ... um ... here. Then cut off the bottom of the page and bring it back to your teacher. Is that clear?

WRITE

3

- Remind students that this exercise mainly tests grammar. Make sure students remember the grammar points they covered in Unit 5 (see the **Grammar review**).
- Students should check that the *meaning* of the second sentence matches that of the first sentence. Point out that they should use a maximum of three words in each blank and then check for any spelling mistakes.
- Make sure that students think about timing – although you might not want to set a specific time limit.

ANSWERS
1 at learning 2 planning to study / going to study 3 probably
4 going to do / planning to do

4

- Check that students have understood the target reader and the reason for writing. Ask for suggestions for how to begin and end this message (see the model answer below for suggestions).
- Check that students understand what their messages must include (*the three bullet points*) and remind them of the importance of following all the instructions.
- Remind students to use *because* and *so*, as practiced on page 60. Ask them to tell you why we use these two words (*to explain a reason*; *to say what comes next*).
- Remind the class that they will need to use language to express hopes, plans, and predictions, as well as conditional constructions.
- Finally, remind students of the word limit and the importance of checking their own spelling, grammar, etc.
- Allow up to 20 minutes for the exercise; remind the class when they have five minutes left.

MODEL ANSWER

Hi, everybody.
On Saturday morning we're going shopping. In the afternoon we might go to the beach because it'll probably be hot. If the weather's bad, we'll watch a movie. I'm going to visit my grandparents on Sunday, so I can't see you then.
Charlie

Feedback and extension

READ

- Some students may have found this task difficult, so spend time answering their questions. Review the questions one at a time and ask students how they were able to eliminate certain answers. Discuss the options and focus attention on where the options were syntactically wrong (e.g., *2A "topics you am be interested in" makes no sense)*.
- An exercise such as this one provides many opportunities to enrich students' vocabulary. Don't allow students to look at their grades and move on – that would be wasting a valuable opportunity. In many cases, students need to know how to correctly use the *wrong* answers as well as the right ones. The more phrases and expressions they can learn, the easier they will find future exercises such as this one.
- It's sometimes difficult for students to understand that they need to learn words in context or in fixed expressions. Encourage them to write down phrases as they encounter them.

LISTEN

- Hand out photocopies of the audio script and ask students, in pairs, to go through it and underline where the correct answers can be found. They can also underline sections that help eliminate the wrong answers. Remind students that the answers are usually in the same order as the items in the exercise. This will help them when referring to the audio script. Check the answers as a class.

WRITE

- Focus on the grammar points in Exercise 3. Write the first sentence of item 1 on the board.
- Ask the class to tell you how this sentence is constructed grammatically (subject "*I*" + verb "*am*" + article "*a*" + adjective "*good*" + noun phrase "*language learner*"). Write this next to or below the sentence on the board.
- Now write the correct second sentence and elicit the grammar used to form it (subject "*I*" + verb "*am*" + adjective "*good*" + preposition "*at*" + *-ing* "*learning*" + noun "*languages*").
- Point out the two ways the same idea is expressed (e.g., *a good learner = good at learning*).
- Go through items 2 through 4 in the same way, asking students to explain first the grammatical construction and second the pairs of expressions; for example, *Her plan is to ... = She is planning/going to ...*
- For students who had difficulty with Exercise 4, go through the grammar points that they need in order to follow the instructions (*going to, might, probably, If ...*).
- Write the following on the board and ask for as many suggestions as possible for each one: *On Saturday morning, we're going to ... ; In the afternoon we might ... ; ... probably ... ; If the weather's bad, ... ; On Sunday, ...*
- If students had a lot of difficulty with their writing, you could now ask them to write another similar message based on this feedback.

WORKBOOK AUDIO SCRIPT

Starter Unit

Track ▶68

Page 80, Exercise 5a

Conversation 1

Eva: Are you ready, Joanna? Hurry up! Mom's ready to take us to school.
Joanna: Is it cold outside?
Eva: Yes, it is! Don't forget your sweatshirt.
Joanna: OK, I have it!

Conversation 2

Joanna: Eva, are you wearing pants or a skirt to school today?
Eva: I'm wearing jeans.
Joanna: Jeans?
Eva: Yes, we're going on a field trip by bus, so I want to be comfortable.
Joanna: Good idea!

Conversation 3

Eva: Joanna, do you have your sneakers? We have tennis club after school.
Joanna: Oh no! Where are my sneakers? I have my shoes, but I can't find my sneakers.
Eva: Here they are!
Joanna: Oh, thanks!

Track ▶69

Page 81, Exercise 2

1 **Dad:** Matt, hurry up! You have five minutes!
Matt: Oh no – I don't have my house key!
Dad: There's a key on the table near the door.
Matt: OK, thanks! See you later!

2 **Felipe:** What's in your lunchbox today?
Matt: Two cheese sandwiches and an apple.
Felipe: Do you have any chocolate?
Mateo: No, I don't.

3 **Mr. Andrews:** Matt, you're 10 minutes late!
Matt: I'm sorry!
Mr. Andrews: Do you have your homework?
Matt: Yes, I do. Here it is.
Mr. Andrews: Good! Now sit down and open your book.

Track ▶70

Page 82, Exercise 4

A

I like listening to music and reading.
I don't like swimming or cooking.
I'm not in the drama club because I don't like acting.
I like languages! I like speaking Spanish.

B

I like swimming and cooking.
I don't like listening to music or acting, but I like reading.
I'm not good at languages, and I don't like speaking Spanish ... or French!

C

I like swimming and listening to music.
I don't like reading, and I don't like speaking Spanish.
I like acting, but I don't like cooking.

Unit 1

Track ▶71

Page 88, Exercises 3, 4, and 6

Conversation 1

Carrie: Hey, Nick, do you know how this works?
Nick: Sure, Carrie, what's going on?
Carrie: I'm just not sure how to view the pictures I've taken.
Nick: Oh yeah. You want to access the "view album" button right here. And then just press the arrows here to go back or forward.
Carrie: Great! Thanks a lot.
Nick: No problem.

Conversation 2

Dan: Hey, Zara, can you help us with this?
Zara: What's wrong, Dan?
Dan: We want to watch this video file – but on a bigger screen. I need to plug in my speakers. Where's the USB port on this thing?
Zara: Oh, I see. It's usually ... look – it's on the side here.
Dan: Oh yes, I see it now. Great!

Conversation 3

Anna: Oh no! Barney, help!
Barney: What is it, Anna?
Anna: I can't remember how to save a new number. Do you know how?
Barney: Sure, just a second. Open the menu, and then you enter the number here. And it pops up on the screen.
Anna: Oh, thanks.

Track ▶72

Page 91, Exercise 2

Annie: What do you think about this new e-reader, Nick?
Nick: I think it's very useful. It's small and it isn't heavy. You can use it to read books on the train.
Annie: I agree. I think it's very useful because you don't need a lot of heavy books. But look at this wrist camera; it's a really creative idea. You can take pictures anywhere!
Nick: I'd love to have one, but don't you think it's expensive? It costs a lot of money!
Annie: I don't know. What do you think about this house robot? I don't think it's very interesting. It's so ugly.
Nick: Oh, I disagree. I think it's cool. I hate housework!
Annie: Look at this computer pet. Now that's really silly! Who wants that?
Nick: Oh ... yeah, I see what you mean ... kind of stupid. But here's something that's really creative. You can see people and images in 3D. It looks like they're real!
Annie: Yes, that's really amazing.

Track ▶73

Page 91, Exercise 4b

words with /æ/: calculator, calendar, camera, laptop, maps, tablet
words without /æ/: compass, games, mail, messages

Unit 2

Track ▶74

Page 100, Exercises 2–5

Carl: Hi, Anna!
Anna: Hi, Carl! Great to see you! This is my friend Josh.
Josh: Nice to meet you!
Carl: You too!
Anna: What's up, Carl?
Carl: Well, I got a good grade on my French test, and now I'm going to the movies with friends!
Anna: Good for you!
Josh: Good job! Are you doing something special to celebrate after the movies?
Carl: Not really, I'm going to guitar class.
Josh: Really? Do you like playing the guitar? Can you play well? I play the saxophone.
Anna: He can't play well yet, believe me. That's why he's taking classes.
Carl: It's true!
Josh: OK, OK.
Carl: What are you doing later? My class ends at six o'clock.
Anna: Josh and I are going ice skating in the park at 7:00. We love skating.
Carl: Oh, me too!
Josh: Do you want to come with us?
Carl: Sounds like fun! See you there.
Anna & Josh: Great!
Anna: OK, see you at the park at seven.

Track ▶75

Page 102, Exercise 4

Fiona: What are you doing tomorrow night? Do you want to go to the movies?
Mario: Sorry, I can't. I'm meeting some friends.
Fiona: Oh, that's too bad! I'm going to the movies with Tony. We're going shopping after the movie. It's Marta's birthday, and we're buying her a present.
Mario: I can meet my friends early. Then I can go shopping with you and Tony later!
Fiona: Perfect! Tony's coming to the movie theater at 5:00 p.m. We can meet at 7:00 p.m. at the mall.
Mario: Sounds great! See you then!

Track ▶76

Page 103, Exercise 4

Woman: Woodland Community Center. Can I help you?
Brad: Hello. I'm calling about swimming classes.
Woman: Hold on ... There are swimming classes on Tuesdays and on Thursdays.
Brad: What time are the classes?
Woman: At 3:00 p.m. or 6:00 p.m.
Brad: Can I sign up for the 6:00 p.m. class?
Woman: The 6:00 p.m. class is full. You can leave your name and number if you want.
Brad: OK. My name's Brad Stinston.
Woman: Can you say that again, please? Simpson?
Brad: No, Stinston. S-T-I-N-S-T-O-N.
Woman: All right. What's your telephone number?
Brad: 733-8025.
Woman: Perfect. We're starting more classes in the summer.
Brad: Oh, OK. Thank you very much!

Track ▶77

Page 103, Exercise 5

1 autumn **2** castle **3** half **4** island
5 knee **6** knife **7** know **8** listen **9** sign
10 walk **11** Wednesday **12** wrong

Unit 3

Track ▶78

Page 112, Exercises 3 and 4

Conversation 1

A: We saw some fantastic wildlife when we were in Kenya last month.
B: Oh yeah? What kind of animals did you see?
A: We saw a group of elephants - a whole herd of them!
B: That's amazing!
A: They came up behind the hotel and started eating fruit from the trees in the garden.
B: How many of them were there?
A: Oh ... about five! It was great! I took some great pictures - and I put them on my bedroom wall.
B: I love elephants. They live for a long time, don't they?
A: Yes - some can live up to 60 or 70 years!

Conversation 2

A: Did you take a lot of pictures on your trip to Canada last summer?
B: Yes, I did. But I lost my camera.
A: How did you lose it? Did you drop it somewhere?
B: No, a grizzly bear took it.
A: Oh no! Really? What happened?
A: We went camping in the mountains and stayed overnight next to a river.
B: Did the bears come into your tent?
A: Yes, so we ran away behind some trees. They went into our tents, but they didn't stay long. When we got back, our bags were gone - with all our food and, of course, my camera. I was so upset!
B: Did they eat all your food? What kind of food do grizzly bears like to eat?
A: They eat fruit, meat, fish - anything really - especially during the summer. Then they sleep a lot during the winter.

Conversation 3

A: A scary thing happened on our vacation in Florida this winter.
B: Oh, yeah? What happened?
A: We found a huge snake in our kitchen.
B: Oh no!
A: I guess it wanted some lunch. When I looked into the kitchen, it was just sitting there behind the refrigerator.
B: What did you do?
A: I was so scared I called the police! And they called the animal rescue patrol.
B: That was close.
A: Apparently there are thousands of wild snakes in Florida. Some say there are about 150,000 snakes there. It's because there are no animals that eat snakes, so the population is increasing all the time.

Track ▶79

Page 115, Exercises 1 and 2

Diane: What should we do to improve the environment? Let's choose one of these ideas.
Linda: OK. How about telling everyone to recycle more plastic and paper? We have a lot of recycling bins in school, but no one uses them.
Ian: That's a nice idea. We could make signs and posters.
Diane: That's not very exciting. Let's raise money to help the local animal shelter.
Ian: What could we do? What about having a dance or a formal party?
Linda: I like the No Plastic Bottle Day. Everyone who buys a plastic bottle has to pay a fine.
Diane: I don't know - that's pretty serious. I like the once-a-week Veggie Day. That means you don't eat any meat and it's healthy to eat vegetables anyway.
Ian: How does that help the environment?
Diane: It saves animals, of course!
Linda: OK. Why don't we write a letter to the school cafeteria and get everyone to sign it?
Diane: That's a great idea!

Track ▶80

Page 115, Exercise 5

1 started, <u>walked</u>, got
2 <u>taught</u>, won, told
3 stopped, <u>thought</u>, was
4 said, began, <u>saw</u>

Unit 4

Track ▶81

Page 124, Exercises 3, 4 and 5b

Interviewer: Good afternoon and welcome. It's two o'clock. Today's show is called "Waste Not, Want Not." On today's show we're talking to Martin Ramsey, who, believe it or not, is building his new home out of recycled materials. We're asking him a few questions about his project. Later, we will see if people think it's a good idea. Welcome to the show, Martin!
Martin: Thanks. It's nice to be here.
Interviewer: So Martin, why are you building your home out of, well, trash?

Martin: I think recycling is so important. In the USA alone, at least 75 percent of our trash can be recycled, but a lot of people don't take recycling seriously.
Interviewer: That's true. According to an article in the newspaper last week, a lot of people think that recycling is too complicated, and so they don't recycle as much as they should. Only 30 percent of all the trash is actually recycled.
Martin: In my opinion, people make a lot of excuses not to recycle. It's wrong to throw things in the trash when we can use them again. That's why I'm building furniture and other parts of my house out of recycled bottles and cans.
Interviewer: Wow! That must be a lot of work!
Martin: It's not always easy, but I think it's fun! I love the challenge.
Interviewer: Fun?
Martin: Yes, friends and neighbors often come to my home with bags full of materials so I can continue building. The local school brought me 1,000 plastic bottles last month. I cut them into pieces and used them to make a strong, colorful wall in my bathroom. They're waterproof too!
Interviewer: One thousand bottles!
Martin: That's nothing! To make the kitchen table and chairs, I need over 5,000 cans!
Interviewer: Incredible! Well, Martin, many thanks for joining us. Let's see what listeners think about your original idea.

Track 82

Page 127, Exercises 2 and 3

Sammy: Sammy's Salads, this is Sammy speaking. How can I help you?
Maria: Yes, hello. I'd like to place a take-out order, please.
Sammy: Sure, of course. What would you like?
Maria: Well, let's see. What's the special today?
Sammy: We have the tomato salad and our chef's salad.
Maria: Um, I'll have the tomato salad.
Sammy: OK. Would you like some chicken on your salad?
Maria: No thanks, I'm a vegetarian.
Sammy: OK, so that's one tomato salad, no chicken.
Maria: Exactly.
Sammy: Your order includes potato chips or bread. What would you like?
Maria: I'm allergic to flour, so I'd rather have potato chips, please.
Sammy: Perfect. Anything else?
Maria: No, that's it, thank you.
Sammy: OK, what's your name and address?
Maria: It's Maria. I live at 13 Aragon Road.
Sammy: Sorry. Can you repeat your address, please?
Maria: 13 Aragon Road.
Sammy: Thank you. That will be ...

Track 83

Page 127, Exercise 5

Sarah: Let's stop here and get something to eat before we get to Marco's house.
Nick: Good idea!
Man: Hello there. Can I help you?
Nick: Let me see. I'd like an egg salad sandwich with lettuce and tomato.
Sarah: Can I have the same but with no lettuce, please?
Man: Of course. Would you like some cold drinks?
Nick: Do you have any soda?
Man: No, sorry. I have cartons of juice or bottles of water.
Sarah: I'd rather have iced tea.
Nick: One bottle of water and one glass of iced tea, please.
Man: OK, that's $7.70.
Sarah: Thank you. Oh, and can you tell us where Marigold Avenue is?
Man: Sorry? Mari*grove* Avenue? Could you say that again, please?
Sarah: Marigold Avenue – M-A-R-I-G-O-L-D.
Man: Oh, yes. It's just around the corner.
Nick and Sarah: Thank you!

Track 84

Page 127, Exercise 6

1 a bottle of milk
2 a package of pasta
3 a carton of milk
4 a box of chocolates
5 a loaf of bread

Unit 5

Track 85

Page 136, Exercises 2, 3, and 4

1
Man: Aura, what do you think this proverb means?
Aura: Home is where the heart is? Well, I think ... um ... well, it means that home is where your family lives. For example, I was born in Colombia, but I moved to the USA when I was three, and America is really my home now. All my brothers and sisters and my mother and father are all here, and, well, this is where my home is now – with my family.

2
Man: Luiza, what do you think this proverb means?
Luiza: I think it means that your home is basically the people and culture that you feel comfortable with. You know, like ... now I live in New York because I'm studying at college here. But I was born in Brazil, and all my friends and family still live there – and I really miss my home. So when I go back to Brazil ... well, it just feels right – the people, the place, and the culture. That's home.

3
Man: What does this proverb mean to you, Carlos?
Carlos: Um ... well, I'm not sure, but I think that it means ... uh ... that if you're happy in a place, that's your home. Home is not a place, really – it's a feeling. I'm originally from Puerto Rico, but I live in Orlando now. I speak Spanish and English and ... well, and I really like it here, but I think that in the future I want to travel, like to Japan, for example. So as long as I feel happy, it doesn't matter where I am!

4
Man: What does this proverb mean to you, Angela?
Angie: I think this proverb means that home is when you're with the person that you love. It doesn't matter where you are – uh, you can be, uh, in any country or any city, but as long as you are with that person, then you feel happy. Like, my family is from Ireland, but now I live in the USA because my dad came here for work and, uh, this is really my home now.

Track 86

Page 139, Exercise 1

Conversation 1

Matt: What's wrong?

Sally: My math homework is so difficult. I'll never get it done!

Matt: Don't worry. I have this great new book. It explains everything in easy steps. Would you like me to lend it to you?

Sally: That would be great! Thanks so much!

Matt: No problem.

Conversation 2

Katie: What's wrong?

Rob: I have a music test tomorrow and I'm so nervous!

Katie: I can practice with you if you like. I'll pretend to be the teacher.

Rob: Oh, that's a great idea. That's really nice of you.

Katie: I know!

Track 87

Page 139, Exercise 2

Conversation 1

Matt: What's wrong?

Sally: My math homework is so difficult. I'll never get it done!

Matt: Don't worry. I have this great new book. It explains everything in easy steps. I'll lend it to you!

Sally: That would be great! Thanks a lot.

Matt: No problem.

Conversation 2

Katie: What's wrong?

Rob: I have a music test tomorrow and I'm so nervous!

Katie: Would you like me to practice with you? I'll pretend to be the teacher.

Rob: Oh, that's a great idea. That's really kind of you.

Katie: I know!

Track 88

Page 139, Exercise 4

Pronunciation

Brazilian	Japanese
English	Mexican
Egyptian	Portuguese
German	Russian
Italian	Spanish

WORKBOOK ANSWER KEY

Starter unit

VOCABULARY 1

Page 80

1 **1** notebook **2** class schedule **3** textbook **4** pencil case **5** keys **6** lunchbox

2 **1** Yes, there is. **2** Yes, there is. **3** No, there isn't. **4** Yes, there are. **5** No, there isn't. **6** No, there aren't.

3 **1** brother **2** mom and dad **3** grandparents **4** aunt **5** cousins

4a **1** a **2** b **3** a **4** a **5** b **6** a **7** a **8** b

5a items checked: sweatshirt, pants, jeans, shoes, sneakers, skirt (items not checked: dress, shirt)

5b hat, socks, T-shirt, jacket

GRAMMAR 1

Page 81

1 **1** am **2** isn't **3** are **4** aren't **5** have **6** doesn't have

2 **1** B **2** A **3** C

3 **1** have **2** don't **3** There's **4** 's **5** have **6** don't have **7** 're **8** 'm **9** have **10** do **11** is

4 **1** have **2** are **3** 'm **4** 's **5** has **6** have **7** are **8** has

5 **1** Sarah has three sisters. **2** I don't have my homework. **3** You don't have much time. **4** They have new bicycles. **5** We don't have our textbooks. **6** Judy doesn't have her lunchbox.

VOCABULARY 2

Page 82

1 **1** f **2** c **3** b **4** a **5** d **6** e

2a **1** f (period) **2** c ? **3** b ? **4** a (period) **5** d ? **6** e (period)

3 **1** swimming **2** acting **3** do homework **4** cooking **5** read a book **6** play tennis **7** listening to music **8** speak English

4 **1** a **2** c **3** b **4** a **5** c **6** b

5a **1** swimming **2** acting **3** speaking Spanish **4** reading **5** listening to music **6** cooking

5b Suggested answers: do homework, play tennis, go to music class

GRAMMAR 2

Page 83

1 **1** are **2** is **3** is **4** are **5** are **6** are **7** old **8** What **9** do **10** you **11** do **12** do **13** does **14** do **15** does **16** he **17** What **18** does **19** Why **20** long

2a **1** Where **2** What **3** Who **4** When **5** Why **6** How long

2b **1** e **2** a **3** b **4** f **5** d **6** c

3 **1** reading **2** cooking **3** listening to music, reading **4** swimming **5** listening to music **6** swimming **7** bike riding **8** cooking

4 **1** What's her name? **2** How old is she? **3** Where does she live? **4** What does she do after school on Mondays? **5** What does she like doing (in her free time)?

Unit 1

VOCABULARY 1

Page 84

1 **1** television **2** console **3** laptop **4** laptop **5** computer **6** smartphone **7** tablet

2 **a** calculator **b** calendar **c** camera **d** compass **e** games **f** mail **g** maps **h** notes **i** videos **j** messages

3 **1** calendar **2** notes **3** mail **4** compass **5** calculator **6** messages **7** camera **8** maps **9** games **10** videos

5 **1** use a social networking site **2** open a web browser **3** chat online **4** log on **5** surf the internet **6** watch videos

READING

Page 85

1 **1** type **2** adjective **3** compare **4** similar **5** before

2 **1** b, c **2** a, d

3 c

4 **1** C **2** I **3** DS **4** DS **5** DS **6** C

5 **1** N **2** A **3** V **4** A **5** A **6** A **7** A **8** N

6 **1** a **2** b **3** b **4** a **5** a **6** a **7** a **8** b

GRAMMAR 1

Page 86

1 **1** They **2** play **3** She **4** They **5** She **6** doesn't **7** do **8** play **9** he **10** don't **11** play **12** Does **13** doesn't

2 **1** routines **2** third **3** before **4** do and does **5** before **6** at the beginning or the end

3 *-s*: sends, plays, uses; *-es*: does, goes, teaches; *-ies*: flies, studies

4 **1** sends (H) **2** plays (T) **3** studies (R) **4** teaches (R) **5** flies (H) **6** goes (R)

5 **1** never **2** hardly ever **3** sometimes **4** often **5** usually **6** almost always **7** always

Page 87

6 **1** a **2** b **3** b **4** b **5** a **6** a **7** a **8** a

7 **1** Do you chat online every day? **2** How often does Steve send email? **3** Does your phone play music? **4** Do you normally play games on a console? **5** How often does your family watch DVDs? **6** Does your laptop have a camera?

8 **1** How often do you chat online? I don't often chat online. **2** How often does she update her blog? She updates her blog from time to time. **3** How often do your friends check their email? My friends regularly check their email. **4** How often do Leo and Vicky post photos online? Leo and Vicky hardly ever post photos online. **5** How often do your parents send you text messages? My parents send me text messages every day. **6** How often does your computer crash? My computer doesn't often crash.

9 **1** He doesn't often send email. **2** I check my email every day. **3** She studies online in the mornings. **4** How often do you chat online? **5** Do you regularly update your blog? **6** I don't often have problems with my cell phone. **7** They go online from time to time. **8** Do you sometimes talk to friends on your cell phone?

LISTENING

Page 88

1 A digital camera B cell phone C tablet

2 digital camera: album, menu, pictures, save, screen, view
cell phone: album, file, menu, number, pictures, save, screen, view, watch
tablet: album, file, menu, pictures, save, screen, speakers, USB port, view, watch

3 Conversation 1 is about the digital camera. Conversation 2 is about the tablet. Conversation 3 is about the cell phone.

4

Conversation 1	pictures, view, album
Conversation 2	screen, watch, file, speakers, USB port
Conversation 3	save, number, menu, number, screen

5 Conversation 1 – Person A (Carrie) doesn't know how to view the pictures she has just taken.
Conversation 2 – Person A (Dan) can't find the USB port to plug his speakers into his tablet.
Conversation 3 – Person A (Anna) can't remember how to save a new number on her cell phone.

6 Conversation 1: Great! Thanks a lot. No problem.
Conversation 2: Oh, I see. What's wrong?
Conversation 3: Just a second. What is it? Thanks.
Not in any conversation: Excuse me. What did you say?

VOCABULARY 2

Page 89

1 **1** webcam **2** monitor **3** speaker **4** headphones **5** printer **6** screen **7** mouse **8** keyboard

2 **1** mouse **2** webcam **3** keyboard **4** USB port **5** microphone

3 **1** IT **2** log on **3** post **4** blog **5** chat **6** text messages **7** webcam **8** screen **9** invention **10** website

Words & Beyond

1 b **2** c **3** a **4** c **5** c **6** a

GRAMMAR 2

Page 90

1a **1** a **2** an **3** a

1b **1** cell, hotel **2** app, umbrella **3** Euro, unit

2 **1** I love computers / Rule b **2** I live in New Zealand. / Rule g **3** My uncle is an artist. / Rule c **4** I use the internet every day. / Rule e **5** The is the best cell phone you can buy. / Rule f **6** We study IT on Thursday. / Rule a **7** I go to school in a big city. The school has 2,000 students. / Rule d

3

zero article	*the*
April	best
Australia	internet
January	moon
Main Street	Netherlands
Tuesday	sun
	United Nations

4 **1** a **2** a **3** – **4** the **5** a **6** – **7** an **8** – **9** the **10** a

5 **1** the **2** the **3** a **4** – **5** – **6** the **7** the **8** an **9** the **10** –

SPEAKING

Page 91

1 **1** reading books **2** taking pictures **3** having fun **4** cleaning the floor **5** making calls

2 **1** do you **2** I think **3** do you **4** know **5** What **6** it's

3

gadget	Nick's opinion	Annie's opinion
e-reader	useful	useful
wrist camera	expensive	creative
house robot	cool	ugly
computer pet	stupid	silly
3D phone	creative	amazing

4 Words with /æ/: calculator, calendar, camera, laptop, maps, tablet
Words without /æ/: compass, games, mail, messages

WRITING

Page 92

1 **1** verb **2** subject **3** verb **4** adjective **5** object **6** adverb

2 **1** virtual, new, old, free, expensive, cheaper **2** never, always, almost never, sometimes, often, usually, hardly ever **3** every day, now and then, from time to time **4** I get (a lot of) texts and email; We share music tips, photos and videos; I buy clothes or CDs

3 **1** I sometimes visit social networking sites. **2** She hardly ever buys computer games. **3** We often buy clothes online. **4** Elisa usually sends text messages. **5** I play games every weekend.

4 **1** Ali often texts her friends. She sometimes plays games. She hardly ever chats online.
2 Leo never plays games. He hardly ever updates his blog. He often downloads music.
3 Mike sometimes surfs the web. He sometimes checks his favorite social network. He never shares photos.

LANGUAGE & BEYOND

Page 93

1 Tom's planner

2 Suggested answers: Tom's time isn't very organized. He isn't specific about some things (e.g., get there "early," leave before 4 p.m.). His planner isn't in the order he has to do things.

VOCABULARY REVIEW

Page 94

1 **1** sweater, jeans, sneakers **2** shirt, skirt, shoes **3** notebook, pencil case **4** textbook, lunchbox, cell phone **5** listening to music, cooking **6** taking pictures, learning Spanish **7** Aunt **8** cousins

2 **1** map **2** calculator **3** compass **4** headphones **5** calendar **6** USB **7** keyboard **8** mouse

GRAMMAR REVIEW

Page 95

1 **1** b **2** a **3** b **4** a **5** a **6** a **7** b **8** b **9** a **10** a

2 **1** a **2** the **3** a **4** the **5** the **6** The **7** a **8** the **9** the **10** the

3 **1** surfing, surfs **2** playing, play **3** send, sending **4** buy, buying **5** watching, watches **6** chatting, chat

Unit 2

VOCABULARY 1

Page 96

1a **1** d (bathroom/shower) **2** c, f (bedroom/bed, desk) **3** b (kitchen/stove) **4** a (living room/sofa) **5** e (dining room/table)

2 **1** apartment **2** house **3** bungalow

3 **1** clock **2** armchair **3** shower **4** lamp **5** television **6** lights. Mystery word: carpet

4a **1** is mopping **2** is making **3** is taking out **4** is hanging up **5** is vacuuming **6** is setting **7** is doing **8** is washing

5 **1** stove **2** picture **3** lamp **4** door **5** walk the dog **6** kitchen

READING

Page 97

1a **1** d **2** c **3** b **4** f **5** a **6** e

2a houseboat, family, busy, household chores, not a lot of space, organized, neat

2b **1** b **2** c

3a **1** I **2** I **3** C **4** I **5** I **6** C **7** C **8** I

3b **1** The Thompsons live on a canal in the Caribbean. **2** There isn't a lot of space on the boat. **4** Linda is clearing the table. **5** Linda is a family friend. **8** The boys argue about the ironing.

4 **1** large/small **2** boring/exciting **3** difficult/easy **4** ugly/beautiful **5** similar/different **6** relaxed/busy

GRAMMAR 1

Page 98

1 **1** They **2** is **3** doing **4** They **5** sorting **6** is

2 **1** Are **2** Yes **3** he **4** setting/clearing **5** is **6** No **7** doing **8** I am/'m **9** is **10** watching

3 **1** SP **2** PP **3** SP **4** PP **5** SP **6** PP

4 Simple present: I never do my homework ... I'm too tired ... You're such a good student ... I go to the gym ... I'm rarely awake ...
Present progressive: What are you doing? I'm listening ... and surfing the net. Are you doing (your homework)? What are you doing (tonight)? I'm studying (for our chemistry test). Are you going (to the gym tonight)?

Page 99

5 **1** 'm listening **2** is reading **3** aren't making **4** 's riding **5** isn't playing **6** is playing

6 **1** have **2** Do you sometimes help **3** is doing **4** swim **5** is shopping **6** are loading

7 **1** b **2** a **3** c **4** a **5** c **6** b

8 **1** want **2** like **3** don't know **4** don't understand **5** need **6** hate

9 **1** are you doing **2** 'm sleeping **3** Do you always wake up **4** I don't always get up **5** I'm studying **6** Are you reading **7** My brother is **8** He's making **9** I'm going

10 **1** What are you doing? **2** When do you normally have breakfast? **3** When do they usually do their homework? **4** What's he doing now? **5** How often does Jake get up early? **6** Is she sorting the recycling?

LISTENING
Page 100
1 ice skating, go shopping, play soccer, ride their bikes, playing the guitar, watching soap operas/television, listen to music, go to the movie theater
2 **1** three **2** no
3 **1** Anna, Carl, Josh **2** go to the movies, play the guitar, ice skating
4 **1** C **2** I, Carl and Josh don't know each other/aren't friends. **3** I, Carl is going to the cinema. **4** I, Josh plays the saxophone.
5 I, Carl's class ends at 6.00. **6** C
5 **1** A **2** A **3** J **4** A **5** C **6** C

VOCABULARY 2
Page 101
1 **1** book **2** bike **3** friends **4** skating **5** television **6** listen. Mystery object: football helmet.
2 play: an instrument, soccer, tennis. go: ice skating, shopping, to the movies. read: a book, a magazine, a text message.
3 **1** the piano **2** soccer **3** text message **4** shopping **5** book **6** to the movies

Words & Beyond
1 remote control **2** argue **3** soap opera **4** mess **5** study **6** feed

GRAMMAR 2
Page 102
1 **1** now **2** tomorrow
2 **1** I'm going **2** 'm not going **3** is leaving **4** I'm going to **5** is starting **6** 're meeting
3 **1** FA **2** FA **3** N **4** FA **5** FA **6** N
4 **1** are you doing **2** 'm meeting **3** 'm going **4** 're buying **5** 's coming
5 **1** C **2** I, Mario's meeting some friends. **3** I, It's Marta's birthday tomorrow. **4** C **5** I, Tony is going shopping tomorrow night. **6** I, Mario is going shopping with Fiona.
6 **1** She isn't going swimming on Tuesday. She's playing tennis with Jo. **2** She isn't going to the movies with her mom on Thursday. She's going to the movies with Marcos. **3** She isn't studying for her math test on Friday. She's going ice skating with Judy. **4** She isn't going ice skating on Tuesday. She's playing tennis with Jo. **5** She isn't helping her mom on Monday. She's studying for a math test. **6** She isn't playing tennis with her mom on Tuesday. She's playing tennis with Jo.
7a **1** Tomorrow **2** Next week **3** tonight **4** Next year **5** This weekend **6** tonight

SPEAKING
Page 103
1 speak **2** on **3** repeat **4** How **5** again **6** this is **7** from **8** message
2 1, 3, 2, 5, 7, 6, 4, 8, 10, 9
3 **1** Can I speak to Tony, please? I'm sorry ..., Yes, of course ... Can I leave ... Thanks a lot. **2** Tony isn't here right now. **3** How do you spell that?
4 **1** c **2** a **3** e **4** f **5** b **6** d
5 knee, knife, know, castle, island, wrong, sign, listen, autumn, walk, half, Wednesday

WRITING
Page 104
1 **1** and **2** too **3** also **4** and **5** also **6** too
2 **1** also **2** too **3** and **4** too **5** also **6** and
3 **1** and **2** too **3** and **4** too **5** also **6** too
4 **1** James is washing the dishes. He's also doing the ironing. **2** We are studying math. We're studying French too. **3** I'm tired and hungry. **4** Alison plays the piano. She also plays the violin. **5** They're going to the movies. They're going to the museum too. **6** It's dark and cold.
5 Where are you going? I'm going shopping.

LANGUAGE & BEYOND
Page 105
Suggested answers:
1 These aren't good solutions because both boys have other things that they are unhappy about.
2 **1** The Metallic Three concert. **2** Dave is unhappy because Sam also has three of his CDs. He's also unhappy because Sam gets a bigger allowance than him. **3** Sam is unhappy because Dave never says when he can pay him back.
3 Dave could tell Sam that he can pay back the money next month. He could offer to buy him a juice more often after swimming. Sam could remember to give back the CDs that he borrows from Dave.

VOCABULARY REVIEW
Page 106
1 **1** h **2** g **3** e **4** f **5** a **6** b **7** d **8** c
2 **1** brothers **2** swimming **3** mp3 player **4** headphones **5** setting **6** plays **7** brush **8** cook **9** ironing **10** closet
3 Watch: a movie, television. Play: basketball, tennis. Read: a book, a magazine. Use: a computer, a mouse, a printer.
4 **1** off **2** out **3** off **4** on **5** out **6** out

GRAMMAR REVIEW
Page 107
1 **1** How often do you write email? I sometimes write email. **2** How often does he update his blog? He updates his blog from time to time. **3** How often does your mom send text messages? She doesn't regularly send text messages. **4** How often do Teo and Raul download apps? They always download apps. **5** How often does she use her laptop for homework? She hardly ever uses her laptop for homework.
2 **1** starts **2** are listening **3** are talking **4** play **5** 's playing **6** are reading **7** studying **8** don't like
3 **1** c **2** d **3** c **4** b **5** b **6** d **7** d **8** b
4 **1** are you doing **2** clean **3** vacuum **4** don't / do **5** 'm meeting **6** 're going **7** are shopping **8** are you doing **9** is taking **10** 'm calling
5 **1** Paco hardly ever goes to the movies. **2** Maria's doing the ironing now. **3** Mom is making pizza for lunch today. **4** I make my bed every morning. **5** My dad's flying to New York on Friday night. **6** Tonight I'm studying for my exams and doing my homework.

Unit 3

VOCABULARY 1
Page 108
1 **1** mountain **2** river **3** lake **4** coast **5** island **6** ocean
2a Water: ocean, river, lake, stream
Land: beach, island, mountain, coast, countryside, savannah, desert, hill
Plants: tree, grass, flower
3a **1** beach **2** desert **3** stream **4** countryside **5** savannah **6** ice sheet **7** forest
4 **1** coast **2** hills **3** trees **4** flowers **5** beach **6** ocean

READING
Page 109
1 **1** all **2** beginning **3** next **4** information.
2 b and c
3 **1** Paragraph 2 **2** Paragraph 2 **3** Paragraph 3 **4** Paragraph 3 **5** Paragraph 4 **6** Paragraph 4
4 **1** c **2** a **3** b **4** c **5** c **6** b
5 **1** Kenya **2** TED **3** cattle / cows, lions **4** shed **5** Nairobi National Park **6** motorcycle lights / solar panel
6 **1** didn't need **2** wasn't **3** helped **4** stopped **5** didn't kill **6** saved

GRAMMAR 1

Page 110

1 **1** did **2** were **3** did **4** said **5** didn't **6** were **7** were **8** was **9** were **10** were **11** she **12** didn't **13** was **14** wasn't

2 Regular verbs: help/helped, like/liked, start/started, stop/stopped, study/studied, travel/traveled

Irregular verbs: be/was, go/went, come/came, do/did, teach/taught, win/won

3 **1** a **2** a **3** b **4** b

4 **1** What did you do last night? **2** How did they feel after the exam? **3** Why did Sarah leave the party – before 11.00 p.m.? **4** Where did she grow up? In Boston? **5** Why didn't you ask Tom to come to the party? I thought he was your friend. **6** Why didn't you come? You missed all the fun.

Page 111

5 **1** did **2** started **3** cleaned **4** won **5** spoke **6** made

6 **1** Did, win **2** did **3** didn't expect **4** was **5** started **6** gave **7** explained **8** Were **9** wrote **10** Did, make **11** didn't reply **12** stopped

7 **1** They started the project last year. **2** They saw a movie about Thailand before they left. **3** She decided to start a campaign. **4** We didn't know about the wildlife problems there. **5** What did *they* discover about the environment? **6** They weren't nervous about their talk. **7** Did you travel to the USA? **8** Did you give a presentation to another school?

8a **1** What did Richard invent? **2** What was the problem? **3** Was he successful? **4** How did he save the lions? **5** Did he save the cattle?

8b **1** He invented lights that flashed on and off. **2** The lions killed the cows and the farmers killed the lions. **3** Yes, he was. **4** He protected the cows from the lions. **5** He made lights that flashed on and off around the cattle shed. Lions are afraid of moving lights.

LISTENING

Page 112

1 **1** important **2** symbols **3** great **4** horrible **5** spelling

2a **1** Big bear! Scared 😲. **2** Saw 5 elephants ☺ **3** She hates snakes – bad experience on vacation ☹

2b a savannah b forest, river c desert

3 **1** ☺ When: last month. Where: Kenya. Animal: elephants. What did the animals do? b (Elephants came into the garden behind the hotel.) **2** ☹ When: last summer. Where: Canada. Animal: grizzly bear. What did the animals do? a (A bear took his camera while they were camping.) **3** ☹ When: this winter. Where: Florida, USA. Animal: snake. What did the animal do? c (A snake came into the kitchen.)

4 Conversation 1: **1** five, **2** 60/70 years. Conversation 2: **3** fruit, meat, fish, anything **4** They sleep a lot. Conversation 3: **5** 150,000 **6** There are no animals that eat snakes in Florida.

VOCABULARY 2

Page 113

1 **1** owl (b) **2** dolphin (f) **3** *ant* (a) **4** snake (c) **5** parrot (d) **6** penguin (e)

2 **1** b **2** b **3** b **4** a **5** c **6** c

3 **1** owl (b, e) **2** spider (c) **3** bee (d, e) **4** bear (b) **5** turtle (a, f) **6** crocodile (a, b, f)

Words & Beyond

1 campaign **2** plant **3** make **4** pick up **5** take part **6** reach

GRAMMAR 2

Page 114

1 **1** were **2** wasn't **3** were **4** was **5** was **6** was **7** were **8** wasn't

2 playing, getting, visiting, stopping, traveling, sleeping, writing, swimming

3 **1** a **2** b **3** b

4 **1** were you all doing **2** I was waiting **3** Sharon wasn't riding **4** Sam and Andy were swimming **5** Were they visiting **6** We weren't talking

5 **1** Was Robbie riding; he wasn't; He was playing; I called **2** We saw; were you going; We were taking **3** were you doing; Were you sleeping; I wasn't; Cara and I were making

6 **1** took **2** were climbing **3** heard **4** were putting **5** didn't know **6** was following **7** turned **8** saw **9** was waiting **10** shouted **11** ran

SPEAKING

Page 115

1a Start a School Recycling Campaign. Raise money for your local animal shelter. Persuade everyone to go "veggie" once a week. Have a No Plastic Bottle Day.

1b They choose once-a-week Veggie Day.

2 Making suggestions: What should we do … ?
What could we … ? We could … Let's … Why don't we … ? How about … ?
React to suggestions: That's pretty serious. That's not very exciting. That's a nice idea.

3 **1** d **2** e **3** c **4** f **5** b **6** a

4a 6, 2, 4, 5, 1, 3

5 **1** walked **2** taught **3** thought **4** saw

WRITING

Page 116

1 Suggested answers: **1** The dog jumped into the lake. **2** The dog was barking. **3** A dog was chasing a rabbit. **4** The dog rescued the rabbit.

2a **1** Then **2** later **3** yesterday **4** later **5** Then **6** After

Correct order: b, c, d, a

3 **1** c **2** a **3** e **4** d **5** b

4 **1** did **2** did **3** Did **4** didn't **5** wasn't **6** Was

5 **1** Last night **2** during the night **3** at first **4** Then **5** At first **6** Later

LANGUAGE & BEYOND

Page 117

Suggested answers:

1 to organize ideas for a new project

2 ✓ Start with a main word or idea.
✓ Draw lines from the words and pictures.
✗ Write one or two key words on each line.
✗ Use CAPITAL LETTERS for important words.
✗ Group similar information in boxes.

3 Chess club: ☺ Low cost; Small room needed only; ☹ Not popular; ?: Length of each session
Dance club: ☺ Very popular; ☹ Big hall; Need a teacher; Need to charge; ?: What day? What kind of dance?

VOCABULARY REVIEW

Page 118

1 **1** map, It's not an electronic device. **2** cell phone, It's not part of a computer. **3** kettle, It's an appliance, not an item of furniture. **4** bed, It's an item of furniture, not an appliance. **5** shopping, It's not a sport. **6** bear, It's not landscape. **7** mountain, It's not an animal. **8** cousin, The others are all male. **9** ant, It's an insect, not a reptile. **10** house key, The others are things you have in the classroom.

2 **1** b **2** b **3** a **4** a **5** b **6** b **7** c **8** c **9** b **10** a

3

birds	insects	reptiles	mammals
owl	ant	crocodile	human
parrot	bee	turtle	lion
penguin		snake	dolphin
			bear

GRAMMAR REVIEW

Page 119

1 **1** was watching, called **2** was eating, saw **3** was hiking, took **4** was swimming, heard **5** were, found **6** was sitting, came

2 **1** a **2** b **3** a **4** b **5** b **6** a **7** b **8** b **9** b **10** a **11** a **12** b **13** b **14** a

3 **1** do you do **2** are you going **3** going shopping **4** get home **5** is she doing **6** going fishing

Unit 4

VOCABULARY 1

Page 120

1a Vegetables: onion, potato, carrot, (tomato). Drinks: mineral water, tea, juice, milk, coffee. Fruit: lemon, banana, apple, (tomato). Other: bread, chicken, eggs.

2 **1** knife **2** bowl **3** frying pan **4** saucepan **5** cutting board

3 **1** e **2** a **3** d **4** c **5** b

4a **1** Beat **2** chop **3** Heat **4** Fry **5** stir **6** pour

5 **1** steak **2** cheese **3** pasta **4** sandwiches **5** butter **6** chips **7** ice cream **8** chocolate **9** salad **10** oranges **11** grapes

READING

Page 121

1 No, he isn't a good cook. He says he's not sure about cooking.

2 a

3 **1** Decide **2** Read **3** Find, read

4 **1** Time **2** Ingredients **3** Things you need **4** Directions **5** Notes

5 **1** b **2** c **3** c **4** b **5** a **6** b

GRAMMAR 1

Page 122

1 **1** some **2** a few **3** a lot of **4** many **5** any **6** a little **7** any **8** much **9** much **10** a little

2 **1** countable **2** uncountable **3** countable and uncountable **4** countable and uncountable

3a Countable: banana, egg, lemon, potato, sandwich, vegetable; Uncountable: cheese; soda, juice, milk, oil, pasta, rice, tea

4 Zero: no
A small quantity: a few, a little, not many, not much
Not a small or large quantity: some
A large quantity: a lot of, many, much

5 **1** There's **2** There's **3** Are **4** don't have **5** Is **6** There isn't

Page 123

6 **1** some **2** some **3** a lot of **4** some **5** not many **6** some

7 **1** an **2** a few **3** not much **4** a little **5** a few **6** a little

8 **1** We don't eat many vegetables. **2** There aren't many good restaurants near here. **3** I don't have many friends at this school. **4** We don't have much cheese. **5** We don't have much homework tonight. **6** I don't have much time to cook at night.

9 **1** are **2** few **3** little **4** no **5** any **6** few

10 **1** Is there any bread? There's a little bread. **2** Is there any cheese? There isn't much cheese. **3** Are there any apples? There are a few apples. **4** Are there any eggs? There are a few eggs. **5** Is there a little tea? There's some tea. **6** Are there any grapes? There aren't many grapes.

LISTENING

Page 124

1 b

2 Facts: 4 (Martin Ramsey is very interested in the environment ... He's building his new home from recycled ... His bedroom and bathroom walls are made from ... His kitchen furniture is made from ...)
Opinions: 3 (He thinks people don't recycle enough ... Some of his neighbors think it's unhealthy ... in my opinion, recycled homes are a good idea)

3 30 75 1,000 5,000

4 **1** 2 **2** 30 **3** 75 **4** 1,000 **5** 5,000

5a **1** F **2** O **3** F **4** O **5** F

6 possible "good ideas" – 3, 4

VOCABULARY 2

Page 125

1 Rebecca: **1** soup **2** orange juice **3** chocolates **4** meat **5** eggs **6** oil
Ethan: **a** bread **b** water **c** pasta **d** jam **e** ice cream **f** cheese

2 Vegetarian: Ethan. Allergic to dairy: Rebecca

3a **1** a bottle of water **2** a piece of meat **3** a carton of milk **4** a jar of jam **5** a box of chocolates **6** a loaf of bread **7** a can of soda **8** a package of pasta

4 **1** box of eggs **2** packages of butter **3** piece of cake **4** loaf of bread **5** bottle of oil **6** packet of rice

Words & Beyond

1 chicken – It's the only meat.
2 coffee – It's the only one that doesn't contain dairy.
3 soda – The others are used for making cakes.
4 milk – The others are used for seasoning food / adding flavor.
5 jam – The others are fruit.
6 eat – The others are verbs connected to recycling.

GRAMMAR 2

Page 126

1 **1** somebody **2** somewhere **3** anyone **4** anywhere **5** everybody **6** everyone **7** everything **8** nobody **9** no one **10** nowhere

2 **1** don't refer **2** affirmative **3** negative **4** singular

3 **1** No one **2** anything **3** anywhere **4** Somebody **5** nothing **6** anybody

4 **1** everybody/everyone **2** anything **3** everywhere **4** nothing **5** Everybody **6** something **7** somebody/someone **8** nobody/no one **9** everybody/everyone

5a **1** everybody/everyone **2** something **3** anybody/anyone **4** everywhere **5** everybody/everyone **6** something

SPEAKING

Page 127

1 **1** b **2** c **3** a **4** e **5** d

1b please, would you like, thanks, I'd like

2 **i** 2c **ii** 4e **iii** 5d **iv** 3a **v** 1b

3 **1** Sammy's Salads **2** 13 Aragon Road **3** (Chef's) salad **4** free **5** allergic **6** repeat

4 **1** b **2** b **3** b **4** a **5** a **6** b

5 **1** Can I help **2** I'd like **3** Can I have **4** Would you like **5** Do you have **6** I'd rather **7** please **8** Sorry **9** Could you say **10** Thank you

6 **1** a bottle of milk **2** a package of pasta **3** a carton of milk **4** a box of chocolates **5** a loaf of bread

WRITING

Page 128

1 4, 3, 1, 2

2 **1** c **2** a **3** b

3 First, Next, Then, After that, Finally

4 **1** First, boil the water. **2** Next, put a tea bag in a cup. **3** After that, pour boiling water onto the tea bag. **4** Then take out the tea bag. **5** Next, add some milk. **6** Finally, stir in some sugar.

LANGUAGE & BEYOND

Page 129

Suggested answers:

1 He is organizing who is sharing rooms in a hostel.

2 **a** 3 **b** 1 **c** 4 **d** 2 **e** 5

3 Room 1 Sol and Luke; Room 2 Adam, Ian and Rav; Room 3 Mica

4 He could ask the hostel for a room on the ground floor for Luke and a quiet room for Mica.

VOCABULARY REVIEW

Page 130

1 Free time activities: go shopping, go swimming, listen to music, meet friends, play the piano, read a book, ride a bike Household chores: clear the table, cook dinner, set the table, load the dishwasher, take out the trash, sort the recycling, walk the dog

2 bee, key, loaf, milk, snake, radio, island, banana, brother, monitor

3 Countable: ant, calculator, desert, hall, hill, printer, sneakers; Uncountable: butter, flour, furniture, grass, milk, trash

GRAMMAR REVIEW

Page 131

1 **1** a **2** some **3** a few **4** a **5** a lot of **6** – **7** a **8** some **9** much

2 **1** was walking **2** saw **3** were passing **4** called **5** wasn't **6** was sitting **7** think **8** was

3 **1** we **2** everyone **3** you **4** everywhere **5** someone/somebody **6** anybody/ anyone **7** anything

4 **1** What are you reading? **2** How long is the class? **3** Are there any eggs in the refrigerator? **4** Do you eat much/a lot of fruit? **5** How often/When do you play soccer? **6** Where did you go last summer? / When did you go to Greece?

5 **1** I hardly ever go to the movies. **2** Maggie is doing her homework in her room. **3** How often do you make your bed? **4** Did you go to the coffee shop yesterday? **5** They were driving to the mall when a car crashed into them. **6** They didn't go to the movies last week.

Unit 5

VOCABULARY 1

Page 132

1 **1** d **2** c **3** b **4** a

2 **1** kind **2** creative **3** brave **4** generous **5** sensitive **6** smart

3 **1** confident **2** brave **3** creative **4** ambitious **5** smart **6** competitive

4a **1** a rude **1** b generous **2** a sensitive **2** b calm **3** a competitive **3** b cheerful **4** a kind **4** b polite **5** a friendly **5** b shy **6** a funny **6** b serious

READING

Page 133

1 **a** triangle **b** circle **c** rectangle **d** squiggle **e** square

2 **1** c **2** b **3** b **4** c

3 **1** circle **2** square **3** squiggle **4** rectangle **5** triangle

4 **1** in a good mood **2** worried **3** on time **4** harmony **5** details **6** loves to get attention

5 **1** calm **2** shy **3** ambitious **4** friendly **5** creative

GRAMMAR 1

Page 134

1 **1** at **2** is/'s **3** singing **4** is/'s **5** dancing **6** are/'re **7** running **8** about **9** Are **10** in **11** reading **12** of **13** about **14** are

2 **1** -ing **2** a noun **3** double **4** remove **5** Never

3 **1** drawing **2** telling **3** reading **4** swimming **5** writing **6** taking **7** creating **8** using **9** running **10** cooking

4 **1** about **2** in **3** in **4** of **5** at **6** at **7** at **8** at **9** about **10** with

5 **1** ... about Alison's grades **2** ... at talking **3** ... in math **4** at reading and writing **5** ... about her history project **6** with studying for tests

Page 135

6 **1** good **2** bored **3** tired **4** worried **5** worried **6** scared **7** excited **8** interested

7 **1** Tired **2** Good **3** Worried **4** Interested **5** Bored **6** Scared

8 **1** at cooking, International cooking **2** of failing, Study group **3** about creating, Web design group **4** of playing, Music group **5** in designing, Apps and games club **6** about singing, Singing club

9 **1** She's terrible at singing. **2** He's good at playing the guitar. **3** She's interested in taking pictures. **4** She's bored with doing homework. **5** I'm excited about starting my new school. **6** She's scared of playing ice hockey

10a **1** We aren't so good at painting. **2** Are you excited about the party? **3** They're worried about changing schools. **4** What is Melissa interested in? **5** I'm scared of snakes. **6** My brother isn't bad at swimming.

LISTENING

Page 136

2a **1** Germany **2** London **3** Australia **4** the USA

2b **1** c **2** d **3** a **4** b

3 **1** India **2** Lebanon **3** Poland **4** Switzerland

4a **1** I, Germany is really my home now. **2** C **3** I, Luiza wants to go back to Lebanon. **4** I, He really likes it in Australia. **5** C **6** I, Angie likes her home because she's with her boyfriend.

VOCABULARY 2

Page 137

1 **1** A **2** B **3** B **4** A **5** B **6** B **7** B **8** C

2 Brazilian, Portuguese, Italian, Spanish

3 **1** Mexico **2** Japan **3** Russia **4** China **5** Italy **6** France **7** Spain **8** Brazil **9** Egypt **10** Germany

4 Mexican, Japanese, Russian, Chinese, Italian, French, Spanish, Brazilian, Egyptian, German

Words & Beyond

1 doodles **2** patterns **3** shape **4** square **5** triangles **6** circle **7** arrows **8** stars

GRAMMAR 2

Page 138

1 **1** am ('m) **2** is ('s) **3** ('m not) **4** I'm not **5** Are **6** he/she is

2 **1** a **2** a **3** a **4** b **5** b **6** b

3 **1** are you going to do **2** probably won't go **3** are going to cook **4** 're going to visit **5** They'll probably come **6** definitely won't play

4 **1** are you **2** might **3** I'll **4** going to **5** probably won't **6** you'll **7** hope

5a **1** I'll definitely learn to drive. **2** We might visit Italy next year. **3** We'll probably learn Italian next year. **4** They probably won't win the competition. **5** Suzanna may/might study science. **6** I'm definitely going to study harder.

SPEAKING

Page 139

1 Conversation 1: 3, 5, 1, 2, 4 Conversation 2: 3, 5, 1, 2, 4

2 (1) I'll lend it to you! (2) Thanks a lot! (3) Would you like me to practice with you? (4) That's really kind of you.

3a **1** Would you like me to help, would be **2** I'll show, That's **3** I can explain, you **4** I can show, That

4

●••	•●••	••●	●•
	Egyptian	Japanese	German
Mexican	Italian	Portuguese	Spanish
			English
			Russian

WRITING

Page 140

1 because, so

2 **1** b **2** a **3** a **4** b

4 **1** Because she is sometimes shy and lonely. **2** So that she'll feel more positive. **3** Because she's going to have an interesting career in art and design. **4** So that she can visit a lot of countries. **5** Because she'll be good at communicating with other people. **6** Because she's going to be successful.

LANGUAGE & BEYOND

Page 141

Suggested answers:

1 helping people, outgoing, good at sports and other activities, patient, kind and energetic, able to speak English

2 (✗) bad at spelling and writing in English, no experience working with children, can't drive, never been abroad, don't like sitting around for long periods, not very good at crafts, can't cook
3 I'm very good at speaking English; I have experience looking after my two little brothers; I am good at riding a bike, so could take the children on bike trips; I am very interested in traveling abroad; I am very energetic and love doing physical activities; I am good at making campfires and cooking food on barbecues.
4 good at speaking English (S); have two little brothers (F); have to use my bike (H); always on time (S); prefer physical activities like soccer (H); can make a campfire (C); love barbecues (H)

VOCABULARY REVIEW

Page 142

1 **1** France **2** the USA **3** French **4** shy **5** Spanish **6** kind **7** brave **8** creative **9** ambitious
2 Across: **3** keyboard **4** Arabic **5** mouse **6** dairy **8** serious **10** bottle **11** listen; Down: **1** reptile **2** countryside **7** laptop **9** kitchen
3 **1** play – The other verbs are connected with cooking. **2** rude – The other personality adjectives are positive. **3** Brazilian – It is a nationality; the other words are countries. **4** stream – It is the only one connected with water. **5** bookshelf – The others can be found on a mobile phone. **6** app store – The others are parts of a computer.

GRAMMAR REVIEW

Page 143

1 **1** playing **2** play **3** solving **4** I'll **5** at **6** often **7** the **8** anything **9** made **10** going to
2 **1** solving **2** computers **3** computer games **4** online **5** learning **6** in **7** at **8** history **9** at **10** in **11** reading **12** project
3 **1** c **2** b **3** a **4** b **5** a **6** a **7** b **8** a **9** b **10** c **11** a **12** b **13** c **14** a
4 **1** Is Sally doing her homework right now? **2** We had a party last weekend. **3** Does Tom usually get up at 6:00 a.m.? **4** Our class visited the zoo yesterday. **5** I probably won't win the competition. **6** Viktor and David didn't watch the soccer game yesterday.
5 **1** What are you doing right now? **2** I don't know the answer. **3** I was watching TV when I heard a strange noise. **4** On Saturdays, I usually play tennis. **5** I started school when I was five. **6** When I was buying lunch, I saw my friend Eva.

Macmillan Education
4 Crinan Street
London N1 9XW
A division of Macmillan Publishers Limited

Companies and representatives throughout the world

ISBN 978-1-380-00779-7

Written by Anna Cole and Michael Terry

Go Beyond First published 2015
First edition entitled *Beyond* published 2014

Designed by EMC Design Ltd.

Cover design by EMC Design Ltd.

On-body design by Dynamo Studio, Co.

Full acknowledgements for illustrations and photographs in the facsimile pages can be found in the *Move Beyond* combined Student's Book/Workbook.

Printed and bound in China

2021 2020 2019 2018 2017
10 9 8 7 6 5 4 3 2 1